The Complete Idiot's Reference Card

Shopping List

Fill in the appropriate blanks (or circle the appropriate choices) before you go shopping or pick up the phone to order. On the phone, you can just read off the list (be sure to include the mail-order company's order numbers). In the store, use it like a grocery list.

I have a (computer make/model):_____.

It has a _____ central processor chip (e.g.: 80386SX, 68040) running at _____MHz (its clock speed).

I've got _____MB of RAM installed.

I'm using _____ (MS-DOS 6.2 with Windows 3.1, System 7.5, etc.) as my operating system.

I want an internal/external (select one), _____ _____ (manufacturer and model number, or catalog number) CD-ROM drive—or just tell them what speed and price factors you're looking for.

What all does that come with? (Write the extras down here, then eliminate anything in the next section if it's included.) Do I get any free stuff, too?

I'll also need:

_____MB of added RAM (only if you need to increase yours).

_____ (make and model CD-ROM controller card, if required, for PCs only)

_____ cable(s)

_____ (make and model sound card, PCs only).

How much have I spent so far?? (Keep the smelling salts handy, just in case.) If you didn't faint or exceed your spending limit:

I'll also need:

_____ (make and model/catalog number) speakers. Will they work all right with my drive?

_____ (make and model/catalog number) stereo headphones.

Shopping List

Does that drive use CD caddies? (If YES) Okay, add a three/five (circle one) pack of caddies, too.

And, I want to get these CD-ROM discs (list by name and catalog number):

_____

_____

I also want (for any additional hardware you might want):

_____

_____

Is everything in stock?

(If not:) When do you expect it?

Five Definitions You Need to Know While Shopping

Access time   How long it takes a CDROM drive to jump to that next bit of data it needs. You'll usually see it measured in *ms* (for *milliseconds*), as in "the drive has an access time of 300ms." Lower numbers are better/faster. Access time is discussed in Chapter 4.

Interface   In CD-ROM-to-computer terms, it's how information is passed back and forth (through a SCSI card and cable, or other interface). What kind of interface does the drive you are considering have? SCSI and other interfaces are covered in Chapter 15.

MPC   Multimedia Personal Computer. In order to claim the name (and wear the MPC logo), multimedia products (CD-ROM discs, drives, or whole computer systems) must adhere to the MPC standard set down by the Multimedia PC Marketing Council. MPC 1 is the older standard. MPC 2 is the most current. The MPC standard is covered in Chapter 5.

Transfer rate   How quickly a CD-ROM drive can move information from a disc to your computer. It is measured in *KB/sec*, for *kilobytes per second*. Higher numbers are better. Transfer rates are covered in Chapter 4.

Internal/External   Refers to where the CD-ROM drive will actually go in your system. Internal drives are installed inside your computer. External drives sit on your desk outside of your computer. Deciding between internal and external drives is discussed in Chapters 3 and 12.

X-rating   CD-ROM speed babble is often babbled in an abbreviated form: 1X, 2X, 3X, up to 6X for some drives. The higher the number, the faster the drive - and faster is better. Chapter 4 has more details.

The COMPLETE IDIOT'S GUIDE TO CD-ROM, Second Edition

by John Pivovarnick

que

A Division of Macmillan Publishing
A Prentice Hall Macmillan Company
201 W. 103rd Street, Indianapolis, IN 46290

This book remains dedicated to the memory of Langston Earley (1953–1993), devoted partner, friend, source of inspiration, and a glorious toy-brain in his own right.

International Standard Book Number:1-56761-606-2
Library of Congress Catalog Card Number: 94-73564

97 96 95—8 7 6 5 4 3 2 1

Interpretation of the printing code: the rightmost number of the first series of numbers is the year of the book's printing; the rightmost number of the second series of numbers is the number of the book's printing. For example, a printing code of 95-1 shows that the first printing of the book occurred in 1995.

Screen reproductions in this book were created by means of the program Collage Complete from Inner Media, Inc., Hollis, NH.

Printed in the United States of America

Publisher
Roland Elgey

Vice President and Publisher
Marie Butler-Knight

Editorial Services Director
Elizabeth Keaffaber

Publishing Manager
Barry Pruett

Managing Editor
Michael Cunningham

Development Editor
Heather Stith

Technical Editor
Wayne Blankenbeckler

Production Editor
Mark Enochs

Copy Editor
Anne Owen

Cover Designer
Scott Cook

Designer
Barbara Webster

Illustrations
Judd Winick

Indexer
Carol Sheehan

Production Team
Steve Adams
Claudia Bell
Chad Dressler
DiMonique Ford
Karen Gregor
John Hulse
Erika Millen
Kaylene Riemen
Christine Tyner
Robert Wolf
Jody York

Contents at a Glance

Contents

Introduction

Oh, it's a cliche-riddled day today. Trying to figure out how to introduce the *second* edition of this book keeps corny thoughts like, "The more things change, the more they stay the same," and, "What goes around, comes around" zipping through my brain.

The More Things Change...

In the year-and-a-bit since I wrote the first edition, things have changed: CD-ROM drives are more popular and come built-in with more computer models; the drives themselves have improved, giving us faster and cheaper drives; and CD-based software has exploded as a market, giving us more and better products to choose from. Hey, even some of my predictions for the future have come true—you actually *can* buy a CD-ROM drive as an option for a laptop computer.

For all that, though, things haven't really changed *that* much. It's still puzzling to decide which drive is best for you. The different system requirements of the various CD-ROM products can still be baffling (even to so-called "professional computer geeks" like myself). Nobody's come up with one sure-fire system that will work easily for everyone.

If you're coming at this fresh, with no exposure to CD-ROM and buzzwords like "multimedia" and "interactive," none of that will make much sense. Don't worry, it will.

If you're coming to this book after reading the first edition—maybe you were lured by the promise of that shiny CD that's glued in the back—thanks for coming back. I'll try to make it worth your while.

Let's get down to basics.

CD-ROM Technology

CD-ROM is an acronym for *Compact Disc Read-Only Memory*. It's an amazing bit of technology. They are kissing-cousins to the music CDs that have turned the term "record store" into an anachronism. In a similar vein, they're revolutionizing the computer industry.

Where once they were clunky, slow, outrageously expensive buggers, CD-ROM drives for computers have become more reliable, faster, and less expensive. That combined with the recent explosion in CD-based software have made CD-ROM products one of the fastest growing segments of the computer market.

Besides all that, they're sooooo cool: animation, photo-realistic images, honest-to-goodness movies on your monitor, and huge elaborate games. The toy-brain in me is fascinated by the possibilities.

How About You?

Something about CD-ROM must be appealing to you or you wouldn't be poking your nose in here of all places. Perhaps you have children, and you want them to benefit from the huge (and hugely entertaining) library of educational games and resources available on CD-ROM. Perhaps you're a kid at heart yourself, and you want to take advantage of all the wild and wonderful games that have come out on CD, or huge reference libraries that fit on one CD. Perhaps you've got a business interest in them: There are huge collections of graphics, fonts, and software available to boost your productivity and put pizzazz in your own multimedia presentations—or All of the Above.

For whatever reason, your fancy's been tickled, and you're looking for help getting started. Well, here it is.

How This Book Will Help

The Complete Idiot's Guide to CD-ROM pretty much says it all. Whether you own (or plan to buy) a DOS-based computer or a Macintosh, this book will:

➤ Explain (as clearly as possible) everything you need to know about CD-ROM.

➤ Walk you through the process of selecting a drive while making sure you get all the goodies you need to use it.

➤ Give you tips on buying the drive after you've chosen it.

➤ Hold your hand while you set the drive up and get ready to run with it.

➤ Give you ideas on what to do with it after you've gotten it up and running.

How to Use This Book

I've broken everything down chronologically, that is, in the order you should do them. You can easily pick up wherever you are in the process of acquiring a CD-ROM drive.

Part 1 is all about CD-ROM drives, what they are, what they do, and what hardware you need to run one. It includes information on features of popular drives and all the doo-hickeys you need to hook one up to your computer. This is the section with shopping lists and buying tips. If you haven't purchased your drive yet, start here.

Part 2 is all about setting up, installing, and running your new drive. There are generic installation and troubleshooting tips for Macintosh, Windows, and DOS-based computers. There's also a chapter devoted to general CD-ROM basics, like turning it on, inserting a disc, finding stuff on a disc, and so on. Read the general information plus the information for your particular kind of computer.

Part 3 is all about the things you can do with your new drive. Even though you may have purchased it with only one specific goal in mind (like a child's education), the variety of CD-ROM discs available jumps by leaps and bounds every day. You may be surprised at all the other stuff you can do with your drive. Everybody should read Part 3.

Part 4 is all snips and snails and puppy dog tails—useful information that didn't quite fit in anywhere else in the book. There are maintenance tips, troubleshooting tips, and everything you need to know about the CD that's glued inside the back cover. Everybody should read this part, too.

Geekazoid Stuff You May Ignore

As if actually expecting you to learn things wasn't bad enough, I'm also going to give you the opportunity to learn *more* stuff that goes above and beyond the call of duty. None of the "geekazoid" stuff is absolutely, positively essential. The world will still spin on its axis, and the sun will rise and set, but it could make using your CD-ROM drive a little easier and maybe even more fun. If you're interested, you'll find this kind of information in boxes like these:

These will explain some of the more technical things about computers and CD-ROMs. You'll find some behind-the-scenes information about the working of CDs and their software presented in a painless way. It may interest you, and it may not. If it does interest you, you may be a potential byte-head.

You can feel free to ignore any or all of these that you care to. They're in boxes and set off to one side so you can easily spot them and easily ignore them if you choose. I would suggest, however, that you read them *some* of the time.

The definitions will help you make a little more sense of what you're reading. All of the definitions, plus a few extras, are conveniently concatenated (guess who got a thesaurus for Christmas?) in the big glossary at the back.

If you're completely intimidated by technological babbling, the Techno-type boxes may give you a headache. Or, they may not. Try reading a few of them, and if they catch your attention, that's cool. Keep reading them. If not now, well, maybe someday.

Byte-head An adjective used to describe some-one fascinated by the technical details of computing. Byte-heads think nothing of popping the hoods on their computers and fiddling with the innards just to see what will happen. Also known as **tweaks**.

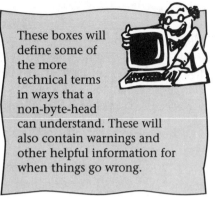 These boxes will define some of the more technical terms in ways that a non-byte-head can understand. These will also contain warnings and other helpful information for when things go wrong.

Acknowledgments

Nobody writes a book in a vacuum (some of us don't even vacuum). I'd like to take a paragraph or two to acknowledge and thank the people who made the work possible:

The usual suspects: my families (both immediate and extended); the crew at Alpha Books (now part of Que—and my head is *still* spinning) who keep me busy and *try* to keep me in line; and especially Faithe Wempen who has reorganized herself into a freelance career— best of luck! Thanks also to Cari Skaggs for mastering the CD.

My thanks to the hardware and software companies who graciously provided evaluation copies of their goodies so I could babble about them.

More thanks to the readers of the first edition whose comments and questions are mainly responsible for the shape of the second edition. New comments and questions can be mailed care of the publisher or e-mailed to **piv@aol.com**.

Very special thanks to the programmers who have kindly consented to share the software and fonts you'll find on the CD at the back of the book.

Extra special thanks to T. Greenfield and Teresa Fallon who created the never-before-seen works of art for that same disc. Thanks for taking it to a new medium as gracefully as you did.

I'm starting to gush. I'll stop.

Trademarks

While on the subject of companies, this book, probably more than any of my other books, mentions a lot of trademarks, service marks, and all sorts of other marks. They denote property and services that belong to people, companies, and legal entities other than myself. Wherever I knew that a product or service mentioned is registered to someone else, I've indicated it by the proper capitalization (as in Apple Computer or IBM).

Even if I screwed up and missed some, everybody retains everything, all rights associated with their names, and I get *bubkes* (Yiddish for "nothing"). I say this to spare myself and the typesetters the hassle of slapping © and ® and ™ notices on every occurrence of names that are somebody else's property, and to keep myself from getting sued.

The application CD Menu V1.3.1 is copyright © 1995 by Henrik Eliasson. It is distributed here by permission of the author.

The application CD Wizzard 3.07 is copyright © 1995 by BFM Software. It is distributed here by permission of the author.

The Christmas Clip Art is copyright © 1995 by Teresa Fallon. It is distributed here by permission of the artist.

The extension Color Tracks is copyright © 1995 by Andy Schafer. It is distributed here by permission of the author.

The application EasyPlay 2.0 is copyright © 1993 by Leptonic Systems Co. It is distributed here by permission of the author.

Large Clip Art is copyright © 1995 by T. Greenfield. It is distributed here by permission of the artist.

MSREC V3.1 is copyright © 1995 by David Mullen. It is distributed here by permission of the author.

PhotoCD Images is copyright © 1995 by T. Greenfield. It is distributed here by permission of the artist.

The application UltraRecorder v2.1 is copyright © 1995 by EJ Enterprises. It is distributed here by permission of the author.

Part 1
License to Shop

James Bond may have his license to kill. Walt Whitman may have his poetic license. Most 16-year-olds may have a license to drive. To any computer junkie worth his or her salt, the most impressive license is the license to shop.

I've consistently maintained that shopping well (for technology or anything else) is half the battle, and, I'm sorry to say, shopping well means doing your home-work before you hit the streets with that credit card burning a hole in your pocket. That way you won't create a three-card pileup in the checkout line. To avoid that tragedy, Part 1 will:

➤ *Explain CD-ROM drives: what they do and how they work.*

➤ *Look at some features to consider before you buy.*

➤ *List accessories, including what you need for setup.*

Chapter 1

The Least You Need to Know

Actually, I prefer to think of this as *Lifestyles of the Terminally Impatient*. I just know that somewhere out there, there's a clutch of folks flipping through pages saying, "Who gives a rat's hindquarters about all this? I just want to play games. Is that so wrong?" Far be it from me to be judgmental—so, no. It's not so wrong.

Because you may be of the "hurry up I've got places to go and games to play" mindset, this chapter is a quick summary of everything you need to get yourself up and running with basic, run-of-the-mill multimedia CD-ROM discs. You can sweat the advanced theory and practice stuff later, if you care to, because it's liberally cross-referenced to the rest of the book.

No fair letting your eyes glaze over at unfamiliar terms and concepts. Here goes!

1. Multimedia Is...

Nowadays, *multimedia* has become a big ol' hefty juggernaut of a buzzword. Every time you open a computer magazine, it's "multimedia" this and "multimedia" that. They all use the "M" word differently and mean different things (rendering the word meaningless, if you ask me). There are multimedia computers, encyclopedias, presentations, and games. A touch-screen tour in your favorite museum (like Philadelphia's Franklin Institute, my own personal favorite) is multimedia.

Just so you know: When I use the "M" word, I mean the mixing of several different presentation media (photos, sound, text, and so on) into a single project. I don't care what the end product is or what it's for—it's still multimedia to me. Maybe that's simplistic, but this is the *least* you need to know. All of Part 1 is salted with references to multimedia, the strain it can put on your computer, and what's necessary to keep it from spraining your computer.

2. The Least You Need to Have...

In theory, all you really need to plunge into the world of multimedia CD-ROM is a computer, a CD-ROM drive that works with that computer, some multimedia CD software, and maybe a sound card with speakers. That's it. In practice, however, there's a little more to it.

For any type of multimedia work, you need a pretty spunky computer. For PCs, that means at least a 286 machine with at least 10MHz of clock speed, a minimum of 2MB of RAM (4MB if you're running Windows), a VGA card and monitor (640 × 480 resolution) that can display at least 16 colors, and a hard drive with a decent amount of room left on it (10 to 20MB is decent). To be at all comfortable, plan on a 386 or 486 with a 25MHz clock speed (at least), with 4MB or more of RAM and a Super VGA card and monitor. To be compatible with the current "multimedia personal computer" (MPC) standard, you'll need more of *everything* (see below).

For a Macintosh, "spunky" means a Mac or Performa with an 68030 or better processor, with 4MB of RAM (8MB or more if you're running System 7.5 or using a Power Mac), a 13-inch color monitor capable of displaying 256 colors, and a hard drive with some room left on it (at least 10MB). You'll also need to add an appropriate CD-ROM drive.

These, however, are *bare* minimums. Chapters 4, 5, and 6 spell out the hardware that will give you "cutting edge" performance.

3. Speaking of the CD-ROM Drive...

For the CD-ROM drive itself, you'll want one as fast as you can get in three specific areas: spin rate, access time, and throughput rate. (All this speed stuff is covered in depth in Chapter 4.)

If you can afford it, you should try to get a drive that spins at least at two speeds—a double-speed drive. It should also have a short access time (300ms or less) and a high transfer rate (300K per second or higher). Triple- and quad-speed drives will give you better performance. Chapter 4 explains all of these speed terms (ms, K/S, and so on).

Speeding up your computer and drive will smooth out the presentation of dynamic data (stuff that changes over time, like video, animation, and sound). It will also keep you from hanging around and twiddling your thumbs while CD-based applications start up or load the next part of a game (or whatever).

Don't forget to read the fine print, either. If you buy CD-ROM software while you're purchasing your new drive, make sure it'll work with both your computer and your new drive. Like any other software, the CD-ROM variety comes with a label that gives you system requirements for using it. Read it closely; make sure your system at least meets the minimum requirements. If it doesn't, or if you aren't sure, skip that CD-ROM title for now. You can always get it later.

Trust me on this: There is nothing more frustrating, irritating, @#$!%@-making than getting an expensive disc of CD software home, only to find that it won't run (or won't run properly) on your system. Chapter 10 talks about the fine print in more detail.

4. MPC = Mighty Pricey Computer?

Actually, no. *MPC* stands for *Multimedia Personal Computer*. It applies only to IBM-compatible machines running Windows. There are certain minimum standards that a computer system has to meet before it can be certified "MPC-compatible." The most recent MPC standard is MPC2. Here's what's necessary to have an MPC2-compatible system:

➤ A 386SX-based PC or higher

➤ Minimum 16MHz clock speed

➤ 4MB of main memory (RAM) configured as extended memory

➤ 30MB hard drive (more is better)

➤ 1.44MB, 3.5-inch, high-density floppy drive

➤ VGA card and monitor with a resolution of 640×480 pixels, 256 colors, or 800×600 resolution at 16 colors

➤ Two-button mouse

➤ Analog joystick port (IBM-compatible)

➤ MIDI port

➤ MPC-compatible sound card

➤ MPC-compatible CD-ROM drive

➤ System software compatible with Microsoft Windows 3.1 (or 3.0 with Multimedia Extension)

5

These are the minimum requirements for your computer to be considered an MPC machine. I think you can, and should, exceed this standard if you can afford it. Chapter 5 explains it all for you.

5. Multimedia Upgrade Kits May (or May Not) Be the Best Choice.

When flipping through your favorite mail-order catalog (or wandering your favorite computer store), you'll see a lot of CD-ROM bundles called *Multimedia Upgrade Kits*. The name is misleading. (You can read my full take on buying bundles in Chapter 9.)

Generally speaking, these upgrade kits (either for PCs or Macs) will give you everything you need to connect a CD-ROM drive to your system, plus a couple of extras (often speakers, headphones, and/or a couple of CD-ROM discs).

What these kits *don't* do is anything about raising your computer to a level powerful enough to deal with multimedia CD-ROM discs. If you have a "slow-ish" computer, installing a multimedia upgrade kit will give you a "slow-ish" computer with a CD-ROM drive attached. In addition to buying one of these so-called upgrade kits, you may still need (and/or want) to invest in some actual system upgrades. Check out some of the system information in Chapter 5 before you decide.

6. You Might Want Some Extra "Doo-Dads" and "Thingamies."

Heads up—you might want to consider some other odds and ends to make your gaming experience the thrashing sensory overload you crave:

➤ Amplified speakers so you can blast sound effects and game music to head-banging levels.

➤ Headphones so you can blast sound effects and game music to head-banging levels without getting your head banged by your parents, spouse, roommate(s), or neighbors.

➤ A joystick or other game controller or an assortment of controllers if you have wide-ranging taste in games. Check out Chapters 7 and 8 for more details.

7. CD-ROM is Easy(ish).

I'll tell you right up front: The most difficult thing about hooking up a CD-ROM drive to your computer will be hooking up the CD-ROM drive to your computer. (Is that a Zen statement, or what?)

To be politically correct, I guess I should say "simplicity-impaired" rather than "difficult." There are two areas where the simplicity of connecting the drive is impaired: dealing with the SCSI (or other) interface and getting your computer (particularly an IBM-compatible) to recognize and access the drive. *SCSI*, if you're wondering, is one of several ways to hook up a CD-ROM drive to your computer. After that, it's all skittles and beer.

Fortunately, I made all the gaffes and goof-ups for you (and how!). There's a chapter (Chapter 13) dedicated to hooking up a drive to your PC. There's another chapter (Chapter 14) devoted to connecting a drive to your Macintosh. There's even a third chapter (Chapter 15) that walks you through a short primer of SCSI and other connections.

Additionally, Chapter 30 focuses on resolving any problems that crop up that aren't covered in the official list of "chapters."

The long and short of it: Even though getting your CD-ROM drive up and running involves a couple of simplicity-impaired tasks, there's just gobs of information handy—and I'll be here to hold your hand through the entire process with tips, tricks, and soothing words (*shhh, there-there*). Don't panic.

8. Does It Play Well with Others?

There's a bewildering assortment of standard claims made about CD-ROM drives in ads and magazine reviews. Stuff like QuickTime compatibility, PhotoCD compatibility, Audio-CD compatibility, and other, equally oblique terms.

Since ads are designed to make you want to buy stuff, they make everything sound important. Depending on what you want to do (or be able to do down the road), some will be more important than others to you. You don't want to pay for stuff you're never going to use, but you also don't want to buy a drive only to find out it *can't* do something you really need it to do.

All of Part 1 spells out what all that advertising double-speak means and puts it into perspective for you before you shell out money for a drive.

9. The Price Is Right.

Bob Barker notwithstanding, the price is only right if you can afford it and if the drive you can afford does all of the things you need it to do, and some of the things you'd like it to do.

It's always difficult to weigh the practical considerations of price versus performance when buying a techno-toy (it is for me, anyway—but I'm a toy-brain). Chapter 10 walks you through the selection process and even gives you a handy-dandy shopping list so you won't forget anything you need.

Because I'm a cheapskate at heart, Chapter 11 is chock-full of shopping tips to help you get the most for your money, as well as ways to protect yourself and your investment.

10. Keep It Clean.

Even more than most computer junk, CD-ROM drives can get very wheezy and sneezy and grumpy when bombarded by dust and other airborne crud (like cigarette smoke and pet hair).

Once you select, buy, and set up your new drive, some easy maintenance practices will help you make sure it stays up and running. These can be as simple as handling the discs properly (by the edges, thank you very much), using covered storage boxes, and cleaning the discs properly if they do get all cruddy. You don't have to be Heloise to keep it clean, and in the process, to keep your drive (and you) very happy. Just read Chapter 29.

Chapter 2

What Is a CD-ROM, and Why Do I Want One?

In This Chapter

➤ CD-ROMs explained

➤ Discs detailed

➤ What CD-ROMs are good for

Do you need a CD-ROM?

That's a question you should ask yourself before you run off to your friendly, neighborhood computer superstore to buy one. If you can't say why (or if) you need it, or what you want to be able to do with it, you probably don't need it. Instead, you *want* it. Most likely because you're suffering from a good, old-fashioned case of Weenie Envy.

Not *that* Weenie Envy, Dr. Freud—the other one.

I'm talking about the envy you feel when the biggest techno-weenie on your block (or in your school, or at work) starts bragging about his spiffy new techno-toy. You feel jealous, so now you have to get one, too—only bigger. So there, *nyah*.

That's not a good frame of mind to go shopping in—you wouldn't go grocery shopping while hungry, would you? And if you have done that, do you remember how big the grocery bill was? The same thing happens when you go computer-stuff shopping, only the bill can be much, *much* bigger.

There are plenty of other ways to justify the purchase of a CD-ROM drive (even if the real reason is Weenie Envy), but you have to know what you're talking about. I can't tell you why you want one; the Amazing Kreskin I'm not, but here are a few of the more legitimate reasons for wanting a CD-ROM drive:

> ➤ You have younger children. Most of the best stuff on CD (educational games, mainly) is for kids.

> ➤ You have (or are) a student. There's a lot of educational and reference material on CD for students of all ages.

> ➤ You're a graphic artist. Not only can you get stock photographs, fonts, and clip art galore on CD, but many of the popular graphics programs (Photoshop, Adobe Illustrator) come on or with CD accessories.

> ➤ You're a game addict. CD-ROM games have the coolest graphics, most complex plots, and wildest special effects.

You may be able to find other justifications by skimming through Part 3, which has a round-up and review of the major categories of CD-ROM software.

Disk/Disc
Two different spellings of the same word. When you see it spelled **disk**, it refers to a computer floppy disk. When you see it spelled **disc**, it refers to a compact disc (CD), which can be either the audio kind (a music CD) or the computer kind (a CD-ROM). Some folks don't make the distinction at all—go figure.

So, What Is a CD-ROM?

CD-ROM stands for *Compact Disc Read-Only Memory*. (Aren't you glad we can just call it CD-ROM?) In really big, broad, general terms, a CD-ROM drive is a lot like your computer's floppy drive: a disc gets popped in; the mechanism spins the disk at high speed (more about the importance of speed in Chapter 4), and then reads the data from the disk; the data gets funnelled to your computer so the machine can make use of it.

How a Regular Disk Drive Works

Before you can compare a CD-ROM drive to a regular drive, you need to know how that regular disk drive works. Here goes:

When a regular floppy drive reads data from a disk, it reads magnetically stored information. The read/write head (kind of like the arm on an old-fashioned stereo turn-table) trundles over the surface of the spinning disk, determining whether or not there's a magnetic charge where it's looking.

The sequence of "charge/no-charge/charge" (or whatever) is sent to the computer as ones (charge) and zeroes (no charge). Each of these zeroes and ones is called a *bit* of information.

A bit is the smallest amount of information a computer can deal with. Bits get sent to your computer in eight-packs, called a byte. Those zeroes and ones are the language of computers (called *binary*), where everything is said in combinations of zero and one.

Bit The basis of how all computer storage is measured, not just storage on a regular diskette. There are eight bits in a byte. A thousand bytes is a kilobyte (abbreviated K or KB). A million bytes is a megabyte (MB). A billion bytes is a gigabyte (GB).

Storage Capacity

Your average floppy disks hold between 360K and 1.4MB, depending on what kind of disks they are. A CD-ROM disc can hold more than 600MB (wow!). If you really want to sound like you know what you're talking about, say "six hundred meg" instead of "six hundred megabytes," and never say the initials "MB."

How a CD-ROM Drive Works: It's the Pits

When a CD-ROM drive reads a disc, it's actually reading a series of microscopic pits scored into the metal wafer inside the CD's plastic coating. The pits and smooth areas behave like the magnetic charges on a floppy disk.

Instead of a read/write head, a laser beam is fired at the surface. When the beam strikes a smooth spot, the laser light is beamed back and registers a "zero." If the light hits a pit, the light scatters: that registers as a "one."

Because lasers are used to inscribe the pits (and later to read them), the pits can be more precisely placed and, therefore, can be packed much more closely together. That's how they can fit over 600MB of information on a CD-ROM disc only 4.5 inches in diameter.

What CD-ROMs Can Do for You

Because CD-ROM discs can handle such huge amounts of data, they're ideal for big, cumbersome files that would be impossible to handle on other storage media. If you wanted to copy a 600MB CD onto high-density (1.4MB) floppy disks, it would take over 425 of those bad boys to copy the information from one CD-ROM.

That high capacity makes it possible for software companies to produce huge, complex games, vast databases of information, and libraries of books or photo-quality images on a single disc. What that does for you is give you access to all the photos, fun, and information you could possibly need—in a (proportionally speaking) teeny-tiny amount of space.

We'll talk a lot about the various kinds of stuff you can find on CD in Part 3, but just to make a point, consider the following:

The Los Angeles telephone directory is about four inches thick, and it weighs about seven pounds. Add the Manhattan, Chicago, and Philadelphia phone books to that one, and you've got about 30 pounds' worth of phone numbers. If there were such a thing, you could fit a national phone book on a few dozen CD-ROM discs—that includes phone numbers for practically everybody.

Which would you rather keep around for easy reference? 'Nuff said.

(By the way, even if there isn't a complete national phone book, one company has come pretty darned close to it: PhoneDisc. Some of their products are covered in Part 3.)

The Least You Need to Know

➤ Generally speaking, CD-ROM drives work in a way comparable to regular floppy drives, except you can't write your own files to them.

➤ The BIG difference between CD-ROM and floppy disks is that floppies store data magnetically (with magnetic charges), and CDs store data by physically etching digital data into the medium (a pit means "one," and a smooth area means "zero").

➤ The laser's precision in packing all that information into a small space lets you store over 600MB of data on a single CD.

➤ 600MB is a lot of information—more information than you could eat with a spoon.

Chapter 3

Different Drives for Different Folks

The very first step in deciding which CD-ROM drive is right for you is figuring out what your choices are and which of those will suit your needs. The next couple of chapters will talk about all the different things you should consider when you're choosing a CD-ROM drive.

This chapter looks at the broad differences between machines. The next chapter explains the potentially confusing but important speed factors that will affect your drive's performance (and price). Chapter 5 looks at a variety of compatibility issues you need to think about.

Don't worry. It isn't as painful as it sounds.

Readin'

Probably (at this point) the most common kind of CD-ROM drive you see in stores, magazines, and catalogs are *CD-ROM readers*. Until not too long ago, there were only CD-ROM readers. They are the drives that earned the name *ROM (Read-Only Memory)* because all these bad boys can do is read the enormous amounts of data from a CD-ROM disk into your computer's memory.

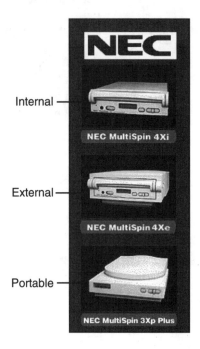

Internal — NEC MultiSpin 4Xi

External — NEC MultiSpin 4Xe

Portable — NEC MultiSpin 3Xp Plus

An assortment of typical-looking CD-ROM readers—these are from NEC.

Reading and Recording

Drives that can write to a CD are called **CD-WO** (for **write once**) or **CD-R** (for **recordable**). Some are even (confusingly) called **CD-ROM recordable drives**. We'll talk about recordable CD drives in a minute. For now, just know that they aren't for average users like you and me—so when I talk about "CD-ROM drives," I mean the more run-of-the-mill "readers" that most of us will be using. If I mean the more advanced and expensive recordable drives, I'll say so.

If you play around with any of the information stored on the CD-ROM (if you alter a photographic image, for example), you can't save the changed file back to the compact disc. Readers only work in one direction: from the disc to your computer. If you want to save any changes, you have to save them to your hard drive or onto floppy disks.

Additionally, the wide variety of drives available can give you as few or as many of the bells and whistles available that you care to have. Most CD-ROM drives also play audio CDs—a bonus for you if you enjoy listening to music while you work at your computer, as I do. (Right now, it's Joni Mitchell's *Turbulent Indigo*—great background music for writing.)

Memory
The amount of **RAM**, or **Random Access Memory**, your computer has. It's the amount of space your computer has to "remember" the program(s) you're working with, as well as the file(s) you're working on. Don't confuse memory (that is, RAM) with storage space—hard drives and floppy disks are not memory.

CD-ROM readers are ideal for people who want to make use of the huge variety of software available on CDs (see Part 3 for a roundup of CD software categories) but don't want to spend an enormous amount of money to do it. CD-ROM readers range in price from as little as $100 to over $500.

Lately, it seems, every electronics and computer company on the planet is releasing their own line of CD-ROM readers. Competition is getting stiff as more and more companies try to cut themselves a slice of the CD-pie. For you and me, that's a good thing and a bad thing, all at the same time.

On one hand, you can bet that once the market fills up with similarly featured CD-ROM drives, pricing wars will begin, and prices will drop even lower. On the other hand, every Tom, Dick, and Harry is trying to cash in on the CD-ROM craze. That means you have more drives to choose from, but also that you have to know exactly what you want and need from a drive before you buy one—otherwise, you could get stuck with a lemon.

The Price War Cycle

Here's how this price-war routine usually runs: Everybody jumps on a techno-logical bandwagon—in this case, CD-ROM—at the current premium price. As machines become equivalent in features and performance, the only selling point left is price. So prices drop.

Soon, some smarty-pants company introduces a more advanced model (for CD-ROM drives, that means it reads faster). Buyers flock to the new, improved, and more expensive gadget. Prices on the older gadgets drop further while companies scramble around trying to make their own versions of the new, advanced (and more expensive) thingy. Then it starts all over again.

Writin'

The other broad class of CD drives are called *recordable drives*. These are the ones abbrevi-ated CD-WO (write once), CD-R (recordable), and such.

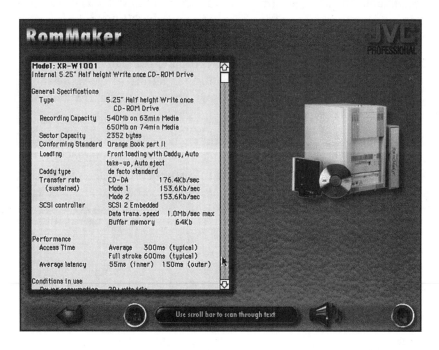

A recordable CD setup, from JVC.

The big difference, if you haven't guessed, is that a recordable drive can record (that is, write) information to a blank compact disc in much the same way your computer writes to a floppy disk. This is a great boon for folks who create big multimedia presentations; they can save their 600MB, "I'm ready for my close-up Mr. DeMille" productions onto one disc for easy transportation. It's better than having to lug huge hard drives or a mountain of floppy disks around when the show has to go on the road.

Special CDs

Recordable drives write to special CDs that contain a layer of dye instead of the metal platter at the heart of ordinary CDs. The laser creates the pits and smooth areas (covered in Chapter 2) in the dye. These discs can then be used as originals, or master discs, for duplication or production of regular CD-ROM discs.

It's also a boon to the folks who create CD-ROM software. After working out all the details of their productions, they can save everything to one CD for testing and reproduction.

As the "Write Once" implies, however, you can only write to a compact disc once. If any problems turn up, you have to chuck the old CD, fix the problem on your hard drive, then copy the whole shmear to a new, blank CD.

Recordable drives are not for the casual user, however. Adding the capability of writing to a CD doesn't come cheaply. We're talking thousands of dollars' worth of "not cheap." For the JVC Personal RomMaker system (shown in the figure at the beginning of this section), for example, current prices start in the $2,000 range—which is roughly half the price quoted in the first edition of this book.

If the prices keep dropping, there's hope that recordable drives may become at least approachable for us common users who want to set themselves up as homespun multimedia moguls.

In-ies and Out-ies

Once you've decided between a reader or a recordable drive (my checkbook is choking on the implication that there's a choice), your next decision is where to put the bloody thing. Again, you have two basic choices: *internal* and *external* (are you getting the belly-button analogy here?).

In-ies

Internal CD-ROM drives, like internal floppy drives, are installed inside your computer's main casing; just the face pokes out (so you can twiddle the controls and insert discs).

The main attraction of internal drives is twofold. First, they don't take up any additional desk space, which is nice if you work in a cramped (or, as in my case, big-but-sloppy) work environment.

Second, they tend to be a little less expensive (by about $25–$75) than the same CD-ROM drive in an external configuration. You don't pay extra for a pretty and protective case because all you see is the face-plate when it's installed.

The main disadvantage to an internal drive is installation: It can be a bit intimidating to someone who's not comfortable poking around in the guts of his or her computer. However, parts of Chapters 13 (IBM-compatibles) and 14 (Macs) are devoted to internal installations for the timid among us. If you're brave enough to try, I'll be here to hold your hand through the process.

Also, once you install the CD-ROM in your computer, if you want to use the drive in another location, you'll need to haul your whole computer along—or you'll have to remove the drive and reinstall it at the new site. Neither is a lot of fun.

Before you decide to go for an internal CD-ROM drive, you should ask yourself a few questions:

➤ Will an internal drive fit in my computer? Is the actual case big enough to hold one? (If yes, you can ask yourself the next question. If no, you've got no choice: get an external CD-ROM drive.)

Expansion bay
An open area inside and (usually) at the front of a computer so you can add internal hardware (such as CD-ROM or floppy drives) to your system. They also (usually) have a support framework built in so the new hardware can be secured inside the bay. They're also referred to as *drive bays*.

➤ Do I have an open expansion bay? Are the innards of your computer sporting the full complement of floppy and/or hard drives, or do you have the actual room to install another internal device? (If yes, you can ask yourself the next question. If no, you've got no choice: get an external CD-ROM drive.)

➤ This one is for IBM-compatible users only—the question doesn't apply to Macs (you'll see why in Chapters 6 and 7). If I have the expansion *bay*, do I have at least one (possibly two, depending on the drive you select) expansion *slots* available for the required controller and/or sound cards? (If yes, carry on. If no, you're system won't be able to handle a CD-ROM drive unless you've already got a SCSI controller card installed for something else.)

➤ If I have the bay and slot(s) available to install an internal drive, do I have an additional plug from my computer's power supply (a power-supply feed) to power an internal drive? Check your computer's manual or pop the hood and look. (If yes, you may continue; if no, you'll need to get an external unit or upgrade your computer's power supply.)

➤ Do I want to be able to use the CD-ROM in more than one location? (If no, you can ask yourself the next question. If yes, get an external CD-ROM drive—and you should probably think "portable.")

> **Expansion card**
> An expansion card is a printed circuit board that, when added to your computer, "expands" its capabilities. Expansion cards fit in expansion slots, also inside your computer.

➤ Do I want to deal with the installation or the cost of having it done for me? (If yes, you can skip the next section and move on to Chapter 4. If no, you should read the next section closely.)

Out-ies

An *external CD-ROM drive* will sit on your desk, close to your computer. That's the main drawback: they take up space. Depending on the size, shape, and how you insert a CD, you may be able to stack it—under your monitor or with an external hard drive—in order to conserve your desk's valuable real estate.

> **PhotoCDs**
> Kodak Photo-CD is the new way to get your photographs developed. When you turn in your roll of film, you get the images on a CD-ROM disc instead of getting a stack of prints back. (We'll talk about PhotoCDs again in Chapter 5.)

Some external CD-ROM drives are purely desktop models, meant to stay on your desk. They aren't really designed for traveling (but you can lug them around if you so choose). Others are designed to be portable. They're smaller and lighter; some can run on optional battery packs, and most offer some extra connection options for working on-the-go. Portable CD-ROM drives offer a variety of features you should weigh (against the price and your needs). Some work with both Macs and PCs that run Windows if you work in a multi-computer environment. Some will connect to your stereo for playing audio CDs, or your television to view Kodak PhotoCDs on any television set. Some also come with a remote control, which makes it an excellent choice for mobile-presentation work.

There are trade-offs, however. Portable CD-ROM drives tend to be slower than the desktop models. (Read more about the importance of the drive's speed in the next chapter.)

So Who Needs What?

I'm so glad you asked. The average computer user (with an average budget) will probably be satisfied with a CD-ROM reader. Unless you really need one and can afford one, leave the recordable drives to the CD professionals—kids, don't try this at home.

The choice of internal or external will really be decided by your system configuration (do you have room to install an internal drive?) and your needs (do you need to use the drive at multiple locations or on multiple systems?).

If you opt for an external drive, you need to decide if you need a portable (at the sacrifice of some speed). You don't need one if you'll be able to leave the drive connected to one system, in one place. Alternatively, you might need the CD-ROM as a computer drive only occasionally—in which case, a multi-use portable might be just the ticket.

Only you can answer these questions. Better take notes. They'll come in handy when we start to work up a shopping list.

The Least You Need to Know

➤ CD-ROM readers are drives that work in only one direction: They read data from a disc and send it to your computer.

➤ Recordable drives work in both directions: They can read discs but can also write (once) to special blank CDs.

➤ Internal drives go inside your computer's housing. You need to have enough room inside to install one, and you need an extra lead from your computer's power supply.

➤ External drives sit on your desk near your computer. They can be bigger machines meant to stay in one spot, or smaller, lighter machines made to transport easily.

Chapter 4

The Speed's the Thing

In This Chapter

➤ XXX: it's not just for dirty movies anymore

➤ Access time

➤ Pushing it through

➤ Cache or cheque?

➤ 2 SCSI 2 Quit

No police officer is ever going to pull you over for having a CD-ROM drive that works too fast. It's not going to happen, my friend. You may, however, get pretty unsatisfactory results from a CD-ROM drive that works too slowly.

The whole issue of the drive's speed should be a big deciding factor for you when figuring out which particular drive you're going to buy. Complicating the issue are all kinds of speed terms that get bandied about in ads for CD-ROM drives, with impenetrable abbreviations and numbers that are hard to interpret. Is this drive really faster than that one, or are the numbers just too confusing?

That's the reason behind this chapter: to demystify and explain all of the speed-related gobbledygook you'll see in advertising and other promotional literature about CD-ROM drives.

X Marks the Spot

The first speed consideration is how fast the CD-ROM drive is capable of spinning the actual compact disc as it reads the data from it.

In the Beginning...

When CD-ROM drives first appeared on the scene, they were (for the most part) the same mechanism as audio CD players, with extra gewgaws added to transfer information to a computer. These first drives (the ones that earned CD-ROMs their reputation for slowness) also spun their discs at the same rate as audio CD players.

Nowadays, these original drives are snail-slow compared to the newer multi-speed drives. In ads, you'll see these one-speed ponies referred to as plain CD-ROM drives (or 1X drives), with no mention of other speeds.

The single speed was fine (if slow) as a ground-breaking invention, but computers are able (and need) to accept data much more quickly. At that basic, single speed, animation read from a CD-ROM seems choppy—less animated, if you will. Any moving image seems to play in jerky slow motion.

Theater Movies vs. CD-ROM Movies

Movies (either live-action or animated) run at a rate of 24 frames of film (individual pictures) for every second of screen time. Videotape runs still more frames per second, so even a short, one-minute-long film or animation (and we're talking real animation—like early classic Disney, not today's Saturday-morning schlock) contains 1,440 individual pictures. Even at CD-ROMs scaled down 15 frames per second, that's a lot of pictures.

All those pictures flash past your eyes and deceive you into seeing life-like motion where there is none. You can understand, then, why any delay in getting those pictures from a CD to your computer screen can result in a less-than-satisfactory video display. It blows the illusion of motion.

The bottom line: avoid single-speed drives. They're going to pass on to the technological "other side," while newer, variable-speed drives take their place.

Double Your Pleasure

The electronics giant NEC pioneered what they call *MultiSpin technology*. It allowed CD-ROM drives to spin discs at two speeds: the regular speed for audio, and twice that for data. Double-speed (or 2X) CD-ROMs smoothed out a lot of the kinks from the original drives.

22

Right now, most CD-ROM drives you'll see advertised are capable of these two speeds. They can play audio CDs (or sounds in general) at the regular rate, while transferring dynamic (moving) images and other data at a speed a little closer to what's optimum for computers.

If your budget allows, you should buy at least a double-speed drive; but even as I'm writing this, the status quo is changing yet again. Most of the CDs I tested for this edition recommend at *least* a 2X speed drive.

3X, 4X, or More X?

Just when everyone got all nice and comfy with the idea of double-speed CD-ROM drives, NEC went ahead and introduced triple- and quadruple-speed CD-ROM readers. No doubt some mad CD scientist or other is working on quintuple- or even sextuple-speed (5X and 6X) drives. (Actually, you can find 6X speed drives now, but they're expensive.)

What does that mean for you?

Well, if you need to have the latest, greatest hardware and price is no object, you should probably go for a quadruple-speed drive (unless higher speeds are available when you're ready to shop). It will give you the standard spin rate for audio discs, twice that for data, and three- or four-times that for data if (and it's a big "if") the authors of your CD software have made their disc compatible with the higher spin rate.

If you're not suffering from a case of Weenie Envy and don't have the top of the line model, a 3X drive will hold you in good stead for awhile.

A Big Ol' But...

Don't think of quad-, quint-, or some yet to be invented warp-speed capability as the be-all and end-all factor when you buy a drive. They're just labels that say the drive is capable of spinning at different speeds.

If you'll forgive a lapse into Philosophy 101: Potential is not the same as actuality. Just because it *can* go faster doesn't mean it *will*. Or, if it does spin faster, it might not necessarily be noticeable to you. There are other speed factors that can render the fastest spin rate practically useless.

In addition to the other drive performance issues (coming right up), the software on the CD has to be written to make use of the multiple speeds of the drive. Not all CD software can.

As for those other speed factors—here they come.

Access Me

It doesn't matter if a compact disc is spinning at a million miles an hour, if it takes the drive minutes or hours to find the next bit of data you need.

Millisecond (ms)
One millisecond equals one thousandth of a second.

Access time is how long it takes a CD-ROM drive to find that next bit of data. You'll usually see it measured in *ms*, as in "the drive has an access time of 300ms," for *milliseconds*. In plain English, that means this drive takes (on average) 300 thousandths of a second to locate a particular chunk of information on a CD.

A Different Theory of Relativity

Time is relative—just ask Einstein. Keep that in mind while you read through all this milli-, micro-, and nano-second jazz. 300ms sounds fast to you and me. Heck, to you and me, that *is* fast, considering how quickly individual seconds seem to pass for us mere mortals. To a computer, however, that isn't fast at all. Consider that your average hard drive has an access time of 20ms. A CD-ROM drive with a 300ms access time is 15 times slower than an average hard drive. Even if that drive were spinning along at a million miles per hour, those 300 thousandths of a second would begin to add up.

When researching or shopping for your CD-ROM drive, be sure to check the access time. If it isn't listed in the ad (even in the fine print), call up the manufacturer or mail-order company and ask—there's usually a toll-free number you can use.

Don't assume that all drives by the same manufacturer have the same access-time rating. For example (just because it was the first ad I found), there are four different models of NEC drives advertised in a mail-order catalog. The access times range from 650ms (very slow) down to 195ms (pretty spunky) for the latest model.

Don't Hurt Your Brain!

Don't get yourself into a dither over all these digits. For access time, just remember that lower numbers are faster and better for you.

Judging by the requirements of today's crop of CD-ROM software, most of them (at least the whiz-bang ones with lots of movies and photographic-quality images) recommend you use them with a drive that has an access time rating of about 300ms or faster for optimum performance.

Pushing It Through

Once your drive has accessed that next bit of data it needs to keep you informed or entertained, it has to move that data from the CD to your computer. How long that takes is called the drive's *transfer rate* or *throughput*.

When you skim an ad, you'll see the transfer rate stated in the almost-runic form: *K/S* or *KB/S*. That stands for *kilobytes per second*. You may see a drive with a stated transfer rate of 300K/S, which would mean that it can transfer 300 kilobytes of data every second.

Double- and triple-speed drives have had the biggest effect on the transfer rate. Regular audio CD players transfer their data (the music) at a rate of 150K/S. Oddly enough, so did the first CD-ROM drives.

Double-speed drives can transfer data at twice that rate, or 300K/S. Triple-speed drives, if my math serves me (hmmm—three times five, carry the one), transfer data at 450K/S, and quad-speed drives at 600K/S. You can see from the leap in the transfer rate why I warned you away from the older, single-speed drives.

As with the access time, don't assume that all drives by the same manufacturer have the same transfer rate. You have to read the fine print to compare. The same set of drives in the ad I mentioned earlier had transfer rates that ranged from 150K/S to 600K/S. They ran the gamut of currently available speeds.

Also, most of the ads weasel a little and say, "Up to (Whatever) K/S." Remember what I said earlier: Just because it can move 600K/S, that doesn't mean it will, or will all of the time. If you plan to make use of CDs that use a lot of movies, animation, or other dynamic data, the higher the transfer rate, the better.

For multimedia uses, a higher transfer rate is more important than a low access time (but too sluggish an access time will also impede the performance of multimedia discs—it's like walking a tightrope, isn't it?).

Multimedia
A big, fat juggernaut of a buzzword that gets used so many different ways, it's become almost meaningless. When I say **multimedia**, I mean software that combines several kinds of data: plain text, photographs, drawings, sounds, and other dynamic data (like animation or video clips).

Don't Hurt Your Brain II!

Unlike with access time (where lower numbers were better), all you need to remember about the transfer rate is that the higher the number, the faster and better the drive.

Because software always lunges forward to make use of the technology available, I wouldn't recommend that you buy a drive with a transfer rate less than 300K/S. If you can afford it (faster is always more expensive), I'd even go for one with a higher rate. If price is a concern, try to get the best drive you can to fit your budget.

Cache or Charge

Even with zippy access and bodacious transfer rates, the presentation of information can still seem choppy when it finally works its way to your screen. One of the ways CD-ROM drives can smooth out the presentation of data is by having a built-in *memory cache* (sometimes called a *buffer*) so the information can just charge through.

My father's secret storehouse of Oreo cookies is a cache. In computer terms, a cache is a chunk of memory set aside to hold frequently accessed data, which speeds up the operation of your system. For a CD-ROM drive, it's memory used for nothing but storing information from a disc. The information is fed to the computer from one end of the cache, while new information is fed into the cache from the disc. It smooths out the data access so there are fewer pauses in the transfer of data. These days, most CD-ROM drives come with a built-in cache. I wouldn't buy one that doesn't.

Generally, you'll see caches of 64K, 128K, or 256K. A bigger cache is better, but I wouldn't let a 64K cache stop me from buying a drive that did everything I wanted at a price I could afford. (I would, however, let a larger cache be the deciding factor between two drives that were otherwise identical. I'd get the one with the bigger cache.)

I'm Too Scuzzy for My Shirt

Many of the CD-ROM drives on the market today are *SCSI* (pronounced *scuzzy*) devices that connect to your computer through a built-in SCSI port (as in a Macintosh) or a SCSI adapter card (added to a PC).

In fact, all CD-ROM drives made for the Macintosh are SCSI devices (to make use of the Mac's built-in SCSI port). For IBM-compatibles, the field is split: you can find SCSI CD-ROM drives and drives that connect through other methods (some sound cards, an IDE controller, a parallel port, and such).

SCSI Abbreviation that stands for **Small Computer System Interface**. It's a way of connecting up to seven SCSI devices to a computer.

However, I feel that the advantages of SCSI (particularly being able to add several more SCSI devices without adding hardware) far outweigh the advantages of other methods. The disadvantages of these other methods (on the whole, they require more work and technical knowledge on your part) make them very unattractive to new users.

In short, I prefer, and recommend, SCSI CD-ROM drives to everybody. They may be a little more expensive up front, but they can save you heartache and money down the road. Currently, there are two flavors of SCSI: SCSI and SCSI II.

SCSI II was devised to make accessing today's bigger hard drives a little faster (by way of faster transfer rates). To reap the benefits of SCSI II's extra speed, you must have a SCSI II card installed in your PC or Mac, and have it connected to a SCSI II-capable device, like a hard drive.

As far as I know, right now there are only a few SCSI II CD-ROM drives. So why the heck am I bothering you with this? Well, just in case you already have a SCSI II card and device hooked up to your computer: You *can* attach a SCSI device (like a CD-ROM reader) to a SCSI II card, or SCSI chain, and still have it work. It won't work faster because of it, but it should still work.

There's an entire chapter devoted to the tacky rococo intricacies of SCSI and other connection methods—in fact, it's Chapter 15. It should contain more than you ever wanted to know on the subject.

The Least You Need to Know

When winnowing down the competitors for the CD-ROM drive of your dreams, these are the speed factors you should keep in mind:

➤ The better drives run at multiple speeds when accessing different kinds of data. You should select a drive that runs at least two speeds. If you can afford three or more speeds, go for it.

➤ The "better drives" are also more expensive—don't let anything I say here blow your budget to heck-in-a-hand-basket. These are merely recommendations. The point is to give you information so you can select the best drive you can afford.

➤ Your multiple-speed drive should have a low access time rating (preferably 300ms or faster). Lower numbers are faster.

➤ Your multiple-speed drive with the short access time should have a high transfer rate—at least 300K/S. Here, the higher the number, the faster the transfer rate.

➤ Your multi-speeding, short-accessing, fast-transferring, CD-ROMming drive should also have a built-in RAM cache. Any size cache is better than none, but the bigger the better.

NOW, YOU TWO PLAY NICE...

Chapter 5

Some Standard Standards and Other Compatibility Issues

In This Chapter

➤ Multimedia Personal Computer standards

➤ ISO standards

➤ Not Ready for QuickTime Players

➤ Alphabet City: XA, HSF, and a HFS besides

Compatability and *standard* are two words you'll see bandied about a lot in the computer press—in magazine reviews and ads, mostly. Compatibility is a fairly simple matter: will this thing work with that thing—yes or no? Standard, on the other hand, is hardly what I'd call a yes-or-no affair.

Ads and reviews of new products will say junk like, "The Whiz-Bang 4250 v1.6μ sets a new standard in cross-platform inter-operability (or some other $2 buzzword)." That isn't a standard—that's ad copy. You only have an honest-to-goodness standard when everybody gets together and says, "Eureka! This is perfect. Everyone should do it this way." And then everybody does.

There are some real standards out there. This chapter is about some of the standards you should know about, and related compatibility issues you should think about, while deciding on a CD-ROM drive for your computer.

M-P-C (See You Real Soon) K-E-Y

This section is for PC-compatible users. If you've got (or are going to get) a Macintosh, you may skip blithely ahead.

MPC is a standard set for *multimedia personal computers* by the Multimedia PC *Marketing* Council in Washington, D.C. The italics on "Marketing" are mine. I added italics to the word because I get suspicious when I see the word "marketing" in a professional group's title.

Marketing groups are formed to sell you stuff. That's what marketing is all about—like the cheese council that spent I don't know how many millions of dollars trying to convince us that cutting grilled cheese sandwiches into strips makes them into something other than grilled cheese sandwiches cut into strips. Follow me?

Regardless of how suspicious I feel about the Multimedia PC Marketing Council, they exist, and so does their standard. If you're adding a CD-ROM drive to an IBM-compatible computer, you'll run into phrases like *MPC-compatible* a lot, so you should know what it means.

Read the MPC Label

The MPC standard is subject to change. The first version of it was much less demanding than the current MPC2 standard. When shopping for hardware and software in person (as opposed to by phone or mail), make sure you know *which* version of the MPC standard the hardware meets. There could be some stuff floating around with old labels on it.

The current MPC standard (called MPC2) has the following specifications:

➤ A 386SX-based PC or higher

➤ Minimum 16MHz clock speed

➤ 2MB of main memory (RAM) configured as extended memory

➤ 30MB hard drive

➤ 1.44MB 3.5-inch high-density floppy drive

➤ 101-key IBM keyboard

➤ VGA card and monitor with 640 × 480 pixel resolution, 256 colors, or 800 × 600 resolution at 16 colors

➤ Two-button mouse

➤ Analog joystick port (IBM-compatible)

➤ MIDI port

➤ MPC-compatible sound card

➤ MPC-compatible CD-ROM drive

➤ System software compatible with Microsoft Windows Multimedia Extension

These are the minimum requirements for your computer to be considered an MPC machine. Naturally, faster equipment is better, as is more RAM and hard disk space. If you buy a new computer that claims to be a multimedia PC, it should meet or exceed these requirements. If the manufacturer paid their fee to the marketing council to have the machine examined and approved, it will also bear an official MPC logo.

If You've Already Got a PC...

...you can check to see if your current computer meets or exceeds the MPC standard by checking the technical specifications in its manual(s) against the preceding list. If you don't really care, don't bother. I won't tell.

The MPC logo isn't like the Good Housekeeping Seal of Approval or a UL listing. It doesn't mean a computer (or a CD-ROM disc) is any good—it just means the machine or product has all the stuff it's supposed to have to wear the name. It's a measure of superficial detail, not of quality. You can find a perfectly good multimedia computer without the seal or a crappy one with it.

The MPC "standard," like a lot of stuff you'll run into while shopping, is a marketing tool. It should actually be called the MPC "minimum standard." If you're serious about multimedia and CD-ROM, you'll actually want to exceed that standard by as much as your budget will allow. You'll notice that the advice I give throughout the rest of the book goes beyond what the MPC standard calls for. That's because this advice is based on real-world experience rather than market-analysis reports and sales figures.

Anyhow, that's the MPC standard.

Coming Soon from Fox, ISO 9660...

"First there was *Beverly Hills 90210*, then *Melrose Place*, but nothing prepared you for the sleazy antics of *ISO 9660*...."

Just kidding. (Actually, if I were still working in Hollywood...*Hmmm*.)

ISO 9660 is a CD-ROM disc format that allows a disc to be used on more than one computer platform. ISO 9660, by and large, has replaced HSF (more on this in a minute) as the popular format for CDs that can be used on more than one type of computer.

ISO stands for the *International Standards Organization.* The ISO researches and sets standards for all kinds of things around the world. They try to cut down on confusion— which, in my book, is always a good thing. In this case, they've set one that describes an internationally accepted format for CD-ROM discs.

Unlike the MPC standard, ISO 9660 is a true standard. Almost any CD-ROM drive you look at will be ISO 9660-compatible. If it isn't, run away! Actually, the compatibility question isn't about the CD-ROM drive, but whether the appropriate ISO 9660 driver software is included so your computer can interpret the format.

Other Compatibility Questions

Other issues you should consider before you buy a drive depend on what you want the drive for in the first place. If you want to use CD-ROMs that include video clips, you need to think double hard about the speed of the drive you buy. If you want to use Kodak PhotoCDs, you have additional things to think about. This section will start you thinking.

Movie Time: Pass the Popcorn

Live-action video clips are turning up all over the place in the world of CD-ROM. CD encyclopedias include film clips to illustrate concepts (like rockets launching) and document historical actions (like JFK's inaugural address). In games, video simulates actions, plays out scenes, or otherwise moves the story of the game forward. Educational programs use them to demonstrate lessons: to show, rather than to tell. You can even find full-length movies on CD like the one in the following figure.

Right now, there are several video formats that are used. The top two contenders (actually, they're more like litigants) are Apple's QuickTime and Microsoft's Video for Windows.

QuickTime runs on Macintosh computers (it's part of the Macintosh operating system, or Mac OS, 7.1 and later) or PCs running Windows (with additional software). Microsoft's Video for Windows runs only on Windows PCs.

If you want to be able to use CDs that use any sort of video clips, look for a CD-ROM drive that can transfer data at 150K per second or faster (300K/S is best) and that has 128K or larger cache. Both will make the video clips appear less choppy while they're playing on your screen.

An actual full-length movie!

A scene from the documentary film "Comic Book Confidential," from the CD-ROM of the same name.

Don't Panic About Video Software!

If you're trying to install a CD that has special video (or other) requirements, it'll install the proper video software (or at least provide it, so you can install it manually). For example, Voyager's *The Resident's Freak Show* (which is very cool, by the way) detected the fact that I didn't have QuickTime for Windows installed on my PC and offered to do it for me. The disc's manual will provide specific information.

Say Cheeeeese!

The Kodak Corporation's latest invention is a new way to have your film developed. Instead of dropping off your film and getting back a packet of 3 × 5-inch pictures, you get your photographs back on *PhotoCDs*.

PhotoCDs give you a nice, shiny, easy-to-store-and-maintain library of your personal and/or business photographs that will stay attractive and presentable (with proper care and handling) for at least 30 years. If you go the extra mile and store them in a light-proof container when not in use, Kodak says PhotoCDs will last 100 years or longer. No more screams of horror as you discover that squirrels have shredded your family's photographic history to make a cozy nest in your attic.

To view cherished photos, you flip through a "roll" of developed film on your computer, like the one shown here. With the Kodak PhotoCD Access Software, you can tinker with the photos: crop them (cut out the uninteresting bits); resize (or scale) the photos; tinker with the color; flip and rotate the image.

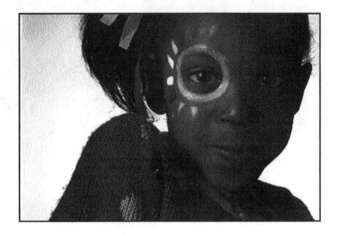

Girl with painted face, by Steve Kelly. From the Kodak PhotoCD Sampler disc.

A Warning

If you change a PhotoCD image, you *cannot* save the changes back to the CD. You have to save the image to a floppy disk or your hard drive—and they can take up lots of disk space. The one shown here, in full size and full color, takes up over 4050K of disk space—the equivalent of about four high-density diskettes. *Yow!*

If you do a family newsletter (as some folks do at the holidays), you can use the PhotoCD images in the documents you create with your word-processing or page-layout programs and print them out like any other graphic.

For design and imaging professionals, the benefits are much the same as those for regular people, only magnified. Folks who keep bazillions of photos can store them on a handful of PhotoCDs.

For non-photographers, you can also buy PhotoCDs full of professional images you can use as you like. Enhanced layout and image-editing software is also available if you want to work the images into graphic designs for ads, brochures, and other glossy productions. (For more about software for use with PhotoCDs, check in Part 3.)

To make use of PhotoCDs on your computer, however, you must have a CD-ROM drive and driver software that are compatible. In technical terms, that means it is *XA Mode 2-compatible*—but don't panic about that either. Most ads for drives will state in clear English: PhotoCD-compatible. (There's more coming up on XA and what it means in the next section—I know you're just shivering with antici-*say it!*-pation.)

If PhotoCD-compatibility matters to you, be sure the drive you get is multisession-compatible. When PhotoCDs were first introduced, you brought in a roll of film, and you got back a CD. When you brought in another roll of film, you got another CD—not because the first disc was full, mind you, but because PhotoCD-compatible drives at the time could only read the first set of images (single session). Anything added later would be virtually nonexistent to your computer because a single-session drive (duh) can't read more than that first session of photos.

Because of improvements to the hardware and software, now you can bring back your old CD when you return that second roll of film. The new images are added to it (thus the term *multisession*) until the disc is full.

Don't settle for anything less than multisession PhotoCD-compatibility. It'll save you money, storage space, and (by reusing the same CD until it's full) be more environmentally friendly.

If you're curious to find out if any of your friendly neighborhood film processors offer PhotoCD developing, you can call Kodak at 1-800-242-2424, extension 36 (or, from outside the U.S., 1-716-1021, extension 36).

To view and use Kodak PhotoCDs on your IBM-compatible, you should have a minimum of a 386 with 4MB of RAM, 4MB of free hard drive space, an 8-bit VGA video card capable of displaying 256 colors, and a monitor to match.

As is always the case with minimums, it's the least you need to have. The more the merrier. For example, a monitor and VGA card capable of displaying 256 colors will let you look at the photographs in nice (if not exactly in CinemaScope/Technicolor) brilliance.

A 16- or 24-bit video card and appropriate color monitor—capable of displaying (respectively) thousands and millions of colors—will let you look at the same photos in all their colorful glory.

To make use of PhotoCDs on a Mac, you should have, in addition to a compatible CD-ROM drive: a color Macintosh with 4MB or more of RAM (more if you're running System 7.5), 4MB or more of free hard disk space, an 8-bit color video card (or built-in video support), and compatible monitor. That's the minimum—the absolute least you need. The recommended configuration includes twice the RAM and hard drive space, and 24-bit color.

XA?

XA is one of the file formats that some CD-ROM discs come in. XA is the shortened form of eXtended Architecture. The XA format allows for better integration of sounds and graphics. It's also the format on which Kodak's PhotoCDs are based, specifically XA Mode 2. KA Mode 2 is common for PhotoCDs and little else. Regular XA is highly uncommon, and you shouldn't lose any sleep over it.

If You Really Want to Know the Details of XA

XA is a formatting standard that interleaves audio and video segments on a CD-ROM disc. Think of "interleaving" like shuffling a deck of playing cards. The cards in one hand are video—in the other hand, audio. When you shuffle the two stacks of cards, you're *interleaving* them. Of course, the real process of interleaving is more complicated and defined than that, but you have the basic concept. PhotoCDs and XA Mode 2 are not interleaved.

Odds are, right now, that XA compatibility will not be an issue for you, unless you're interested in using Kodak PhotoCDs (in which case, you should check out the previous section). Otherwise, XA CD-ROM discs aren't terribly common. You may need to add hardware (like an XA board) to your PC to access XA discs other than PhotoCDs.

Treasure of the (High) Sierra Madres

The *High Sierra Format* (or *HSF*, for short) is another CD-ROM disc format. It allows CD-ROM discs to be used on more than one computer platform (IBM-compatible is one platform; Macintosh is another). A disc in HSF can be just as easily used in a Mac as a PC. How many other things can you say that about?

For manufacturers, at least, High Sierra format is more cost-effective. Rather than making an individually formatted disc for every computer platform, they need only produce one disc format and sell it to everybody.

HSF has been pretty much replaced by the ISO 9660 format, but you may find some older CDs in the old format. So, you don't need the excruciating details of what High Sierra Format is or does, you do have to know whether your CD-ROM drive is compatible with it. For the record: Almost all modern Mac/PC CD-ROM drives manufactured in the past couple of years are HSF (and the related ISO 9660 format, discussed earlier in the chapter) compatible. The question isn't about the drive itself, but whether the appropriate driver software is included so your computer can interpret the format.

> **HSF and HFS**
> Don't confuse HSF (High Sierra Format) with **HFS (Hierarchical File System)**. The Hierarchical File System is what allows a Mac to have a folder inside of a folder inside of a folder inside of a folder... and so on. They're two different ideas entirely.

The Least You Need to Know

➤ The MPC standard is a set of minimums—don't settle for anything less. You should exceed their requirements, if you can.

➤ The MPC seal does not mean quality; it just means the product meets the MPC standard (has the features it specifies).

➤ ISO 9660 compatibility is a must for your CD-ROM drive.

➤ If you plan to use CDs that incorporate video clips, make sure the drive you buy has a transfer rate of at least 150K/S—but 300K/S or higher will be better.

➤ If you want to use and view Kodak PhotoCDs, make sure the drive is multisession PhotoCD-compatible (or XA Mode 2 compatible, in techno-speak).

➤ XA and HSF are other disc formats. You don't need to know what they are, you just need to know whether your drive and/or driver software can handle them.

Sounds Like...

I'm sure I said this somewhere else, but it bears repeating: CD-ROM drives are direct descendants of audio CD players. They've just got extra hardware thrown in (that's why you can't just unhook the CD player from a stereo and hook it up to your computer).

Tipping our hats to the CD-ROM drive's parentage, this chapter is all about the different kinds of sounds you can get out of that bad boy once you get it hooked up and (literally) ready to rock and roll—or blues, or jazz, whatever your preference.

Throwing the Book at You

Fans of J. R. R. Tolkien's *Lord of the Rings* trilogy are probably aware that the story of the magic ring is recorded in the *Red Book of Westmarch*. Tolkien fans probably aren't aware that sounds on audio (and some data) CDs are stored in Red Book audio format.

Red Book is the official name for Compact Disc-Digital Audio (or CD-DA) guidelines as written by the Sony and Phillips corporations. I guess the guidelines are published in a big red book, hence the nickname.

You don't really need to know any of the technical details about the Red Book format. You should know, however, that a drive capable of playing audio CDs can (or its driver software can) read Red Book sound. CD-ROM discs that have music in Red Book format can often be played in audio CD players. (Wayzata Technology's *Loon Magic* CD-ROM has a haunting score that I often just listen to while working.)

But Don't Go Nuts!

For goodness sake, though, *don't just start popping CD-ROM discs in your audio CD player* just to see if it works. Your audio CD player will try really hard to make music out of data, and the yowl you'll get won't be pretty. Check the CD-ROM disc's manual to see if it can be played as an audio CD, too. They usually state it quite clearly.

Red Book audio (and other CD-ROM sound formats like Green Book, and so on) is *digital*—that is, it's recorded as a series of digits (zeros and ones) that are turned back into audible sound by your CD-ROM drive.

Audiophilia

Well, that sounds vaguely obscene, doesn't it? It isn't—not at all. I'm an admitted audiophile and darn proud of it. I love music. At best, my taste in it is described as "eclectic"—though some would venture that I have no taste in music. To them I say: *thhhppptt*. (For those who keep track of this sort of thing, and you know who you are, right now I'm listening to K. D. Lang's *Ingenue*.)

Deciding whether or not to get a CD-ROM drive that's capable of playing audio CDs is pretty much a "Hobson's Choice"—that is, not a choice at all. There aren't many around that won't also play audio CDs for you. You'll have a harder time finding one that doesn't.

If you intend to get a drive that can play audio CDs so you can have good background music at your desk (since you can't play *Myst* or *Doom* all the time), you definitely need to get your hands on some speakers appropriate for your new drive.

You need to add speakers because, while most CD-ROM drives can play audio CDs, they don't (on the whole) have the gizzards to let you actually hear the bloody things.

The speakers (or even a pair of headphones) get the music from your drive to your ears, where it'll do you the most good.

The kind of speakers you get will depend entirely on how your drive is set up to deal with audio CDs—and that, my friends, can vary a lot from machine to machine. (Don't worry, I'm not deserting you on that grim note. Read on.)

Amplify This

When you buy speakers for your CD-ROM drive, deciding what kind is a function of what kind of amplification is built into the drive.

If it has a built-in amplifier (the advertising copy will specify if it does), then you'll be able to use any old pair of speakers you can find. The geeky way to ask for them is to ask for *passive speakers*. They're called passive because they don't have to do anything except sit there and let you listen to tunes. All of the amplifying work is done for them by the drive's built-in amplifier. You adjust the volume of the audio CD you're playing by fiddling with the volume control on the drive. Drive amplification is usually weak; you may want active speakers (coming up next) anyway.

If you get a drive that doesn't have built-in amplification, you'll need to get a pair of *active speakers*. Active speakers, unlike passive ones, have an amplifier built-in to replace the one missing from your drive. It boosts the signal from your CD-ROM drive so it can be played at a volume higher than a whisper. With active speakers, you fiddle with the volume of audio CDs by adjusting the volume control on the speakers—the drive may not even have a volume control.

When you're listening to audio CDs with your CD-ROM drive, you may or may not have to juggle your speaker's connection around.

Mac users may need to plug their speakers into the drive's speaker/headphone jack—unless your speakers are designed with enough audio in/out jacks to allow you to connect them to the drive audio-out jacks and your Mac's audio-out (and maybe -in) jacks, all at the same time. Apple's AppleDesign Power Speakers let you do just that.

PC users may or may not need to re-plug their speakers, depending on whether or not their CD-ROM drive's audio-out jack is connected to their sound card's audio-in jack (you may need to buy a special cable to accomplish this, too). If you aren't sure what you have, check your manuals. There's more information on choosing speakers coming up in Chapter 9.

Sounds Like Sound Sampling

If you remember anything from your high school science classes, you may remember all that stuff about sound: how sound travels in waves; how it has to travel through something, like air (which is why science fiction movies that have ships swooshing through space are a crock); how it has amplitude, resonance, reverberation, and all sorts of other two-dollar words to explain why sound sounds the way it does.

If you're getting a CD-ROM drive only to play intense games, use multimedia software, and listen to the occasional Bonnie Raitt CD, you don't really need to know any more about sound than you already do. If, however, you want a CD-ROM so you can create your own multimedia extravaganzas, you may want to learn more about sound.

The technical specifications of the different sound formats for the different kinds of computers (like Windows WAV files or Macintosh SND resources) go way, way beyond the scope of this book. (Besides, if you're not interested in them, they're kind of dull.)

You should know, however, that all kinds of software exist for creating and editing sound, and it's available for most computer platforms. The applications range from the basic recording utilities that come with most sound cards for PCs, the Sound Control Panel for Macintosh, to a variety of high-powered utilities that let you create and modify general sounds or create and modify musical sounds.

WAV and SND
WAV, as in sound wave, is the format for Windows sounds. The format for Macintosh system sounds is called SND, as in, well, sound.

You might want to take some interesting sound-effects from a CD-ROM game (for example) and convert it to a very cool alert sound for use on your Mac or Windows machine. Or you may want to buy CD-ROM discs of musical clips to include in your own multimedia productions and presentations.

How to Clip Sounds

There are three ways to get a sound from a CD into your computer:

First: If you're using a Mac with an internal Apple CD-ROM drive, you can simply use your Sound Control Panel. Select **Sound In** from the control panel's pop-up menu and then click the **Options** button. The Sound Control Panel will let you choose the internal CD-ROM drive as your audio source. It gives you great sound quality.

Second: If the speakers you purchase have an audio-out jack, you can plug that into your PC's sound card or your Mac's microphone jack (you may need to buy an additional cable). Mac users can use the Sound Control Panel to record. Windows users can use the Multimedia Player to record. PC users, check your sound card's manual. You may have gotten software that allows you to record sound files.

Third: If you've got a microphone, point it at your speakers and record by the method appropriate to your machine. It won't give you as good a quality sound as the first two methods, but it works.

Regardless of the final use (an alert sound or musical accompaniment in your presentation), sound files can be *enormous*. So that they don't take up any unnecessary storage space, sound editing software will often let you convert your sound files to smaller files (sacrificing some sound quality), in addition to letting you cut out the extraneous portions.

The very cool sound programs let you take a sound you've *sampled* (that is, recorded with your computer) and tinker with its *wave form* (the actual sound wave) to turn it into another sound entirely. That really appeals to the toy-brain in me.

For the multimedia-minded, there's a section on authoring tools in Chapter 27. If that's not enough to get you started, there are also some excellent books that cover all aspects of multimedia creation, animation, sound, and MIDI (computer-synthesized music). Some even come with CDs full of useful software (like editing tools, authoring tools, sound resources) that you can use to set yourself up as a multimedia mogul.

Check your local library, computer store, or book store for the titles suited to your needs. As you start clipping sounds, though, keep in mind the copyright laws. Using someone else's voice or music without permission (especially in something you intend to sell) is highly illegal. You want to become a clip artist, not a rip-off artist.

The Least You Need to Know

➤ Most CD-ROM drives can also play audio CDs.

➤ You need speakers or headphones to hear music CDs.

➤ If your drive has a built-in amplifier, you can use *passive* speakers. If it doesn't have built-in amplification, you need to use active speakers.

➤ If you want to create your own sounds for multimedia projects, get yourself a good book on Multimedia, Digital Audio, or MIDI to learn the ins and outs of creating audio on computers.

Chapter 7

Necessary Accessories

In This Chapter

➤ Improve your memory

➤ Cables and cards and bears (oh my!)

➤ Looking and sounding your best

Selecting a CD-ROM drive is only half the battle. There are some to-go-with items that are either required to make use of the full power of your new drive, or nice (but not required) to make your drive that much more effective.

This chapter is about the necessities. The next chapter is about the niceties. Deciding which accessories are necessary and which would just be nice isn't an easy job. It's a lot like the signs on Owl's door in *Winnie-the-Pooh*: "Ples ring if an rnser is rqird. Plez cnoke if an rnsr is not reqid." Knock or ring? Only you know what you want to be able to do with your CD-ROM, and therefore, only you know if an "rnser is rqird."

What I deem necessary, you may not. What I deem a nicety, you may require. For that reason, I'll be sure to give my reasoning; you, as always, should make up your own mind.

More Power!

I love Tim Allen of *Home Improvement* (insert suitable grunts here). To him, every problem in the world can be solved if you just give things more power.

In many cases, of course, he's wrong; things he tinkers with tend to blow up. In the case of you and your CD-ROM drive, however, he may be right. Your computer probably could use more power.

We're not talking about electricity here. We're talking about power in the form of *Random Access Memory*, or *RAM*. You add RAM to your computer by adding (or replacing) *SIMMs*.

Single Inline Memory Modules
A SIMM is a collection of memory chips on a small card. When the card is installed in your computer, it increases the amount of RAM available for computing tasks.

Not So Fast with the SIMMS There, Pal...

Before you buy *anything*, check the technical specifications section of your computer's manual. Not all computers use SIMMs—older ones use DRAM, SIPs, or other monsters from the deep. Oh, and by the way, RAM comes in different speeds, too, and you have to buy the right speed for your computer. Read all about it later in this chapter.

To your computer, RAM is power. The more you have, the more (and bigger) applications you can run, you can create bigger documents, and (most important in this case) the funkier the CD-ROM discs you can play around with.

Here's why.

Opening Windows

On a 386 machine, you need a minimum of 2MB of RAM to run Windows in its enhanced mode. (Notice I said "minimum." To do anything substantial, you need at least 4MB.)

It's the same for using CD-ROM discs that comply with the MPC standard (discussed back in Chapter 5 if you're skimming) under Windows. Technically, it can be done with 2MB of memory, but animation and video clips (which eat up RAM like it's popcorn) won't be as smooth as they could be with a little more RAM elbow-room. If you have only 2MB of RAM and find that animation and video clips are choppy—or run too slowly with frequent pauses while your computer reads them from a CD—you should consider upgrading to 4MB or more of RAM.

If you want to use some really wild CD titles (like Voyager's *The Residents' Freak Show*), you might want to consider 8MB or more of RAM. (Really, I'm not making this up.)

You can find out how much RAM you have installed in your PC by watching the test it puts itself through every time it starts up, or by typing **MEM** at any C:\> prompt (or **CHKDSK** if you're using a version of DOS earlier than DOS 5).

Minimum vs. Maximum

2MB is a minimum. The maximum amount of RAM you can install is limited only by the capacity of your PC and your operating system's capability to access it. Check your PC's manual for its RAM capacity—it should be listed in the Technical Specifications section of your manual.

The Macintosh Mind

For a Macintosh running System 7.5, you need from 4–8MB of RAM (depending on what you install). A Power Mac needs 16MB or more.

Depending on what else you do with your Mac, even that may not be enough. With all the extensions and other doodads (fonts, control panels, and so on) I have installed in mine—plus the ones that some applications add—the System eats up almost 5MB of RAM (and that's on a good day).

How Much RAM Have I Got?

You Mac users can find out how much memory is installed in your Mac and how it's being used by selecting the **About This Macintosh** option under the menu.

Consider, then, that some of the "Oh, my gosh, I didn't think it was possible to do that" CD-ROM disks like *Myst* (from Broderbund) requires a minimum of 4MB of RAM, and *The Journeyman Project* (from Presto Studios) requires 8MB of RAM, you really ought to think about adding more if you've only got 2–4MB.

The bottom line is: You need more power. It can only make your computing life simpler and more productive.

Pump Up the RAM!

Fortunately, SIMMs and other types of RAM are easy to buy and install on your own. However, they can be pricey—and those prices fluctuate wildly.

Before you buy more RAM, you need to know:

➤ The make and model of your computer

➤ The computer's maximum capacity

➤ The kind of chips the machine takes

➤ The speed of the SIMMs (or other chips) your machine requires

➤ How much RAM you want to install

➤ The name and version of the operating system you're using (DOS 6.2, Mac OS 7.5, and so on)

All this information (except how much RAM you want to install) should be available in your computer's manual in the Technical Specifications section (or there may be a section on adding RAM).

To find out which version of operating system you're using, Mac users can select **About This Macintosh** from the   menu. PC-compatible users can type **VER** at the C:\> prompt.

An Easy Way to Decide How Much RAM to Get An easy way to determine how much more memory you should add to your computer is to go software looking (not shopping). See what CD-ROM titles strike your fancy—ones you're likely to purchase when you have your drive up and running—and then meet or exceed their memory requirements. That way, when you actually buy those tasty-looking CD-ROM discs, you won't be disappointed to find that you don't have enough memory.

A Cheap Trick for Mac Users

Mac users have the option of increasing their RAM with software. Two products are available that trick your Mac into thinking it has more RAM installed than it actually does.

RAM Doubler from Connectix is one. It's a system extension that effectively doubles the amount of RAM in your Mac—go from 8MB to 16MB for about $50.

OptiMem from the Jump Development Group optimizes the way your Mac and open applications use memory, allowing it to do more stuff all at the same time. OptiMem is even compatible with RAM Doubler, so you can use *both*.

If you intend to install memory by yourself, I recommend you order from your favorite mail-order company. When you call, they are very knowledgeable and will help you select what you need; many of them also offer installation guides, videos, and even tools that make installing and removing chips easier.

Of course, if you're leery of doing it yourself, you can always bring your computer into your local computer service center and ask them to upgrade your memory for you. You'll pay more, but it's worth it if the idea of doing it yourself gives you the heebie-jeebies.

More power to you.

Interface Needs

Depending on how you buy your CD-ROM drive—either by itself or in a ready-to-run bundle—you may need to get a few extra thingammies to connect it to your computer.

Ready-to-run bundles are usually packaged for specific computers. They include (or should include) everything you need to get your drive set up and running.

With drives sold by themselves, that isn't always the case. For example, some of the NEC line of CD-ROM readers are packaged so that they can be purchased for either Macintosh or PC use. When you buy the drive, you must also purchase an appropriate interface kit.

Interface
Basically, a connection that allows a user and a computer (or a computer and another device) to exchange data reliably when they interact. In peripheral-to-computer terms, it's how information is passed back and forth (through a SCSI cable, and so on), or how these devices are physically connected to each other.

If you buy a CD-ROM drive alone (without all the interface doodads), you may also need to purchase:

For Macintosh	For PC
SCSI cable	SCSI or appropriate cable
Driver software (only if it doesn't come with the drive)	SCSI adapter card (or sound card with built-in CD-ROM controller)
	Sound card (optional with a SCSI interface, but you really should have one)

If your CD-ROM drive doesn't come with an appropriate cable, you have to buy one to hook up the drive to your computer (either a SCSI cable or one appropriate to your controller).

If your PC doesn't have a SCSI card or port already, you'll need a SCSI adapter card (Macs already have one built in), or a sound card with a built-in CD controller, or (depending on the drive you choose) a whole 'nother kind of controller altogether.

Driver A small bit of software that tells your computer how to deal with a new piece of hardware.

Most all CD-ROM drives come with driver software written especially for that drive, so you really shouldn't have to worry about it.

By the Way...

Later on, if your driver software seems inferior, slow, or otherwise unsatisfactory, software companies are beginning to release their own driver software and enhancements, which can do more for (and with) your drive than the original driver. Driver software is covered in Chapter 17.

PC owners should consider getting a sound card and speakers. (This is one of those options I had a hard time calling either a necessity or nicety; I couldn't decide, so it's covered in both chapters.) It will give you much better sound from your CD software than the tiny, tinny little speaker that's built into your PC.

Many CD-ROM programs have original musical scores that sound just awful without a sound card. If you plan to play games, do presentation work, or use educational discs, a sound card and speakers can really enhance the experience.

Mac owners, your sound support is built-in; don't sweat it. You'll probably want to add a pair of speakers and/or headphones, though.

Monitors in Your Face

Another tough call here: a monitor. *"Duh!"* you say? Well, hear me out.

Yes, I know you probably already have a monitor. A computer isn't much bloody good without one. It's hard to see what you're doing otherwise. What you might want to consider is a new monitor. If you have a *monochrome* (one-color, like amber or green) monitor or a *gray-scale* monitor (that shows shades of gray instead of different colors), you should probably invest in a nice color monitor that displays at least 256 colors. It may be necessary for you to buy a video card that's appropriate to this spiffy new monitor, too. When in doubt, ask.

Mac users, while you're at it (buying a new monitor or checking your current monitor to see if it's up to par), make sure the one you'll be using has at least a 13-inch screen. (Most computers these days come with a 14- or 15-inch monitor.)

How Big Is It?

Monitors, like television sets, get measured diagonally, rather than top-to-bottom or side-to-side. Why? I don't know. I guess it's easier to do that than expect math-idiots like me to interpret square inches on a monitor.

Talk About Cutting Corners!

Hey, Mac Users! You actually lose about an inch of display area on your monitor. A 13-inch monitor has about 12 inches of display. It doesn't change my recommendation that you have a 13-inch or larger monitor— I just thought you should know.

Again, it's a question of getting the full effect of your multimedia CDs. Most are designed for color (some won't run without color). A lot specify a 13-inch, 256-color display for Macs, or a VGA or Super-VGA monitor for PCs.

For Macintosh, some CD software requires a 13-inch or larger color monitor. If you try to run a game that requires a 13-inch monitor on a 12-inch monitor—well, speaking as one who's tried it, it stinks. At best, you miss vital details or clues. At worst, the game controls are pushed off the edge of your monitor where you can't get at them, and you wind up staring at the screen unable to do anything. How *very* frustrating.

On the Other Hand...

Of course, you can always just avoid the CD software that makes special demands on your system, such as more RAM than you have, a better monitor, sound, and so on.

You *can*, but you'll be cutting yourself off from the coolest of the CD software available now, and probably from all the over-the-edge, pushing-the-envelope stuff that'll be coming out as more software companies turn their attention to CDs.

Don't say I didn't warn you.

The Least You Need to Know

➤ More RAM will enable you to run the coolest CD software (even the practical CDs) more smoothly and with fewer hassles.

➤ Before you buy SIMMs, make sure you check to see what your computer can hold (its maximum memory capacity), and what kind and speed SIMMs it requires. There's nothing worse than getting your hands on some bad RAM, man.

➤ Make sure your CD-ROM drive comes with (or you order separately) all the cables, cards, and software you need to run the drive.

➤ A bigger color monitor couldn't hurt either.

➤ When in doubt about anything, ask. You're spending some serious bucks, here. It's no time to get shy.

Chapter 8

Optional Options

In This Chapter

➤ Son of Sound Card

➤ Speaking of speakers

➤ Heading for headphones

➤ Wrap that rascal: caddies

There are times when it's appropriate to pull back the reins and say, "Enough is enough. I'm not going to buy everything in sight." Then there are times to say, "What the heck, the sky's the limit. *Gimme, gimme!*"

If going shopping for a CD-ROM has got you feeling like a two-year-old in a toy department, you can do one of two things:

➤ You can wait until that feeling passes.

➤ You can indulge yourself intelligently and buy yourself things that will actually come in handy.

If you're going to wait until the feeling passes, maybe you should skip this chapter because it's all about decadent, indulgent things that'll come in handy (but aren't really essential).

The initial investment in CD-ROM hardware can be daunting. If you don't feel like springing for everything up front, you can always tack these goodies on later (or drop hints that they'd make wonderful gift ideas).

Sound Cards: Déjà Vu

Okay, okay, I know I talked about sound cards in the "necessary" chapter, and here they are again in the "optional" chapter—so which are they, anyhow?

Mac Alert!

Don't forget: Mac owners don't need to bother with a sound card. Sound support is built into Macs from the get-go.

Well, *I* think they're a necessity for PC owners, but I'm not going to bully you into getting one. If you back out of a sound card in your initial purchase—because you've exceeded your budget or really don't think you'll need one—it's not like you won't ever be able to change your mind. Security won't stop you in the store and say, "Wait a minute there, pal. You had your chance, and you blew it. Put that back." They *will* let you buy one later.

Not to belabor the point, but adding a sound card will improve your enjoyment of any CD-ROM disc that includes music, sound effects, or the spoken word. It'll also spice up any non-CD software you have and use that contains music or sound effects. You'll feel like you're playing a completely different game.

'Nuff said?

When choosing a sound card for your PC, let your needs and your budget be your guide. Remember that stereo cards will sound better than mono (and will also be more expensive). Likewise, 16-bit cards are more expensive than 8-bit cards, but they're also more versatile and, in most cases, sound better. (You can't play 16-bit sounds with an 8-bit card.) 16-bit sound cards are becoming the standard, but let your budget be your guide.

Creative Labs' SoundBlaster cards and 100% SoundBlaster-compatible cards by other manufacturers are pretty much the industry standard for PC sound. You can find an assortment of them for street prices ranging from under $100 to about $250.

I wouldn't go for a card that didn't do stereo. Stereo is a necessity—it's just way cool for games and for fully enjoying the music you get on a multimedia CD. Whether you buy 8- or 16-bit is more of a gray area. If your budget allows for 16-bit, I'd say go for it—especially if you're doing more than just playing games.

The old saying about getting what you pay for is true: A cheap sound card will probably sound tinny and cheap—and an expensive sound card will still sound cheap with cheap speakers.

Speaking of Speakers...

Most CD-ROM readers are capable of playing audio CDs, but none of the CD-ROM readers have built-in speakers (well, not *yet* anyhow). In order to get that lovely music out of that box and into the air, you need speakers. The kind of speakers you need depends on the kind of CD-ROM reader you've chosen.

If the drive you want has a built-in pre-amp that will amplify the signal before it gets to the speakers (discussed back in Chapter 6), you can buy a pair of little, inexpensive speakers like the ones made for Walkman cassette players. These speakers don't have any bells and whistles and no controls to speak of, just a plug for plugging them into your drive, your sound card, or your Mac's audio-out jack.

If the CD-ROM drive doesn't have a pre-amp, then you need amplified speakers. Oddly enough, these are speakers that have their own amplifiers built-in. They require power (either from batteries or from being plugged in), and have volume controls. Usually, pre-amp or no, you get better sound from amplified speakers.

Cheapskate Alert!

Specially designed computer speakers can be bloody expensive! I've seen some that list for as much as $400. Yikes! What sets "computer" speakers apart from your run-of-the-mill Walkman-type speakers is that they contain extra magnetic shielding to keep your floppy disks (and hard drives) from getting scrambled by errant magnetism.

However, if you're basically cheap (like me), you can make do with run-of-the-mill $40 speakers. They won't sound as good, and they won't have any additional jacks or cables to do funky wiring to your CD-ROM drive and computer (also mentioned in Chapter 6), but they are cheap and you can save up for an expensive set.

Remember: you absolutely, positively *have to* keep unshielded speakers as far away from your computer and disks as their wires will allow. Nasty things could happen to your data if you don't.

Unless you buy speakers designed for computer use, with extra audio-in and -out ports and cables, you may need to do some cable juggling with them. When running software full of music and sound effects, you may need to connect the speakers to the audio-out jack on your sound card (or the built-in port of your Mac). That will give you richer, louder sound.

As you're kicking back, enjoying a quiet music CD, you might have to connect the speakers to the audio-out or headphone jack on your CD-ROM drive. Then you can chill out to something calming, like a CD from the Narada Collection. It will soothe those nerves that got jangled by gunfire and bits of gore flying everywhere while playing *Doom*.

Most PC sound cards allow you to connect your CD-ROM to them with an audio cable so you can play audio CDs through your speakers without juggling plugs. Your CD-ROM drive will pass the music from an audio CD through the sound card (without fiddling with it) directly to the speakers. You may need to buy a special cable for the connection, so check your CD-ROM drive and sound card manuals for details.

As with the sound card itself, you get what you pay for with speakers. Since the two are so closely related (they're practically incestuous!), try to strike a balance that fits your budget: cheap sound card with cheap speakers, mid-priced to mid-priced, expensive to expensive. Great $500 speakers won't make up for a cheap sound card, and cheap speakers will hobble an expensive sound card.

A Kind of Hush

Chillin' may not be your thing. You may prefer to work with Aerosmith or Blind Melon blaring from your CD. Or you might like to play around with noisy games in the wee small hours of the morning. Even Rickie Lee Jones, the mistress of chill, can be too much at 2 a.m.

Your family, your neighbors, and even your cat might appreciate it if you took the personal stereo concept to the next level and kept it to yourself.

Headphones!

As with speakers, you can plug headphones into your sound card for CD software—and for audio CDs, too, if your sound card is connected to your CD-ROM drive—or directly into your CD-ROM drive's jack.

On a Mac, you plug into the computer's sound-out port for CD software or directly into the CD-ROM drive for audio.

If you don't want to hassle with unplugging your speakers to plug in your headphones, you can get a pair of speakers with—what a great idea—their own headphone jack! I'm all for fewer hassles, and I'm willing to pay a little more money for fewer gray hairs.

Cheapskate Alert! II

There are no special requirements for computer headphones, except that the plug fits into the audio jacks on your computer and/or CD-ROM drive. You probably have an appropriate pair lying around the house already: the ones from the cheap cassette player your Aunt Bertha gave you on your last birthday; the ones from your GameBoy you never use. Any pair will do. Why spend more money?

Caddies: Wrap That Rascal!

As part of their dust-deflecting design, some CD-ROM drives won't accept a naked CD (or as we used to say, *nekkid*, which is somehow more unclothed than just plain naked—go figure). Instead, discs need to be put into a *disc caddy* before they can be inserted into a drive.

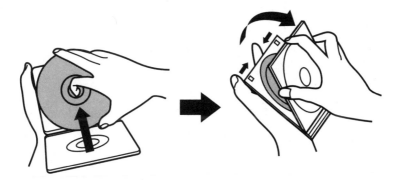

Your basic disc caddy.

The caddy protects the workings of your drive from any dust, dirt, or other crud that may have accumulated on the disc while it was in storage. Additionally, the drive's built-in dust brushes can clean off the outside of the caddy before it makes it inside the drive.

Cheapskate Alert! III

You can clean a compact disc without investing in an expensive cleaning device. In fact, you *shouldn't* use one of those cleaning kits with your CD-ROM. See Chapter 29 for maintenance details.

With most drives that require you to use a disc caddy, you'll get one in the box with the drive. One. Uno. Ein. Gosh, could they spare it?

If you didn't know it from the song, "One is the loneliest number." It's also pretty tedious. If you want to switch between a game CD and a music CD (or any other CD, for that matter), you have to remove the caddy from the drive, remove the disc from the caddy, put that disc back in its box (to keep it from getting dirty), take the new CD from its box, put that CD in the caddy, and then finally slap it in the drive. Talk about gray hair. You'll have gray hair before you get through that little process a few times.

Before you run to the checkout line, peek and see if the drive you're getting uses CD caddies. If it does, as long as you're in the store (or on the phone) shopping, throw in a couple of extra CD caddies. The hair you save may be your own.

I've seen caddies packaged individually for about $13 in stores, and I've gotten them on sale for about $7. They're cheaper by mail order (most things are), and if you buy them in packs of three or more, they're even cheaper.

Put It Away

If you haven't guessed by now, dust is a major threat to CD-ROM drives (it can really booger up the reader's ability to interpret data from a CD). Caddies eliminate some of the threat. You can also eliminate more of it by storing your disks properly. "Properly," in this instance, means out of the way of dust.

To keep your discs clean, be sure to store them in their plastic jewel boxes when you're done with them. Or, if you bought enough extra caddies, you can store the discs you use regularly in their own individual caddies.

Keeping the discs in their boxes or caddies will keep them free from dust, and either method will probably do you fine, until you have to keep track of more than a dozen or so CDs.

Then you might want to think about some kind of storage box. Storage boxes, shelves, racks, and such have the advantage of keeping your discs (and even their caddies) clean, with the added benefit of letting you keep them in some kind of order. That should appeal to the Type A personalities out there. My CDs are the *only* things that are organized on my desk.

Strictly Personal Preference Stuff

This is a personal prejudice, so feel free to ignore it. I just don't trust those CD storage units that hold naked CDs. It seems like asking for trouble—I can see myself spilling a can of sticky soda right into the open storage bin.

I recommend you pick a storage unit that lets you store your CDs in their original jewel boxes or caddies (or both, since caddies and jewel boxes are the same size). Maybe I'm paranoid. Maybe I'm clumsy. That's what I recommend.

Miscellany

There are other gizmos available, too. You may or may not want to consider some of them.

If you're buying a portable drive, you may want to consider:

➤ A padded carrying case if you'll need to take it on the road with you—or a new carrying case that will hold your laptop, the drive, some CDs, and whatever else you need to fit into one bag.

➤ A smaller padded CD storage case for carrying a few essential CDs with you wherever you go.

➤ An extra SCSI (or other) cable so you don't have to completely undo and redo your drive's hookup when you take it with you.

➤ A battery pack (if appropriate) or a set of long-life rechargeable batteries so you can have music (at least) anywhere.

And keep your eyes peeled. Folks are always coming up with new and exciting (or new and silly) stuff all the time. You never know when someone will invent something that has your name (and needs) written all over it.

The Least You Need to Know

➤ In spite of how badly I think you need one, you can live without a sound card. Things just won't sound good, though.

➤ Speakers will supplement your (*ahem*) sound card, and let you listen to audio CDs when you aren't running CD software.

➤ Headphones will let you listen to your software or audio CDs without disturbing those around you.

➤ Extra disc caddies (if your drive needs them) will make changing discs a simpler proposition.

➤ A storage box will keep your discs and/or caddies organized and free of dust.

➤ There are other accessories designed to ease the life of a portable CD owner. If you're one (or are going to be one), you might want to consider them, too.

Chapter 9

Bundles O' Fun

In This Chapter

- ➤ Buying bundles
- ➤ Honing your BS detector
- ➤ Look for the label
- ➤ When in doubt...

While you're in the store, or on the phone with the mail-order company ordering your new CD-ROM drive, you're going to feel an overpowering desire to buy CD-ROM discs. Trust me, you will.

Besides, if you don't get at least one disc, how will you know if the drive works? Right? Of *course*, right!

In this vulnerable state of disc-deprivation, you could make a serious mistake. Here are some tips to keep you from getting burned and/or very frustrated on your first go-round with buying computer CDs.

Package Deals

Here's the easiest way to satisfy that yearning to buy CD-ROM discs with your drive: seek out a drive that you like that comes bundled with software you think you'd like to have.

Bundle(d)
Literally, a bunch of stuff lumped together in a single package. Computers and other hardware often come bundled with software. Sometimes other software gets bundled with a particular piece of software—such as games that come free (or at least cheap) with a utility package.

Bundles of software are often added to increase the perceived value of a CD-ROM drive or other computer product. Keep in mind that we're talking about *perceived* value, not *actual* value. Never *ever* let the amount of bundled software decide which CD-ROM drive you're going to purchase. More often than not, the more stuff that comes with a product, the less current (and/or desirable) the main product seems to be.

Let me explain.

Remember back in Chapter 4 when we looked at the different speeds that drives come in—how when a new product breaks new ground, the prices drop on the old products while companies try to rush their own new product to market? Well, the prices drop because the product (in this case, the CD-ROM drive) isn't top-of-the-line any more, and the companies have a lot of old merchandise to move. They drop the prices to sell off the old product and (if people still aren't buying) increase the perceived value by bundling a bunch of stuff with the drive to make it look like it's a better deal than it actually might be. (This isn't *always* the case, but it happens.)

By the Way...

Consider this a lesson in Machiavellian marketing. It isn't necessarily bad or evil, you just have to be careful and know what you want and/or need. Once in awhile, you can get some really great deals.

If you shop for a drive based on what comes with it rather than what the drive itself does, you can wind up with an obsolete bit of hardware that just cannot meet your needs.

To avoid getting burned, don't even consider the CD-ROM bundles at first. Shop for the drive alone. Weigh the drives against each other, based on your budget (a very important factor) and the performance issues we've been talking about all through the first part of this book (especially speed).

Once you've decided on the drive that gives you the most bang for your buck (it does most everything you want at a price you can afford), *then* see if you can find that drive in a bundle.

If you can find the drive you want, at a price you can still afford, and still get a bunch of extra goodies thrown in for free (or sort of free), the bundle is a fantastic deal for you. Congratulations! If not—well, you can always buy some of the individual CDs that attracted you to the bundle in the first place.

Shopping by mail order? Check the catalog for special "with the purchase of any CD-ROM drive" offers. Many mail-order places will let you pick up a bundle of CD titles at discount prices, just for buying your drive from them. Many also let the offer stand for 90 days after you buy the drive.

My Spider Sense Is Tingling

Did you ever wonder where Spider Man's spider sense is located? He gets awfully excited when it tingles. Just curious.

The lesson of the bundle is a good place to start honing your BS detector before you spend money on a CD-ROM drive or any other major computer-related purchase.

The computer marketplace is cutthroat—people will say practically anything to part you from your hard-earned dollars. When prices suddenly drop or things start being sold with a lot of "free" stuff, you need to ask yourself, "Why is that?"

It might be to disguise the fact that there's an out-of-date something (or several somethings) buried there in the bundle. It could be any number of things: a painfully slow CD-ROM drive, a major application that's about to come out in a "New and Improved!" version.

On the other hand, it could be a brand-new (and fabulous) product used to try to lure users away from the competition by increasing its perceived value. Or pricing on one particular product (or line of products) may drop to remain competitive in the dog-eat-dog marketplace.

As my (and everybody's) mother likes to say, "If it sounds too good to be true, it *probably* is." *Probably* is the operative word here. When you see something that sounds too good to be true, don't just buy it. Examine it. Ask questions. Weigh your options. Don't just look that gift horse in the mouth—count its teeth.

Even if it is a case of, say, old software (something that's about to be released in a new version), you can work it to your advantage. Often, if you've bought an old version of an application right before a new version comes out, you get the new version at an extraordinarily low price—sometimes even for free. Anyway, old hardware, if it isn't too old and it meets your needs, can be a great bargain.

The point isn't to make you cynical and jaded (like me, I'm afraid), but to help you educate yourself before you buy. Economically speaking, times are too difficult to go blindly throwing wads of cash around.

You don't want to throw away good money for an inferior product masquerading as a bargain; nor do you want to pay full price for anything when you can get a real bargain (on a bundle, with mail-order pricing, or some other money-saving option). Curb your impulse to shop and think before you buy: it can (literally) pay to be an educated consumer.

The Fine Print

If the bundled software you got with your drive (if you got any at all) isn't quite your style, and you still want to buy something to take your new drive for a spin, don't be a victim of drive-by shopping.

When you shop for CD-ROM discs, you need to have some information at the tips of your fingers—or better still, written down on a piece of paper for easy reference. (You don't have to understand what all this stuff means, just what it is.)

CD-ROM Shopping Checklist

Taking this information with you when you shop will keep you from buying something that won't work with your computer or CD-ROM drive. It will not, however, guarantee that you'll like what you buy or that the product will do what it promises. So be sure to take your personal taste and your BS detector along on your shopping expedition.

➤ Your computer's make, model, central processor chip number, and its speed. For example: a Harmony 386SX Turbo, 33MHz or a Macintosh LC III, 68030, 25MHz.

➤ Your operating system and version number (for example, MS-DOS 6.2, Windows 3.1, or Macintosh System 7.5).

➤ The amount of RAM installed and how much of that RAM is available after you've launched your operating system, shell program, or memory-resident programs (such as PC drivers or Mac extensions). PC users use the MEM command at the C: prompt. Mac users use About This Macintosh under the   menu.

➤ Your computer's manual will say whether or not you have a math co-processor installed.

➤ Monitor size and type (like a SVGA that runs at 640×480 with 256 colors or 14-inch Mac monitor running 256 colors).

➤ What speed your drive is—that is, 1X, 2X, 3X, and so on.

➤ The amount of free space on your hard drive (yeah, like I have any).

No Keeping Secrets!

If you're going to hint around for CD software as a gift, you should either name specific titles that will run on your system, or you should provide the "hint-ee" with the information from this chapter's CD-ROM Shopping Checklist. That way, whatever they get you will run on your system.

It will run on your computer, but that's no guarantee that you'll like it. If you don't want what they got you, you can always say you already have it and ask for the receipt so you can exchange it. (I use all these evil little tricks. They work.)

Every CD-ROM software package (like any software package) will have a label on the back or side of the box, with a list of the *system requirements* you need to meet before you can use the software. They'll be the minimum requirements, too.

Those Minimum Daily Requirements

Just like the "minimum daily requirements" for vitamins and minerals are just enough to keep you from getting rickets or scurvy, the minimum system requirements are the absolute least you need to run a particular piece of software. By no means does that mean the software will run well, just that it will run.

There is no such thing as "close enough for government work" when it comes to meeting the demands of the software. If you don't meet them, don't buy the disc(s). It's that simple.

Just so you have some experience before you go dashing off to the computer store, here are some sample system requirements for popular CD software products.

To run Broderbund's *Math Workshop*—one of the new crop of gee-whiz educational games—on your Macintosh, you need to have the following (and this is taken right off of the box, too):

"**System Requirements:** 8-bit video support (256 colors or shades of gray); Color or grayscale monitor; 4 MB of RAM with 2.5 MB available; Hard disk with 220 KB free space; CD-ROM drive; System 7.0.1 or higher; Sound Manager 3.0 (uses 80 KB of free space on hard disk—version included on disc); QuickTime 1.6.1 for Parent's Video Guide (uses 850 KB of free space on hard disk—version included on disc); Printer support: works with most popular printers (monochrome and color)."

(I put it in quotation marks so you wouldn't think I—or my editors—would ever lay such a long, badly punctuated, grammatically suspicious run-on sentence on you—well, except maybe this one.)

On the PC side of the store, you might run into something like the requirements of Voyager's *The Residents' Freak Show*—a multimedia, well, freak show. It requires (and I'm quoting the box again):

"486SX-25 or higher processor, 640 × 480 256-color display (accelerator recommended), 8 MB RAM, MPC2-compatible CD-ROM drive and sound card with speakers or headphones, Microsoft Windows 3.1, MS-DOS 5.0 or later."

They don't want much, do they?

If your machine isn't up to their standards, well—don't buy them. They'll only break your heart anyway—or make you spend a lot of money to upgrade your system to meet their needs. What about *your* needs?

When in Doubt...

My rule of thumb when packing for a trip is, "When in doubt, leave it out." It keeps my suitcase from getting too heavy, or worse, having to lug *two* of them anywhere.

My rule of thumb when shopping for software is, "When in doubt, check it out." In short: ask.

Up Close and Personal

If questions of compatibility arise in a store, ask a handy clerk if a such-and-such CD-ROM will run on a such-and-such computer. The clerk won't know the answer unless they're *really* good. Most aren't. But they may have a demo copy of the software squirreled away for their break-time enjoyment, and (if you pout) maybe the clerk will let you look at the manual.

Software manuals often repeat the system requirements inside, usually with a lot less terse statements. You'll also see if the requirements on the box are from a somewhat mind-altered plane of reality.

For example, the manual for the time-traveling adventure *The Journeyman Project* tells you that there are actually *three* versions of the game on the disc: one that will run with 5MB of memory (unlike the 8MB it says on the box), one for 8MB, and one for 16MB.

In this case, if you had only 5MB or 6MB of RAM, you might have decided to risk buying the game rather than being ticked off that you don't have 8MB. It pays to ask.

Far and Wee

If you live in the wilds of Florida and tend to shop for computer junk by mail order, the catalog in your hand may be pretty stingy with the system requirements for the software you want to buy.

Feature of the Month—Yeah, Right.

Don't think that because a particular product makes your favorite catalog's cover month after month, it must be a pretty spiffy, whatever it is. Your BS detector should be beeping like crazy.

All a cover photograph (or a two-page splashy "feature article") means is that the company that makes that particular doohickey shelled out big bucks for the star treatment. It doesn't mean the product is better; it just means it's got a bigger advertising budget behind it. (Which, I suppose, is better than having a bigger behind behind it.)

Don't buy it blind. Pick up the phone, call the catalog's 800 number, and say, "I'm thinking about buying such-and-such a CD. I have a this-n-that computer. Can I use it?"

Unlike most in-store personnel, mail-order phone reps have computers in front of their little faces all the live-long day. Since you aren't actually handling the product before you buy it, much less trying out a floor model, mail-order houses know that you're going to have questions.

The good mail-order companies have a big, fat database of product information on their sales computers, so their phone clerks can answer almost any question that might crop up in the course of a sale. Don't be afraid to ask. They don't mind answering the questions.

I've talked to a lot of mail-order clerks and (not being the shy type) got nosy. Most mail-order companies would much rather answer a pile of legitimate questions before a sale than answer a lot of annoying questions afterward.

They'd certainly rather answer those questions than deal with all the fuss, frayed nerves, and paperwork involved in a product return or exchange. That cuts into their profit margin.

Tattoo it somewhere you'll see it—especially if you're one of those guys that refuses to stop to ask directions when lost: **WHEN IN DOUBT, ASK.**

The Least You Need to Know

➤ Hardware/software bundles aren't always (sometimes, but not always) the great deal they seem to be.

➤ Shop for the CD-ROM drive you want and then see if you can find it in a big, fat bundle of free stuff.

➤ When buying your first CD-ROM discs, be sure you know what your system has. Copy the list from this chapter and take it with you when you go shopping.

➤ Always read the system requirements information on software boxes (for CD or any other kind of software).

➤ If you don't meet or exceed those requirements, don't buy the software. It's that simple.

➤ When in doubt, ask.

Chapter 10

Making a List and Checking It Twice

In This Chapter

➤ Decisions, decisions

➤ Pulling it all together

➤ Platform blues

➤ My shopping list

Well, kiddies, it's time—how to put this delicately—to shop or get off the pot.

By now you have all the information you need to make an informed, intelligent decision about the CD-ROM drive you want to own. It's time to pull all that information together and put it to work by coming up with a shopping list.

If you've been taking notes, now is a good time to haul them out and start looking them over. Circle items in your notes that are important to you. Write them over on a clean list so you aren't confused, distracted, or swayed into deficit spending by items you've deemed less important.

How Much Is That CD in the Window?

Before you go any further, set a budget. Be realistic; specify exactly how much you can afford to spend.

I know (for me, at least) it's very easy to go off half-cocked—start shopping, and run *way* over my budget just because I didn't think it through completely. Write down your budget figure and stick to it—or better still, try to get everything you need under that figure.

If your budget is tight, shoot for the necessary items, the ones you absolutely need to get your CD-ROM drive hooked up. Leave the niceties until later when your budget's had a chance to heal itself.

The Power of Choice

If you've been keeping track of functions and features you want your drive to have, you now have to try to get as many of them as you can while staying within your budget.

Where Will It Go?

The first choice coming your way is whether you're going to opt for an internal or external CD-ROM drive. Remember: In order to install an internal drive, you have to have an open expansion bay available inside your computer. For PC users, you'll also need one or two open expansion slots for a controller and/or sound card.

Internal drives are nice because they don't take up any additional desk space, but they aren't easily removed and transported. External drives, especially portable, are easier to travel with, but take up valuable desk space. Chapter 3 has more detailed information for you chapter surfers.

Speed Demons

Based on the recommendations I made back in Chapter 4, if you want to make the best use of the current crop of CD-ROM software, get a multiple-speed drive, 2X or better, capable of at least the following speeds (if you can afford better, go for it):

➤ An access time rating of 300ms or better. (Lower numbers are better.)

➤ A sustained transfer rate of 300K/S, or better. (Higher numbers here are better.)

➤ At least a 64K cache, but 256K is better.

Anything slower means you'll be buying obsolete technology. Anything faster means you'll be current for at least a little while (it's hard to say how long, as fast as this technology changes).

She's Gotta Have It

Once you've decided where it goes and how fast it goes, you need to set yourself some guidelines for what things your drive must be able to do and which things you can live without.

The easiest way to do that is to take a piece of paper and draw a line down the middle. Label one half of the page **Gotta Have It** and the other **Nice If I Can Get It**.

Down the "Gotta Have It" side, list all the functions and compatibilities your drive *has* to have (described in detail in Chapter 5). Does it need Audio CD or multi-session Photo CD? Should it comply with or exceed the MPC standard? Do you want a PC- or Mac-only drive, or one that works on both platforms?

If there are any compatibility issues you're sure you can live without, write them down in the "Nice If I Can Get It" column.

It's really hard to know what you'll want to be able to use in the future. Right now, you may not have any place locally that develops film into Photo CDs, but one may open up two days after you get your drive. Therefore, the rule of thumb for compatibility issues is simple: The more the merrier.

Unfortunately, the merrier, the more expensive. Try to get as much built-in compatibility as possible in the drive you select, especially if you really don't know how you'll be using it in the future. You don't want your blossoming interest in CD-ROM to be limited by a drive that can't do what you want it to do.

Off the Rack or Made to Fit?

With the speed and compatibility essentials in mind, you should track down the drive of your dreams—only the drive, mind you.

Pore over the magazines aimed at your computer platform, compare prices in reviews to those in mail-order ads versus stores in your area. When you find the drive, *then* you can look to see if that drive is available in a "ready-to-run" bundle.

If you can't find the bundle, you can always piece together a custom bundle; many mail-order companies offer substantial savings on CD-ROM software bundles when you purchase your drive from them. You might also be able to finagle a double-whammy if you can find the drive you want in a bundle with CD-ROM discs *and* get additional CDs at a discount—talk about the thrill of the hunt.

Piecing together a bundle assures you that all the software you get is software you're likely to use, but be sure you get all the things you'll need to get the drive hooked up and running. Don't sweat the small stuff until you have the big stuff taken care of.

The Big Stuff

Here's a breakdown by computer system of the *least* you need to buy. You can, of course, get more. Buy less, and you may not be able to use your drive.

Minimum Macintosh

Mac users get off pretty easily because Macs already have built-in SCSI and sound support. The least you need to buy is simple:

➤ CD-ROM drive

➤ SCSI cable

➤ CD-ROM driver software

➤ Speakers and/or headphones (for vibrant sound)

All of these (except possibly the speakers and/or headphones) should come with the drive you select, or (in some cases) as a separate Macintosh interface kit for that drive. If you select a bundle, you should get all of these features, and then some. With an internal drive, you may also need support rails, and the cables will vary. Ask before you buy.

DOS Minimums

To hook up your drive to a DOS machine, *without* adhering to the MPC standards, you need:

➤ CD-ROM drive

➤ CD-ROM driver software

➤ SCSI (or other) adapter card

➤ An appropriate cable for your adapter card

➤ Sound card (if you want to hear the sounds in your CD software)

➤ Speakers and/or headphones (for vibrant sound—I like that word: *vibrant*)

➤ For an internal drive, you may need additional hardware to install

If your PC has only 1MB or 2MB of RAM installed, you should also upgrade to 4MB (or more) of memory. Otherwise, you'll be very limited in the CDs you'll be able to use. With only 1MB or 2MB, you won't be able to use any CD-ROMs that rely heavily on graphics or photo-quality images—well, you might be able to use them, but they probably won't be fast or pretty... or even pretty fast.

MPC Minimums

Running MPC CD-ROM software under Windows means you'll have access to a whole range of MPC-standard software—if your system complies to the MPC standard (see Chapter 5 if you're not sure your system is up to it).

If your computer is up to snuff, you'll need to purchase:

➤ MPC-compatible CD-ROM drive

➤ SCSI (or other interface) cable

➤ CD-ROM driver software

➤ SCSI (or other) adapter card

➤ MPC-compatible sound card

➤ Speakers and/or headphones

➤ For an internal drive, you may need additional hardware to install.

The MPC standard requires 2MB of RAM configured as extended memory. That's nonsense. If you can't run most DOS-based CD-ROM software on a PC *without* Windows, how the devil are you going to get MPC software (which relies heavily on graphics) to run *with* Windows? You won't.

Upgrade to as much memory as will reasonably fit in your computer (and your budget), but at least 4MB.

My Shopping List

If you didn't know it already, I made myself go through this whole process of deciding which drive to buy, how to buy it, and what to get with it, just before I started writing about it. That way, I'd know the obstacles and pitfalls lying in wait for you.

I even repeated the process for the second edition. For this go-round, I was concerned with getting a drive to hook up to my PC because frankly, it was a pain in the hindquarters to unhook the drive from the Mac (where it stays mostly) and *shlep* it over to the PC (a whole six feet away), and I just didn't do it willingly.

I made the mistakes, so you won't have to. Nice of me, huh?

To help you make up your shopping list, here's my shopping list. It's everything I bought and why I bought it. Maybe it will help you, or maybe it will just help to sate your insatiable curiosity.

What I Got

Drive: NEC MultiSpin 3Xp (external and portable)

Interface: n/a (The 3Xp came with the appropriate SCSI cable.)

SCSI adapter: n/a (It's built into Macintosh, and I already have one in my PC.)

Sound card: SoundBlaster 16 (for the PC)

Driver software: n/a (It was *supposed* to come with the drive. I'll give you the sob story in a moment.)

Miscellaneous: 2-foot SCSI cable (more about why later)

Speakers/Headphones: Nope. Already had them.

Why I Got It

This time, I selected the NEC MultiSpin 3Xp for a couple of reasons. First, it's not the latest, greatest, and fastest drive—it's triple speed, and there are 4X drives out there—but the PC isn't my primary computer. I got the fastest portable drive that fit my $500 budget.

Second, I chose the portable model because it's also Mac-compatible and I may want or need to take it on the road with my PowerBook. If the need arises, I still need to shell out additional bucks for an appropriate cable and battery pack, but I'll burn that bridge when I come to it. Mail order and overnight delivery have made me cocky. I might regret it.

You know how I feel about having a sound card in a PC by now, so I won't belabor the point. I chose a mid-range (not the cheapest, but not the most expensive) Sound-Blaster on the recommendation of a friend who has one and likes it.

The speakers and headphones I already had worked fine (they're cheap, but functional). I may spring for a better set of speakers; I just didn't want to spend the money now.

The two-foot SCSI cable was for connecting the CD-ROM drive to my Mac's external hard drive—on another off chance that I might want or need to be *really* decadent and have both drives up and running on my Mac at the same time. It could happen.

The CD-ROM's cable ends with a 25-pin SCSI connector. My Mac's external hard drive has a 50-pin SCSI port—and you can't plug the one into the other; they don't match (as you can see in the following figure).

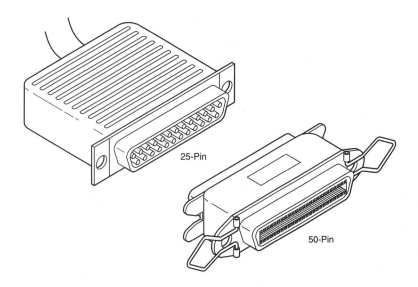

The 25-pin SCSI connector is more common with Macs—it's the size of the SCSI port on the back of all Macs. Most IBM-compatible users will run into 50-pin connectors.

In order to connect them, I had to buy a short piece of cable with an appropriate 25-pin connector on one end (to plug into the original cable) and a 50-pin connector on the other (to plug into the hard drive).

Cable Babble

When talking about cable, *short* is a relative term. The cable in a SCSI chain cannot total more than about 18 to 20 feet—any longer, and the signal starts to break down and bizarre things happen. You can install a signal booster, but they're an additional expense, so avoid them if you can. Keeping the total length between 6–10 feet will avoid problems with weak signals altogether.

You should always select a SCSI cable that is as short as possible, while still giving you enough cable to make a firm connection. Two feet is about as small as they come; I wouldn't buy one longer than five or six feet at most. Chapter 15 covers this stuff in more detail.

Cables, in general, can drive you insane if you don't know what you're looking at and/or for. When in doubt (which is, for me, most of the time), ask before you buy.

If you opt for an internal drive, this won't be a problem. If you get an external drive, and it's the *only* SCSI device you're connecting, it shouldn't be a problem. If you go for another sort of controller card (built into a sound card, for instance), it also won't be a problem.

Other Stupid Things That Happened

I ordered the drive from one of my usual PC mail-order places (I won't say which because this wasn't their fault). I figured, PC place, ordering a PC-compatible drive, and one of the NEC models that doesn't require an interface kit, I should be in like Flynn. Wrong.

The drive came completely decked out for a Macintosh installation without any PC-compatible driver software. The mail-order place couldn't do any more for me than give me NEC's technical support and customer service numbers. I spent what felt like *hours* on hold with NEC trying to get it straightened out. It never happened. Somewhere in hour three of listening to Muzak and "All customer representatives are busy with other calls...," I remembered that I already had driver software from buying the interface kit for the first edition of this book. I tried it. It worked. And I got on with my life.

The other stupid thing I did was try out the drive with a CD that my system wasn't up to handling. Completely wrong. The CD called for a 486; mine's a 386. It wanted 8MB of RAM; I've got 6MB. It was very sad. Which is *why* I stress that if your machine doesn't meet the system requirements on any software box, don't buy the software. It's an invitation to frustration.

Anything else I need to say on the subject is simple: Don't let this happen to you! It will mean I was not an idiot in vain.

Your Shopping List

This Mad-Libs kind of shopping list is scripted for a mail-order purchase. All you really need to do is fill in the make/model/catalog numbers of the stuff you want to order, and then just read it off over the phone. They'll never know what you're doing. Trust me.

If you're doing the shopping in person, you can use this as an easy reference shopping list for yourself, or just hand it to the sales clerk.

Raise Your Right Hand and Repeat After Me...

If you're physically going into a store, you should practice saying this over and over, at various levels of forcefulness, before a slick salesperson gets his or her hooks into you: "I can afford to spend $_____, and nothing you can say will make me spend more."

Cheat Sheet (Fill in the Blanks)

I have a (computer make/model) _____.

It has a _____ central processor chip (for example: 80386SX, 68040) running at _____MHz (its clock speed).

I've got _____MB of RAM installed.

I'm using _____ (MS-DOS 6.2, Windows 3.1, System 7.5, and so on) as my operating system.

I want an internal/external (select one) _____
_____ (manufacturer and model number, or catalog number) CD-ROM drive. If you don't have a make or model in mind, ask for your speed and compatibility requirements.

What all does that come with? (Eliminate any of the following that may be included.) Do I get any free stuff, too?

I'll also need:

_____MB of RAM (only if you need to increase yours).

_____ (make and model SCSI adapter or other controller card, PCs only).

_____ Appropriate cable (if it isn't included with the drive).

_____ (make and model sound card, PCs only).

How much have I spent so far? (Keep smelling salts handy, just in case.) If you didn't faint, or exceed your spending limit, you may also need:

_____ (make and model/catalog number) speakers. Will they work all right with my drive?

_____ (make and model/catalog number) stereo headphones.

Does that drive use CD caddies? (If YES, then) okay, add a three- or five- (circle one) pack of caddies, too.

I want to get these CD-ROM discs (list by name and catalog number):

_____

_____

_____

_____

_____

_____

_____

_____

_____

Do I get a discount on any of these for buying them with the drive? (If you don't ask, you don't get, right?)

I also want (for any additional hardware you might want, like a scanner, and so on, as your needs and budget allow—see Chapter 31 for ideas):

_____

_____

_____

Is everything in stock?

> If not, when do you expect it? _____

> If yes, when will I receive it? _____

The sales clerk (if he or she is working on commission) should thank you profusely for putting a child/spouse/life-partner through medical school, and promise you a lifetime supply of aspirin, should you need it.

If you take your time and proceed carefully using this list, you may not need the aspirin—at least, not because of the CD-ROM drive.

The Least You Need to Know

➤ Set a dollar amount for your budget and stick to it.

➤ Based on your budget, get the best drive you can with the amount of money you have to spend.

➤ Use the shopping list so you get everything you need.

➤ Stick to the shopping list so you don't go wild in the store (or on the phone with the mail-order place) and careen off into deficit spending.

➤ Don't repeat my mistakes—they're of the obvious and humiliating variety.

➤ If you must make a mistake, err on the side of caution. If that isn't your style, be creative and bizarre. At least you'll have a mistake you can learn from and be proud of.

Shopping Without Dropping

There's an art to shopping. It's a thing of beauty when you're able to get a great deal on a gadget or doohickey that will be a joy forever—or at least until a better one comes along.

It isn't necessarily an easy thing, though. Good shopping takes effort. Just ask anyone in a mall on Christmas Eve. It's too easy to be taken in by a slick ad, a pretty package, a salesclerk's wink.

Manufacturers and salespeople want you to buy what they have to sell. If they have to exaggerate the positives a little and overlook the negatives a lot, well, that's salesmanship.

This chapter is devoted to making you a little cynical when it comes to shopping—not just for your CD-ROM drive, but for any techno toy. As Lily Tomlin says: I worry that no matter how cynical I get, it isn't enough to keep up.

Before You Go Shopping

Go shopping—not to *buy* anything, but to see what's available in your local stores and at what price. As I recommended in Chapter 9, you should see what CD-ROM software catches your fancy, take note of its system requirements, and make sure you meet them.

If you're attracted to the real gee-whiz software, you may have to add more RAM or buy a faster CD-ROM drive than you originally intended. It could happen.

Write stuff down. Remember the make and model of drives, what's included (especially in bundles), and prices. That will make it easier to comparison-shop in catalogs or in other stores.

Make a Friend

If a salesclerk helps you out while you're just looking, write down his or her name, too. If you later decide to buy the CD-ROM drive (or whatever) at his or her store, ask for the same clerk to help you. Many salesclerks work on commission—make sure you buy the drive from the clerk who sold you on it. You'll make a friend, besides.

The reason you write everything down (especially the price and features) is that you can't do serious comparison-shopping if you don't have all the facts.

If, say, you forget to write down details like the access speed and transfer rate of a particular drive, when you comparison-shop (maybe, from a catalog) you may wind up buying a less-expensive drive that is also less of what you need—not as fast, not Photo-CD-compatible, and so on.

Price comparisons only work if everything else (features and speed) are equal.

Before You Buy

Because somehow someone found out you own a computer, you've wound up on a billion mailing lists. Today you got a catalog the size of the Manhattan Yellow Pages from the company Mega TechMonger, Inc., and already the pages are dotted with drool. Since CD-ROMs and multimedia are big buzzwords right now, there are CD readers everywhere in the catalog, along with whiz-bang CD software.

RUN AWAY! Fast.

Catalogs are designed to make you want stuff. Forget about what you want; you know you want everything. Shush that inner child that's stamping its feet and screaming, "Gimmee! Gimmee!" Now is the time to think about what you *need*.

You've decided on a CD-ROM drive and the to-go-withs to get it up and running—probably some CD software, too. Keep focused on that alone; when you're in the mood to buy, well, you'll buy. If you can't get through the supermarket checkout without buying some gum, a couple of trashy tabloids, and a bouquet of wilted flowers, you definitely have to curb your impulse-shopping.

An Easy Tip

Here's a tricky tip that's always done well by me: I keep a little list by my computers. When, in the course of human events, it becomes apparent that I need something to make my computing life easier or more productive, I add it to my list. When there are a couple of things on the list, I'll look them over to see if they're things I actually *need*—because I know I'm a toy-brain. If I don't really, *really* need it, I cross it off the list. If there's anything left on the list, I gird my loins and prepare to shop.

When I'm in the mood to shop, a couple of things keep me focused on the shopping task at hand. First I'll take a quick check of my finances to see how much I can afford to spend, then whether or not I have the cash (or the space left on a credit card). I set my price limit first. Only then will I pull out the Mega TechMonger catalog and see how much what I need costs.

If I can't afford it, I put the list and catalog aside and start saving up for it, either by setting aside the cash or paying down a credit card. There's nothing more frustrating than obsessing over a new computer gadget that I can't afford.

On rare occasions, I can afford it (or must—sometimes you just have no choice). Then I start my pre-shopping drill—a couple of simple steps to make myself an informed shopper, save time and money, and (also a good thing) tick off any sneaky or manipulative salesclerks.

I go through this process with everything I buy, from software to complete computers. The more expensive the purchase, the more thorough the homework.

Ask the Geek Who Owns One

I know a lot of computer users: Geeks of a feather... and all that. When I start lusting after something like a CD-ROM drive or other big-ticket item, I'll collar them and pump them for information.

Here's what I ask them:

➤ What's the make and model of yours?

➤ Where did you get it?

➤ What did you pay for it?

➤ Were you happy with the product, and if not, why?

➤ Were you happy with the company you bought it from, and if not, why?

➤ If you had it to do all over again, would you buy the same thing? If not, why?

I always go to the people I know (whose opinions I respect) first. That gives me a place to start looking, either with products and companies to look at or products and companies to avoid like the plague.

The Reviews Are In

Whether or not I've wrestled an opinion out of people I know, my next step is to go to the magazines: *PC Magazine, MacUser, PC World, Macworld, PC Computing,* whichever one is appropriate to the computer I'm looking to buy for.

I'll pull out back issues and see if they've reviewed the particular product I'm interested in, or if they've done a round-up review (like *10 Double-Speed CD-ROM Drives Compared*). I'll read everything on the product, or class of product, I can find.

Two Grains of Salt

I don't read magazine reviews to buy the products they recommend. I find that most magazines have *way* different priorities from mine. You know, "If you're looking for a color laser printer, we recommend the high-speed Kibitzer 3000 Phase-Shifting Palette Cruncher, a steal at $395,675.95." Yeah, sure. I'll run right out and buy two.

I read reviews and round-ups for the factual information: components, speed, price, problems. The opinion stuff is just opinion, after all, and totally subjective. I give the reviewer's opinion a fairly low weight in my buying decision.

After I weigh all the reviews from my friends and magazines, I sit down and decide what I'm going to get.

Settling for the Best

Sometimes, circumstances dictate that you settle for a product that meets fewer of your needs than another. Price is usually the deciding factor here.

In general, I try to get the most for my money that I can. I'd rather spend a little more money for something I'll "grow into"—and meet my future needs (real or imagined)—than spend less money on something I'll have to replace in six months. It's better to wait the six months and get exactly what I need rather than throw good money after bad in an effort to make do.

So, the advice here is: Get as fast and spiffy a CD-ROM as you can while staying close to your budget. If you can't afford to buy something you can grow with, you might be better off waiting until you can.

When You're Ready to Buy

So you've weighed your options (and your wallet or purse), listened to your friends, and read the reviews. You're ready to put your money where your computer is. Where do you go?

With computer companies trying to penetrate the so-called "consumer market" by putting computers and peripherals into more traditional stores (as opposed to "computer stores"), your shopping opportunities have increased dramatically. Each kind of store has its own advantages and disadvantages. Let's look at each kind, talk about the differences, and then you can choose the shopping experience that best suits your needs.

The Educational Market

Apple largely pioneered the educational market with the Apple IIe and the first Macs. To this day, they still have a very strong educational distribution channel, and they discount heavily. IBM and other PC vendors have tried to duplicate Apple's success in the educational market, so options abound.

If you work in education or your child goes to a computer college (that is, a school where they require all students to have a computer), you might be eligible for special educational pricing on computers, software, and peripherals. Good for you!

Before you do anything else, find out what kinds of deals are available for faculty, staff, or students (depending on which one you are) for hardware and accessories. Sometimes all you need to do is flash your student or staff ID in the college store, and you get deep discounts on everything.

On some campuses, you may have to contact a computer company representative directly or place orders through a specific staff member. Check with your school first for details. You have nothing to save but money.

Malls, Stores, Superstores

With the way shopping has evolved in this country, you're most likely to find a store that sells computers, accessories, and software in or near a mall.

You can find systems and all the to-go-withs (software and accessories) in Sears, office supply chains (like Staples, OfficeMax, and so on), and in shopping "clubs" (like Sam's Club). You can find the whole range of computer doo-dads in local computer stores and in national chain "super stores" like Micro Center and Computer Warehouse, and other regional variations that have been springing up everywhere.

Proximity is the main advantage of shopping locally. If you're lucky to be in an area with a lot of stores, you can comparison-shop (and even buy pieces) at different stores. If your local store claims, "We'll beat any advertised price," you should definitely take them up on it.

Shopping locally offers you some advantages: You can often "test drive" software and hardware, question a salesperson, and (should something go wrong) return defective merchandise without having to ship it across the country for repair or replacement.

The disadvantage of local stores is simple: overhead. Part of every dollar you spend in a retail store goes to pay rent, utilities, sales staff, mall security... you get the idea. Prices may be appreciably higher.

Superstores try to offset the cost of overhead by eliminating glossy surroundings and making up the difference with sales volume: They sell more stuff at lower prices. "Super" and other computer stores with a warehouse-like atmosphere generally also have a better-informed sales and technical support staff. Many even have walk-in service centers for the products that they sell. I really, *really* like the ones that have it all.

In non-computer stores (like Sears), you might not have access to a knowledgeable salesperson—that can be trouble. If the clerk doesn't know what you're talking about, how can he or she offer you merchandise that meets your needs—or that even works with your computer?

Of course, the closeness of the store to your home makes it easier to return or exchange things, but how much running back and forth are you prepared to do?

There are ways to protect yourself:

➤ Select a reputable store—one that's been around a while and is likely to still be around. A great returns policy is meaningless if the store has gone out of business.

➤ Before you buy anything, check the store's returns policy. Get it in writing if you can.

➤ If a clerk offers to make an exception to the returns policy for you (because you're so nice), definitely get it in writing, and be sure to get the clerk's name.

➤ If you can, pay with a credit card. You can always ask the card company to withhold payment if a dispute develops.

➤ Try to make your purchase on a weekday or when the store will be open for the next two or three days. If you discover a problem while the store is closed, you'll have to sit and grind your teeth until they open again.

➤ Save all your receipts and don't fill out warranty/registration cards until everything is working satisfactorily. Some stores won't accept returns unless everything (even little slips of paper) are in their original condition.

Mail Order: An Overnight Affair

You've seen them (or you soon will) scattered throughout the computer magazines: mail-order companies that sell everything you could possibly want for your computer, including complete new systems. Their prices are good, and many offer overnight delivery for almost immediate gratification.

The advantages of going the mail/phone order route are numerous. You'll generally find lower prices because they aren't maintaining glitzy stores. You can also save money on sales tax if you're ordering across state lines (at least until the Feds or State governments figure out a way to plug the loophole). Philadelphia has a 7% sales tax. On a $300 CD-ROM drive, I'd pay an extra $21 in tax if I bought one there. That's the price of a cheap CD-ROM disc.

A lot of mail-order places have a knowledgeable staff to take your order. They can help you make up your mind and answer any simple questions you might have. In addition, many mail-order places have toll-free technical support lines you can call to ask heavy-duty questions before (and after) you buy. I like that.

The disadvantages, however, are just as numerous. For one, you can't try things before you buy them. Before you pick up the phone, you have to know pretty clearly what you want. Also, returns policies are a little more strict. Many places charge a "restocking fee" (except on damaged or defective goods), and you must call for permission to return things.

There's no way to judge a mail-order company's reliability from their ads. You can, however, get hints—read their policies closely. If it looks like they're nickel-and-diming you to death with service charges and restocking fees, run away. If they have a 900-number for ordering, run away. 900-numbers always seem vaguely slimy to me. I mean, really: making you pay $2 a minute for the privilege of spending your money with them—*ack!* And don't get me *started* on the subject of pay-as-you-go technical support.

Not Really a Plug, but...

I've been lucky. I've dealt with some of the larger companies (MacConnection, PC Warehouse, MacWarehouse) and have had pretty good experiences. MacConnection helped fix a problem that was a result of my own (*blush*) stupidity, with no hassle (and no extra charges). PC Warehouse accepted a return gracefully. Needless to say, they've all had repeat business from me.

Mistakes happen. It's how mail-order companies correct these mistakes (yours or theirs) that is the measure of their greatness. I'm usually willing to pay a little more at a place (mail order or walk-in) with excellent service. A painful shopping experience is still painful, even if you save a buck.

When shopping by mail order, there are also ways to protect yourself:

➤ Ask your computerized friends who they've dealt with and who they've kept dealing with. Ask them why, too.

➤ Check the magazines. Consumer columns and "Letters to the Editor" are often ways of hearing horror stories about shady companies.

➤ Scour the fine print in ads. Don't pay extra for using a credit card, don't pay more than $6 to $10 for overnight shipping, and *certainly* don't pay for the privilege of placing an order.

➤ Don't pay by check. Even reputable places hold your check until it clears the bank—that's only prudent. Once they have your money, however, you have no recourse. Use a credit card so you can at least try to withhold payment should a dispute arise.

➤ When you're placing an order, take names. Write them down. Have the salesperson confirm your order. Be clear, and be sure you've understood (and have been understood) to avoid any confusion over what you ordered.

➤ Take notes, too. Good notes will help you sort out a problem with the company, or document a claim with your credit card company should you need to withhold payment.

I Read It in the Want Ads

If your budget won't allow you to buy new, don't despair. Bargains can be had in the used-computer market. You can find ads for used equipment in the want ads of your local newspaper (or local computer newspaper or newsletter, if you have one). In the Pennsylvania, Delaware, and New Jersey area, we have *The Delaware Valley Computer User*. It's good, and it's free!

Other good sources: bulletin boards at your local supermarket, high school, college—and, if you use a modem, a local electronic bulletin board.

You can also turn up leads on used stuff if you belong to a computer user's group. The real byte-heads in these groups are always upgrading their equipment and selling off the old stuff.

The advantage of buying used is price. You can get some real bargains. The disadvantages are the same as for buying a used car from a classified ad: You don't know the person you're dealing with, there's usually no manufacturer's warranty, and (if you don't know a good bit about computers) you can pay way too much for a real lemon. Used technology is usually a step or two behind current—that's why it's up for sale in the first place.

User's group
A club that focuses on the needs and concerns of a particular computer, software, or aspect of computing. They're all over the place, and they're great to join.

There isn't a lot you can do to protect yourself after the purchase, unless your local laws provide protection. Even so, resorting to the law is mighty tiresome. It's best to protect yourself before you hand over the cash.

➤ Try out the CD-ROM drive—preferably at your home, for a few hours (if not for a day or two)—before you buy it.

➤ Check for signs of damage or abuse. Heck, check for dust: Anyone who tries to sell you something without cleaning it up first has no idea of how to take care of things.

➤ If you don't know what to look for, bring someone along who does. Buy him or her a nice lunch as a bribe.

➤ Ask if you can have a 30-day warranty (in writing) in case the dingus blows up when you get it home. If not 30, try for 15, 10, or 7 days—even 48 to 72 hours. Anything to give you a little extra leeway.

➤ Make sure you get a transfer of ownership (just a signed note saying what you bought) if the hardware is still under a manufacturer's warranty, or if you want to re-register the software in your name.

Computer Brokers

No, these aren't people who break computers for a living. These are companies that buy up other companies' (and individuals') computers and peripherals, refurbish them, and resell them. Or they're companies that lease computer systems, then sell old models when they upgrade their line of machines. They're like used-car lots for computers.

The advantage of going through a broker to buy used equipment is that (since they refurbish the machines) they usually offer limited warranties.

You can find them advertised in large metropolitan newspapers (you can pick up the *New York Times* just about anywhere these days) or in *USA Today*. Computer resellers are cropping up everywhere there are businesses that lease computers, so you may even be able to find them listed in your local Yellow Pages. Treat them the way you would any mail-order company, taking the same precautions listed earlier.

CD-ROM, the Universe, and Everything

When you're shopping by any non-traditional method (anything except a store or mail order), make doubly sure you're getting everything you'll need to connect whatever you're buying (in this case, a CD-ROM) to your computer.

The shopping list in Chapter 10 should come in handy. If you pick up anything from the want ads or somewhere else, just eliminate it from your list. You'll know automatically what's left to get.

The Least You Need to Know

➤ Don't buy on impulse; do your homework.

➤ Protect yourself however you can when you make a purchase.

➤ Don't forget the savings to be had if you qualify for educational-market purchases at your school.

➤ Take extra care to examine and test things you buy used, from whatever source.

➤ Select a CD-ROM drive (or any hardware) with an eye toward your future needs, as well as your present needs.

➤ Saving money is good.

➤ Blowing your budget is bad.

Part 2
The Setup

If you followed the advice given in Part 1, you should now be surrounded by boxes and bags of CD-ROM-type stuff. This part of the book is devoted to helping you get all that neat stuff out of its packages and onto your desk, or into your computer—without a lot of hassles.

In Part 2, you'll find the straight scoop on:

➤ *What to do before you unpack everything*

➤ *General advice for installing external and internal drives (PC and Macintosh)*

➤ *Some scuzzy talk (not of the "potty mouth" variety)*

➤ *Plus, a step-by-step guide to firing up that bad boy for the very first time.*

Chapter 12

Don't Touch That Screwdriver!

In This Chapter

➤ Damage control

➤ Checking checklists

➤ The point of no returns

➤ Location, location, location

Before You Start Scratching Your Head

More experienced computer geeks may find the way I've broken things down here (and in the following chapters) slightly convoluted.

In my own defense I have to say that, like Hamlet, I am only mad north by north-west; east to south I can still tell a PC from a Macintosh.

Here's the method to this madness: trying to keep general information, PC, and Mac installations stuff neatly segregated (so you don't have to plow through junk you don't need) led to *some* repetition and *some* cross-referencing of information.

To keep from getting lost, everyone should start here, then jump to the chapter appropriate to their installation: PC-compatible in Chapter 13; Macintosh in Chapter 14. Afterward, either sort of computer user may need some of the information in Chapter 15 (which deals with SCSI and other interfaces).

If your installation chapter doesn't include every bit of information you need to proceed, it will direct you to the chapter that has the missing scoop in it. In the event of a loss of cabin pressure, oxygen masks will drop down from the overhead compartment—put one snugly over your mouth and nose and continue to breathe normally.

Starting Here, Starting Now

By now, unless you've been reading ahead (you cheeky monkey), you should have brought home—or had delivered, if you went the mail-order route—all the gizmos and doodads you need to plunge feet-first into the world of CD-ROM.

If you're like me (and I know that you are), you're just champing at the bit to get going. Stop that. It's bad for your teeth.

Before you start plowing through boxes and bags and packing material, going completely berserk, there are a couple of things you should do first. If you actually went to the store, bought stuff, and brought it home with you (as opposed to ordering from a mail-order company), you can probably skip ahead to the next section called "The Box Step."

Book 'Em, Dano...

Doing what it says here (or in any how-to book, for that matter)—rather than rushing in and doing what you think (or worse, guess) you should do—is technically known as *doing it by the book*.

It's a good technique to master, especially if you feel uncertain or have a strong enough ego to admit that you don't know what the heck you're doing. Ego aside, I haven't quite gotten the knack of it. I still tend to shoot first and read manuals later—especially where new toys are concerned. Don't let this happen to you.

With your excitement firmly in check (take a couple of deep, cleansing breaths), the very first thing you should do is examine the shipping cartons for any obvious signs of damage. You know: crush marks with the imprint of a size-15 clodhopper in the middle, tire treadmarks, signs of water damage, suspicious signs that your boxes have been opened and repackaged.

Actually, the very best time to inspect your packages for signs of damage is while the delivery person is standing right there, so you don't actually accept delivery until you're satisfied that the package(s) don't look damaged. If there are any major signs of damage—like the package is smooshed flat—you should refuse to accept delivery, or ask the driver to wait while you check to see if the contents are damaged. It isn't a guarantee that there still won't be something wrong inside the package (unless you've got X-ray specs that work), but it's a start.

If things look okay, allowing for the usual wear-and-tear on a box that's been shipped, you can move on to the next step.

If things look somehow wonky, you have a couple of options. You can refuse delivery if the driver is still there, and then immediately call the company you ordered it from and tell them it was damaged in shipment, you refused delivery, and you want a replacement.

If the mail-order place has a policy of requiring a *return authorization number* (sometimes called an *RA* or *RMA*, for short), and if the driver is amenable, call the mail-order place while the driver waits. Ask the customer service folks how they want you to proceed. It might just make everybody's lives a little easier.

Alternatively, you could also just note the damage on the form you sign to accept delivery (documenting that the goods, if damaged, were damaged *before* you received them), and then carry on with the installation to see if the damage affected the drive (or whatever). You can exchange it with the mail-order company later if the CD-ROM is too boogered to boogie.

If the driver's already gone, well, you may as well carry on and check to see if the damage affected the drive (or whatever). You can still raise a fuss with the mail-order company to get a replacement.

Speaking of carrying on...

The Box Step

Step, together; right, together; back, together; left, together. (That's the real box step. When I was about 6, I stomped the heck out of my poor mother's toes learning that. Sorry, Mom.)

Next on your list of things to do: find the mail-order company's invoice or packing slip. (Retail shoppers, you should find your itemized sales receipt.)

Carefully take everything out of the shipping boxes (or the bags you carried things home in). Don't open any of the product packages yet (you know, don't take off the shrink wrap, and so on). If you need to return or exchange something at this stage of the game, the unopened package will make that easier.

Customer service The people whose job it is to straighten out their company's mistakes and to help you deal with your own mistakes. A good company's Customer Service Department will fix their own mistakes quickly and with no additional hassle to you. A *great* company is one that will fix *your* mistake quickly with no additional hassle to you.

Check for any signs of damage to the contents (those of you with the X-ray specs can skip this). Then check the actual contents against your invoice or receipt; make sure you received:

➤ Everything you ordered

➤ Everything you were charged for

If something turns up missing, check the boxes (or bags) again to make sure something isn't hiding in the packing material or hiding down in the corner (this *always* happens to me).

If it's still missing after you do body-cavity searches on the boxes/bags in question, call customer service at the mail-order company (or store) where you bought it and let them know.

The Box Step Redux

After you've verified that everything you ordered is present and accounted for (or have called to deal with missing items), you should read each product package to make sure that what you ordered is right for your computer.

Look for a System Requirements label or section on the box. Double-check to make sure you can use the bloody thing with your computer before you open it. If it looks like you can use it, open the product package; make sure everything you're supposed to have is included there, too.

Some companies will put a printed packing list at the top of the box. Others will include a page at the front of the product's manual (or other documentation) saying what you should have. Make sure you got everything you were supposed to get.

Returnability Warning!

Don't fill in registration cards yet, or write in or on the manual. If there's software involved, don't open the envelope covered in fine print yet, either. All of these can push you past... *the point of no returns*. (Insert ominous music here.)

If everything is there, great! If not, you should be burning up the phone lines trying to get the store or mail-order company to make things right.

The Point of No Returns

Does all of this cautious, step-by-step checking seem tedious and anal-retentive to you? Well, it is, but you should really be certain that everything is as right as you know it can be before you cross *The Point of No Returns*.

That's the point where you can no longer get your money back, exchange the product for another one of the same species, or get a completely different product.

Spotting the line of demarcation between returnable and non-returnable is as vague and ill-defined as crossing the line into the Twilight Zone (all together, *do-do-do-do, do-do-do-do*). Policies vary from store to store and from one mail-order company to the next. The best thing to do is ask before you buy anything, whether on the phone or in person.

Some sure signs that you've crossed the point of no returns:

➤ Writing on or in the manual, or otherwise defacing it (spilling coffee on it, breaking the spine, and so on)

➤ Filling in registration cards

➤ Opening software envelopes

Note that these particular cautions only apply if the product isn't defective—you want to return it because you bought the wrong thing or accidentally ordered two things that do the same thing (I've done that). If it weren't for the fact that you don't need it, the gizmo would be perfectly acceptable. The company you bought it from is going to want to sell it to somebody else. If it isn't salable, they probably won't want to take it back.

Broke is Broke

If you want to return a product that's broken, or defective, that's a whole 'nother story. It shouldn't matter what you opened, filled in, or wrote on. "Broke is broke." An even exchange for one that works shouldn't be a problem for anyone.

Location, Location, Location

Once you've rested up from all of that strenuous package opening, it's time to clean up your act: unearth that corner of your desk where you plan to place your new CD-ROM drive, or give yourself the elbow room so you can painlessly install an internal drive.

If you're hooking up an external CD-ROM drive to a Macintosh (or you already have the sound and interface cards installed in your PC), you need enough room to set up the drive and to finagle it around so you can get at the connectors in the back. You also need to lay out the manual(s) that accompanied the drive so you can refer to the specific installation instructions for the drive you purchased. You may also need some tools (like a screwdriver—check your drive's manual for details), and you'll need to get at any software that came with the drive.

For an internal drive—or to also install sound and/or interface cards in a PC—you'll need even *more* room. You not only need to lay out all of the above, but you also need room to pop the hood on your computer, more tools, installation hardware (like a mounting bracket, if appropriate; check your drive's manual for details), and the cards—all within easy reach.

In short: Clear the decks around your computer.

Help Is on the Way!

More detailed installation help is covered in the next three chapters. Chapter 13 covers general PC installation. Chapter 14 covers Macintosh. Chapter 15 covers the peccadilloes of the more common Mac and PC interface schemes.

When you've cleared off your work area (I needed to use a shovel—I'm *such* a slob), you may as well (*ack!*) dust the area, too. Just a cloth moistened with some mild cleaner will be fine.

I Got Yer Dust Right Here!

I know, I know. I hate housework, too—but as long as it's clear, it may as well be clean. Dust and dirt are real bogeymen to CD-ROMs in particular, and computers in general. Think of it as "preventative maintenance"—that sounds a lot more technical than dusting.

When the area is cleaned up, set up your tools and get ready to roll. Be sure you have at hand all the manuals that came with all your new doodads. You'll be referring to them.

In the meantime, take five. Put your feet up and have a nice beverage. You've earned it.

The Least You Need to Know

➤ When you start talking about a big dollar investment in hardware, you can't be too careful. Check your packages for obvious signs of damage before you accept delivery or pay for them in a store.

➤ Make sure you received everything you ordered and/or paid for by checking items off of your invoice or store receipt.

➤ Be sure everything that was supposed to come with each product is also there. Check the items against the packing slip (if there is one) or the *What's in the Box?* (or whatever they call it) section of the manual. But don't *write* in the manual while you're doing it—no check marks, or Xs, or anything.

➤ Prepare your work area before you start to work.

➤ Take five before you get down to the actual installation. I mean, all this excitement! I'm feeling *ferklempt*.

Strictly PC

If you've actually been doing what I've been suggesting (as opposed to reading this book on a bus), then you have the space around your computer cleared off, with your tools, cards, cable(s), and your CD-ROM drive all within easy reach.

Tool Time

Speaking of tools (insert appropriate Tim Allen grunts here), a nice computer tool kit will include everything you need to do this sort of job: screw- and nutdrivers, that claw-thingy that picks up screws and small stuff you drop into the crevices inside your computer—all sorts of handy things to have. You can pick up a tool kit for $20 to $30. If you plan on doing more installations on your own, why not treat yourself to a practical gift?

If you're smart, you'll also have all the documentation that came along with each piece of hardware on hand for easy reference. I don't even *pretend* to know how to install every bit of hardware made for every make of computer.

What you'll get here is a plan of attack, an organized and easy way to hook up an external or internal CD-ROM drive to your PC. If what I say runs counter to what it says in your manual(s), ignore me and follow the manual.

For the hard-of-headlines, this chapter is about hooking up a CD-ROM drive to a DOS-based PC. If you have a Mac, boy are *you* in the wrong chapter. Skip ahead to Chapter 14.

All right, class. Stay together now. Roll up your sleeves and get ready to work.

It's Just One Thing After Another

That isn't a complaint, it's a strategy. If you're adding a CD-ROM drive to your PC from scratch, you've not only got to deal with the drive itself but also a controller card and/or a sound card, too.

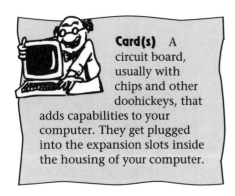

Card(s) A circuit board, usually with chips and other doohickeys, that adds capabilities to your computer. They get plugged into the expansion slots inside the housing of your computer.

Cards are often referred to as "expansion" cards or "adapter" cards because the addition of the card(s) expands the capability of your system, or "adapts" your system to different technology.

Cards come in three different "sizes": 8-bit, 16-bit, and 32-bit. The difference between them is twofold: 16-bit cards transfer information faster than 8-bit cards, and 16-bit cards have twice as many connectors (the gold-toned "fingers" at the bottom of the card) as 8-bit cards. (32-bit cards transfer information even faster than their 16-bit cousins.)

When you add cards to your system, sometimes you run the risk that they're incompatible or otherwise conflict with each other. To make it easier to detect a conflict, we'll install only one thing at a time and make sure each works before we move on to the next. If things get screwy, you'll know which thing caused the problem.

If you install everything at once and then nothing seems to work, you won't know *what* is causing the trouble. Take it easy; make it easy—another motto of mine.

Popping the Hood

Now would be a good time to drag out the manual that came with your computer (if you can find it). You need to look up how the hood is fastened to your computer. A lot of PC hoods (lids, covers, whatever word you're comfy with) are held on with a couple of screws at the back. Some "easy-access" models just pop off—but in my experience, never very easily.

Before you actually pop the hood, be sure the *power is turned off.* Leave it plugged in, though. The power cord plugged into a grounded (three-prong) outlet will ground the system even though the power is off.

Follow your manual's instructions for taking off the cover of the CPU. When it's off, set it aside. Put the screws (if any) in a handy container so you'll know where they all are later.

Before you reach for anything else, touch the metal casing of your PC's power supply (it's usually a silver-looking boxy thing tucked into one of the back corners of your computer). That will discharge any static electricity that may have built up in your hair or on your clothing.

Simply Shocking!

Discharging static electricity is a good idea before you ever mess around with your computer's innards. A static shock (the kind you get when you touch metal after scuffing around on carpeting) can damage the chips inside your computer, or on the card you're trying to install. Bad news.

Pick a Card...

Just so we're all doing the same thing at the same time, let's start with your sound card. If you don't have one (or already have one installed), you can skim ahead. Fish it (and its manual) out of the pile of junk at your elbow.

The Hardware

With the hood of your computer off and any static on you discharged by touching metal, complete the following steps:

1. Choose the slot in which you want to install the card.

2. With the appropriate tool (usually a screwdriver or nutdriver, depending on the fastener), loosen the fastener and remove the plate behind the slot you've chosen. Be careful not to drop anything inside; you *could* damage the delicate components.

3. Set the plate and fastener aside.

4. Remove the sound card from its protective wrapping, making sure you don't handle it by the gold connector at the bottom. To be safe, hold it by the edges.

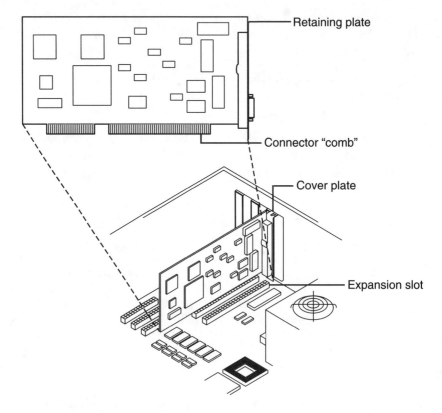

Slide your card into an empty slot.

5. Position the card so its retaining plate fills the spot where you removed the cover plate.

6. Position the card's connector above the slot, resting it lightly in the slot.

7. With the card in position, press down firmly on the end of the card near the retaining plate, until it's seated in the slot.

   (Some cards are a tight fit. If you push one end and it popped out when you pushed in the other, don't panic. You'll just have to ease it in gradually. Push one end in a little and then push the other. Then push down on the whole card until it's seated properly.)

You Can Be Pushy

These cards look fragile—just a piece of plastic with some chips and solder stuck to them. In one sense, they are fragile—they'll break if you push to one side or the other rather than straight down when you're installing them.

On the other hand, they *are* designed to be pushed into the expansion slots. If you're careful about the direction you push, these puppies can stand the pressure. Be gentle but firm, and you'll be fine.

8. Press down on the opposite end of the card (gently but firmly) until that end is seated in the slot.

9. Check to see that the card is seated in the slot properly by pressing down firmly on the length of the card.

10. Replace the fastener from the cover plate to hold the card in place. (I don't know what you should do with the cover plate you removed. I keep them. They're like the little cans from 35mm film. I've got quite a collection of both. If you come up with a use for either, let me know.)

Done!

The Software

Your sound card will, no doubt, come with driver software and probably some testing software, too. Before you can use your spiffy new sound card, you'll have to install the driver software and test the card to be sure it's installed and functioning properly.

Consult your sound card's manual for specific testing and installation procedures. It may recommend that you test the card *before* installing the software, or after. (The manual for SoundBlaster sound cards, for example, says to test the card *before* installing the software.) Follow the manual.

Before you power up your computer to test the card or install the software, carefully check inside to make sure nothing is left inside (screwdriver, screws, metal plate, or anything) that could short out your computer. Don't worry about replacing the cover (you aren't done in there, yet). Just be careful not to touch or jiggle anything inside while the power is on. Things will go boom!

Driver A small bit of software that tells your computer how to deal with a new piece of hardware. With PCs, many hardware drivers are memory-resident programs. As the name implies, they live in your computer's memory (RAM). The driver will load automatically when you start up and will be available to you whenever you need to use the piece of hardware it controls.

105

When your PC is up and running, your manual will probably tell you to insert the first (or only) software disk in your A: drive and type **A:\INSTALL** at the command prompt. The installation software will start. Follow the directions either on the screen or in the manual to complete the installation.

For most novices (without a lot of other gadgets already installed in your computer), the default or automatic installation will probably be sufficient for your needs. When the installation is complete, you'll need to reboot your PC.

Reboot To restart your computer when it's already on. Whenever you need to reboot your PC, you should always try to do a soft boot, that is, restart it by using the **Reset** button (if your PC has one) or by pressing the key combination **Ctrl+Alt+Del**. Either method is much less stressful to your computer than turning the power off and then back on, and less stress is always a good idea.

Once you've installed your software and tested the card (or vice versa), and you know that everything is working fine, you can move on and install the controller card, if you need one.

If things aren't working fine with the sound card, retrace your installation steps and/or refer to the troubleshooting section of your card's manual for help in tracking down the problem. If that fails, you may need to call the card's technical support number—that will also be in the manual. Chapter 30 contains troubleshooting tips and advice on getting help from technical support.

Be aware that some sound cards also double as controller cards for the CD-ROM drive. If that's the sort you have (your manual will tell you), you can skip merrily ahead to the appropriate section on hooking up the drive.

Control Issues

The steps for installing your CD-ROM drive's controller card are the same as those given earlier for the sound card, whether you're installing a SCSI or any other type of controller. I won't repeat them here, and we'll spare a tree or two in the process.

Be certain that you read the card's installation directions in the manual just in case they disagree with mine. If they do, follow the manual. You may also have to set some switches on the card before you install it. Another case of "check the manual."

For non-SCSI cards, you may have a set of DIP-switches to set the card's IRQ or DMA settings—the *who?* The *what?* Don't panic. That's all explained in Chapter 15. If this is the very first time you're installing something in your computer, chances are you won't need to fuss with them. If you *do* need to change them, skip ahead to Chapter 15 now and do it *before* you install the card. It'll be easier that way.

You might also want to attach the controller's cable before you install it if it isn't permanently attached (many aren't). It's fairly simple: A small, rectangular, plastic connector usually fits over a matching set of gold-colored pins on the controller card. Be sure to check out the "First Pin Babble" box in the "Internalizing Your CD-ROM Drive" section.

Also, remember to turn off your PC before installing anything, and touch the metal casing of your power supply to discharge any static electricity on you before you touch anything else.

When the installation of the card is complete, make sure you didn't leave any tools or screws inside, then you can turn on your PC again and install the driver software for the controller card.

Inserting the first disk in your A: drive and typing **A:\INSTALL** is still a good bet for the installation process, but double-check your manual just to play it safe. Humor me. When the software installation is complete, you'll need to reboot your PC: hit the **Reset** button or press **Ctrl+Alt+Del**.

If your PC won't start up, check the troubleshooting section of the controller card's manual to resolve the problem. (We know it's probably the controller card because your system started with just the sound card, right?)

Since you haven't connected the CD-ROM drive yet, you'll probably get an error message or two during your system's *POST* routine—POST stands for *Power-On Self-Test*. It's that little song and dance your PC goes through every time it starts up. The most likely error message will pop up when the controller's driver software loads. Since there's nothing to control yet, your system may abort when it tries to load the driver. Don't panic! The situation will resolve itself as soon as you hook up your CD, which is next on our list of things to do.

If your system starts up and everything else seems fine, you may proceed to hooking up the drive. If you've got an external drive, you may or may not want to put the top back on your PC. You may have to go back in, and you may not. I'd leave it off for now because you never know what will happen, but it's up to you.

Hey, Look Me Over

All that remains is to hook up your drive and any accessories you may have. While your CD-ROM drive is footloose and fancy free—that is, not hooked up to anything yet—it's a good time for you to look that bad boy over and familiarize yourself with all the buttons, switches, dials, and ports you'll be dealing with.

Port A techno-geeky name for where computer-type things plug into each other.

Variations on a Theme

An external, SCSI-based CD-ROM drive will (usually) have two SCSI ports on the back. You just added the SCSI port (on the SCSI adapter card) to your PC. If you're using another type of controller, you may have only one port.

Your sound card will probably have a sound-in port for a microphone, a sound-out port for speakers or headphones, a volume control dial, and perhaps even RCA-type jacks for hooking up your sound card to a stereo amplifier. Consult your manual for the specific ports available on your sound card.

Face Front!

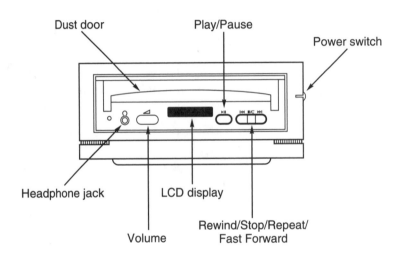

My CD-ROM front view. Yours may look different.

On the front of your CD-ROM drive (as in the figure), you should have some or all of the following, regardless of whether you have an *internal* or *external* drive. The only noticeable difference is that an internal drive won't have a power switch or a fancy case:

➤ **Dust door** Covers and protects the internal mechanism from dust and other crud. This is where you'll insert your CDs (or CD caddies).

➤ **Headphone jack** You can plug in a pair of headphones for private listening— or speakers, for less-than-private listening.

➤ **Volume control** Controls the volume of audio CDs (duh).

➤ **Play controls**   Controls an audio CD. They work like the standard buttons on an audio CD player: play, pause, stop, forward, and reverse. Many drives have them; many do not.

➤ **Status display**   If you've got one, it'll let you know what your CD-ROM is up to at any given moment.

Huh? What? Speak Up!

Your CD-ROM drive's volume control will have no effect on your PC's volume when you're using a CD-ROM disc. The drive's volume control is for adjusting the volume when you're listening to audio CDs through headphones or speakers connected to the drive's headphone jack. To adjust your PC's volume for CD-ROM discs, use the volume control on your sound card.

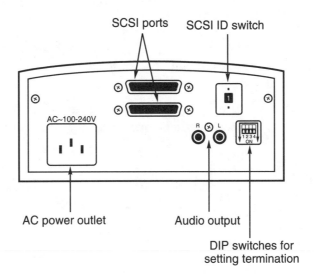

My CD-ROM's backside.

Turn your drive around to examine the rear, and you'll discover one of the great truths of the universe: The backsides of things are usually much less attractive than the fronts. (I guess that's why they're in the back.)

The dominant feature of the back of an external SCSI drive (like the one shown in the figure) will be the two *SCSI ports*. You'll use one of these to connect your CD-ROM drive to the back of your PC (or to another SCSI device, like an external hard drive, if your SCSI port is already occupied).

Daisy chain
A string of SCSI devices, from two to seven, connected to each other and (ultimately) to your PC.

The second SCSI port is for connecting another SCSI device to the CD-ROM drive (if, say, you wanted to add another SCSI device later on) in a *daisy chain*.

An internal drive will have pretty much the same features as an external drive, but the SCSI connectors will look *very* different—just a gold-colored bunch of pins in a rectangular formation. Their position on the drive will vary, and you may only have one port. So you'll need to look in your drive's manual to see what's where.

Similarly, drives that use a different sort of controller will also look different. There are *many* variations, so read your manuals carefully.

The *AC power* outlet is where you'll plug in the drive's power cord for an external drive (if yours isn't permanently attached). On an internal drive, it'll be an odd-looking, geometrical shape with four pins inside.

Nearby you may also find your drive's on/off switch (external only). Or you may not. A lot of companies are finally realizing that it isn't convenient to reach around the backs of all these gadgets to turn them on and off. Your switch may be right up front or on the side of your drive. Internal drives won't have one; they turn on when you turn on the computer. When in doubt, check the manual.

If your drive isn't SCSI-based, you won't have to deal with the SCSI ID and termination stuff covered in the next few paragraphs. Feel free to skim ahead.

DIP switch
A small switch, or set of switches, that resemble teeny-tiny light switches. They're *so* small you need to flip them with the point of a pencil or something similar. You use them to change certain features and functions (such as setting the SCSI ID number of an internal CD-ROM drive) of computer peripherals.

The *SCSI ID switch* (which may be a push-button affair, a rotary dial, or a set of *DIP switches* on your drive: check your manual) is where you set the drive's ID number. As long as you're here, you may as well set it. The SCSI ID number should be a number from 1 to 7. It doesn't matter what number, as long as it hasn't already been assigned to another SCSI device.

If you don't have any other SCSI devices hooked up to your PC, pick a number, any number (as long as it's from 1 to 7). If you do have another SCSI device connected (like an external SCSI hard drive), check to see what its ID number is and pick something else for the CD-ROM drive. I can't stress this enough: **You cannot have two SCSI devices with the same ID number.** It'll give your computer a nervous breakdown.

There will also be a way to set your drive's *termination*. In the preceding figure, it's a set of DIP switches. On your drive, it could be that—or a push button, a switch, or something else entirely. Check your drive's manuals for details on your method of termination.

If your CD-ROM drive is the last item in a daisy chain, or the *only* SCSI device connected to your PC, the termination should be **ON**. The CD-ROM drive should also be the only external device that is terminated in the chain. This is true for internal and external drives. Chapter 15 offers more details.

Terminator/ Termination
An electronic widget that tells your computer that it has reached the end of the line— that there are no more SCSI devices for it to look for. The last device in a SCSI (daisy) chain should always be terminated.

If you're squeezing the drive somewhere in the middle of an existing daisy chain, its termination should be **OFF**.

If at First You Don't Succeed...

If you follow these termination rules explicitly and your PC won't start up (or acknowledge that you have a CD-ROM drive), you may have to finagle the termination some. The rules of SCSI are flaky at best. See Chapter 15 for more SCSI advice.

Finally, there should be a pair of *audio-out jacks* so you can connect your CD-ROM drive to a stereo system amplifier and play your audio CDs at head-banger volume, if you choose.

Once you've located the various doodads you need to connect and control your drive (and looked up the ones you had trouble finding in your manual), you're ready to start hooking it up.

Plugging Right Along

The first thing you should do is turn off your PC and all of your peripherals (printers, external hard drives, and so on). You should *never* connect or disconnect any cable while there is power running through your PC. It could damage the device, you, or all of the above.

If you're hooking up an external drive, proceed to the next section; if you're hooking up an internal drive, skip the next section and go to the section called "Internalizing Your CD-ROM Drive."

An External Hook-Up

Everything turned off? Next, dig out the actual cable you'll use to connect your drive to your PC. The cable will be two or three feet long. At each end, there will be a *male* connector to connect it to the *female* ports on the back of the drive and on your controller card (or another external SCSI device, if you're creating a SCSI chain).

Male The business end of a cable (or a port) that's got an arrangement of pins (usually 25 or 50 for a SCSI cable) that plug into a female connector or port of similar configuration.

Female The business end of a cable (or a port) that has an arrangement of holes that match up with the arrangement of pins in a male connector (or port).

If you find the whole concept of male and female connectors and ports elusive, you probably should have paid more attention in health class.

On the back of your CD-ROM drive, you'll plug one end of the cable into one of the two ports— or the only one. The other end will plug into the port on the back of your PC where you added the controller card.

Don't worry about plugging in the connectors wrong—you really can't. If you look closely at one of the connectors, you'll see that the pins are shielded with a (sort of) rectangular cowl of metal that's wider along one side than the other. The port on the back of your PC (or on another SCSI device) is the same lopsided shape, making it almost impossible to plug things in the wrong way.

If you're chaining several SCSI devices together, you can also plug the other end of the CD-ROM drive's cable into the second SCSI port on an external SCSI device.

Many newer model CD-ROM drives make use of the more compact SCSI 2 connectors and cables. Don't be alarmed if you've got a drive that does—you can use the cable regardless of whether you've got a SCSI 2 adapter or not. You will, however, need to be careful to get the proper type of cable (with a SCSI 2 connector at one end and a 50-pin connector at the other) if you want to use the drive in the middles of SCSI chain. Chapter 15 covers SCSI chains in more detail.

Pick a Port

With some SCSI-based CD-ROM drives (and other SCSI devices), it doesn't matter which of the drive's two SCSI ports you use. With others, it does. Check your manual to see if you should use a particular SCSI port for your initial connection.

Be sure the connections are tight at either end. Most cables these days come with some sort of fastener: clips that snap in, small screws you tighten with a screwdriver, or post-type screws you can tighten with your fingers. Not too tight, mind you. You may want to unhook the drive at some point.

If your CD-ROM has a detachable power cable, now would be a good time to attach it to your drive. Then plug the prong (male) end into an appropriate power outlet.

Your drive is officially connected, but you can't use it yet. You need to install the software that tells your PC how to deal with the scads of information it'll be receiving from your new toy.

Internalizing Your CD-ROM Drive

Installing an internal CD-ROM drive (or anything) in your computer is probably easier than you think, but it can be nerve wracking the first time you try it.

If you don't think your nerves or skills are up to the challenge, there's no shame in paying to have your CD-ROM drive installed by a trained professional. *Debt before dishonor*, that's my motto (it's tattooed somewhere too embarrassing to say).

When you've steadied your nerves (take a few deep breaths), the first thing you need to do is touch something metal, again, to discharge any static electricity on you. Make it a habit. The metal cover on your computer's power supply is a good thing to touch because it's metal and it's grounded.

Next, locate the expansion bay where you're going to install the drive. It'll be at the front of the machine close to the floppy drive.

You can pop off the face plate where the drive will go —they're usually just held in place with clips. Removing it will let you slide the drive in so it's level with the front of your PC.

With some computer models, you may need to install a support frame or rails to hold your drive. Generally, you attach the frame to your drive, and then the whole thing snaps or screws into place. These frames and rails also vary, so check your manual.

Try fitting the drive in place, but before you fasten it permanently inside your PC, make sure you can get at the drive's controller and power connections. If you can, fine. If not, make your cable connections before you screw or snap the drive in place.

The first connection you should make is the power connection. You'll find a power cable coming from the PC's power supply. It'll look something like the one in the following figure. Plug it into the power socket on the CD-ROM drive.

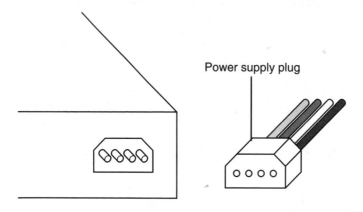

Power supply plug

Plugging in the power supply is a no-brainer. It fits only one way.

Next, find the *controller (ribbon) cable*. It'll be about 2–3 feet long, gray, and flat like a ribbon—that's why it's called a (duh) *ribbon cable*. It should already be attached to the controller card, if you've been following my advice, so you just need to find the loose end.

Before you attach the ribbon cable to the SCSI port on the drive, make sure you check the drive's manual to find out where *pin 1* is located on the drive's port. It's usually described in relation to the power socket (the end closest to the power socket or farthest away from it). Some very kind manufacturers actually label the pin for you.

This is important. With some connectors, it's possible to plug it in incorrectly, and the drive won't do anything.

First Pin Babble

Here's why pin 1 is important. When your computer receives and sends information to your CD-ROM drive, it always sends and receives it in the same order. The first bit shoots out along pin 1, the next bit along pin 2, and so on. If pin 1 is accidentally connected to, say, pin 50 of the cable, you're completely inverting the information being sent along the cable. Neither your CD-ROM drive nor your computer will be able to figure out what the other is talking about.

When you locate pin 1 on the drive, look at the ribbon cable: it looks like a bunch of really thin wires that someone poured a plastic coating over. That's because it's a bunch of really thin wires that someone poured a plastic coating over. One side of the ribbon cable (as in the following figure) will have fine print running down it, a line of dots, or a red stripe. The wire that's under that line and/or fine print is the one that should be connected to pin 1 on the CD-ROM drive. Think of it as wire 1 if that helps.

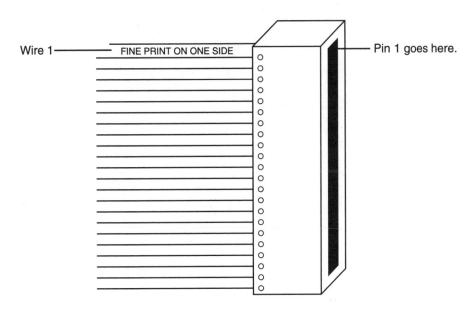

Wire 1 ———— FINE PRINT ON ONE SIDE ———— Pin 1 goes here.

A ribbon cable resembles, not surprisingly, ribbon.

Make sure the printing runs down the same side of the cable where pin 1 is located on the CD-ROM drive connector. You may have to turn (or gently twist) the cable to make the connection, but that's okay. That's why the cable is as thin and flexible as it is.

It *should* be, but if the other end of the ribbon is not already attached to your controller card, you'll need to connect it. The same pin 1 rule applies here, too. Kinder manufacturers make them so you can *only* plug them in the correct way. I wish *more* manufacturers would do that.

When that's done, everything is (or should be) connected. If you haven't done so yet, you can screw or snap the drive into place. Now would be the time to fire up your PC and install the driver software. You may want to install the software with the hood still off of your computer, just in case you need to troubleshoot or otherwise mess around with it again.

Don't Set Yourself Up for a Bad Hair Day

If you do power up with the top off your computer, make sure you've re-moved all of your tools (especially metal ones) from inside, and make *extra* sure you don't reach inside and touch anything while power is running through your system. You could fry your computer. Worse, you could fry yourself. Neither is a very pleasant prospect, and Don King's hair isn't really very attractive, now is it?

Soft Goods

If you haven't done so already, turn your PC back on—don't worry about powering up the CD-ROM drive yet (we'll do that in a minute).

Locate the disk(s) of software that came with your CD-ROM drive—how much software you have to install is a mystery to me. If your drive came with a controller card and/or sound card, you may have only one set. If you bought things separately, you could have up to *three* sets of stuff to install (for a sound card, controller card, and the drive itself).

To be absolutely safe, you should make a backup copy of the disk(s) and put the original(s) in a safe place. Work only with the backup copy.

Back It Up, Baby

If you don't know how to copy disks, you can look it up in your computer's manual. It's very easy. So easy, in fact, that you have no excuse not to do it.

Insert the disk (or the first disk) in your A: drive and type **A:\INSTALL**—probably. As always (and I'm sure you're tired of hearing this), check your manual for the specific installation instructions for your drive and software. When your software is installed, you'll need to reboot your system to load it into memory so your PC can make use of the new driver(s). If you want to try out your drive immediately, instead of doing a soft boot, turn off your PC, turn on the CD-ROM drive, and then turn your PC back on.

If things aren't working, you need to backtrack through the installation procedure and see where things went wrong. Odds are (50-50, at least) that it's some sort of controller problem. Check out Chapter 15 for the skinny on SCSI and other controllers. You may also want to consult the troubleshooting chapter of this book (Chapter 30) and the ones in your drive and/or controller manuals.

If you're ready, why don't you skip ahead to Chapter 16, and I'll help you get started. In the meantime, here's the least you need to remember from this chapter.

The Least You Need to Know

➤ When in doubt, check the manual.

➤ Never plug (or unplug) anything into your PC while it's turned on. Shut everything down before you start to play with cards or cables.

➤ Cards are fragile, but not that fragile. Don't be afraid to push on them to install them—just be sure you're pushing straight down rather than to either side; otherwise, you could break the card.

➤ Your CD-ROM drive must have a different SCSI ID number from any other SCSI device attached to your PC.

➤ If your CD-ROM drive is the last device in a SCSI chain, it must be terminated. If it's in the middle of a SCSI chain, it should not be terminated.

➤ Other controller types vary greatly. Check your manual carefully.

➤ You must install your driver software before your PC can do anything with your new cards or drive.

➤ Turn on your external CD-ROM drive before your turn on your PC. Internal drives turn on automatically when you power-up your PC.

➤ Enjoy!

Chapter 14

The Macintosh Hook-Up

In This Chapter

➤ Making connections

➤ Chaining up daisies

➤ Let me drive

Ahh, the moment of truth. Are your palms sweating? Do you have the latest Sting (or whomever) CD handy to see how your new drive also handles audio CDs? Well, don't get too far ahead of yourself. There's the little detail of hooking everything up and installing software before you can go that far.

Remember: This chapter is about hooking up a CD-ROM drive to a Macintosh computer. If you've got a DOS-based PC, you can read this if you want, but you'll be doing things a little differently. See Chapter 13 for PC installations.

First Things First

If you followed my advice in Chapter 12, you've already got things laid out beside your Mac: your tools, the drive, your manuals, and the software.

If you're hooking up an external drive, you can put it pretty much on the spot it's going to occupy on your desk. If your setting up an internal drive, you've got it handy but out of the way until you pop the hood on your Mac. Have you checked your drive's manual to see what, if any, tools you'll need (like a small Phillips-head screwdriver, maybe?).

We're ready to roll.

Before you touch any of it, pick up that manual and read through its chapter on connecting the drive to your Mac. The stuff I'm giving you is, at *best*, general instructions—if anything you read here clashes or disagrees with what it says in the honest-to-goodness manual, follow the manual. I gladly bow to its superior knowledge.

Hey, Look Me Over

While your CD-ROM drive is footloose and fancy free—that is, not hooked up to anything yet—now would be a good time for you to look it over and familiarize yourself with all the buttons, switches, dials, and ports you'll be dealing with.

Port A techno-geeky name for where computer-type things plug into each other.

If you're connecting an external drive and it's been awhile since you had a gander at the back of your Mac, it might be a good idea to brush up on those ports, too. If you aren't familiar with them, you can look them up in the Macintosh Reference manual that came with your Mac.

The Port Report

A CD-ROM drive will (usually) have two SCSI ports on the back. Most Macs have seven ports: an ADB port (for your keyboard), a printer port, a modem port, a video port (for your monitor), a sound-in port (microphone), and a sound-out port (speakers). However, some of the Performa lines (like the 550) have *two* ADB ports, and some of the Quadras and Power Macs have additional ports for networking and audio-visual connections. All the ports on the back of your Mac are labeled with easy-to-interpret icons (pictures) underneath each port for easy identification. Check your manual for details.

Face Front!

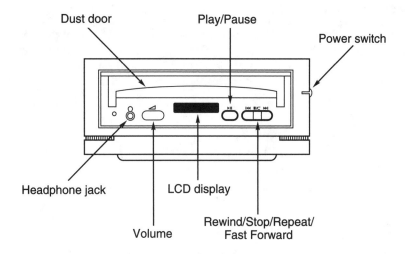

My CD-ROM front view. Yours may look different.

On the front of your CD-ROM drive (as in the figure), you should have some (or all) of the following items, regardless of whether you have an internal or external drive. The only noticeable difference is that an internal drive won't have a power switch or a fancy case.

➤ **Dust door**   Covers and protects the internal mechanism from dust and other crud. This is where you'll insert your CDs. Yours may have a pop-out tray instead, or just be a slot where you insert the CD.

➤ **Headphone jack**   You can plug in a pair of headphones for private listening—or speakers for less than private listening.

➤ **Volume control**   Controls the volume (duh). If your drive doesn't have a built-in amplifier, you won't have a volume control.

➤ **Play controls**   Controls an audio CD. They work like the standard buttons on an audio CD player: play, pause, stop, forward, and reverse. Many drives have them; many do not.

➤ **Status display**   If your drive has one (many don't), it'll let you know what your CD-ROM is up to at any given moment. The display messages are usually abbreviations or symbols, and vary from machine to machine. Check your drive's manual for specific display messages.

Volume Control Alert!

Your CD-ROM drive's volume control will have no effect on your Mac's volume when you're using a CD-ROM disc. The drive's volume control is for adjusting the volume when you're listening to audio CDs through headphones (or speakers connected to the headphone jack).

To adjust your Mac's volume for CD-ROM discs volume, use the Sound Control Panel in the Control Panels folder in your System folder. You can get at it easily by selecting the **Control Panels** item in your menu. System 7.5 users can also just select the **Sound Control Panel** from the list of control panels that pops up when you select **Control Panels** in the menu.

About Face!

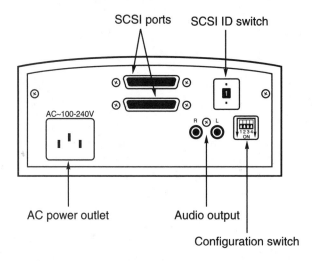

My CD-ROM's backside.

Turn your drive around to examine the rear, and you'll discover one of the great truths of the universe: The backsides of things are usually much less attractive than the fronts. (I guess that's why they're in the back.)

The dominant feature of the back of an external drive (as in the preceding figure) will be the two SCSI ports. An internal drive will have pretty much the same features as an external drive but will look a little different, and may be in different locations.

You'll use one SCSI port to connect your CD-ROM drive to the back of your Mac (or to another SCSI device, like an external hard drive). The second SCSI port is for connecting another SCSI device to the CD-ROM drive (if, say, you wanted to add a second CD-ROM drive or another hard drive later on) in a *daisy chain*.

With an internal drive, the SCSI connectors will look very different—just a gold-colored bunch of pins in a rectangular formation. Their position on the drive will vary, and you may only have one port. So you'll need to look in your drive's manual for a diagram that explains what is where.

> **Daisy chain**
> A string of SCSI devices (from two to seven) connected to each other and, ultimately, to your PC.

The AC power port is where you'll plug in the external drive's power cord (if yours isn't permanently attached). On an internal drive, it'll be an odd-looking, geometrical shape with four pins inside.

Nearby, you may also find your drive's on/off switch (or you may not). A lot of companies are finally realizing that it isn't convenient to reach around the backs of all these gadgets to turn them on and off. Your switch may be right up front or on the side of your drive. Internal drives won't have a switch; they turn on when you turn on the computer. When in doubt, check the manual.

The *SCSI ID switch* (which may be a push-button affair, a rotary switch, or a set of *DIP switches* on your drive: check your manual) is where you set the drive's ID number.

As long as you're here, you may as well set it. The SCSI ID number should be a number from 1 to 6. It doesn't matter what number, as long as it hasn't already been assigned to another SCSI device. **DO NOT use the numbers 0 or 7**; they have already been assigned to your Mac and your Mac's internal hard drive.

> **DIP switch** A small switch, or set of switches, that resemble teeny-tiny light switches. They're *so* small you need to flip them with the point of a pencil or something similar. You use them to change certain features and functions (such as setting the SCSI ID number of an internal CD-ROM drive) of computer peripherals.

If you don't have any other SCSI devices hooked up to your Mac, pick a number, any number (as long as it's from 1 to 6). If you do have another SCSI device connected (like an external hard drive), check to see what its ID number is and pick something else for the CD-ROM drive.

You can find out the SCSI ID number of external peripherals by looking (if you can get a peek at the back) or by using *SCSI Probe*, a free and very handy control panel available on most online services (America Online, CompuServe, eWorld, and the like) and from Mac User Groups (MUGS). SCSI Probe has saved my butt a *number* of times.

Terminator/ Termination An electronic widget that tells your Mac that it has reached the end of the line—that there are no more SCSI devices for it to look for. The last device in a SCSI (daisy) chain should always be terminated.

Your drive (internal or external) will also have a way to set its *termination*. In the figure, it's a set of DIP switches. On *your* drive, it could also be a push button, switch, or something else entirely. Check your manuals for details.

If your CD-ROM drive is the last item in a daisy chain, or the only additional SCSI device connected to your Mac (other than your Mac and internal hard drive), the termination should be **ON**. The CD-ROM drive should also be the only external device that is terminated in the chain.

If you're squeezing the drive somewhere into the middle of an existing daisy chain or installing an internal model, its termination should be **OFF**.

Rules Were Made to Be Finagled

If you follow these termination rules explicitly and your Mac won't start up (or acknowledge that you have a CD-ROM drive), you may have to finagle the termination some. The rules of SCSI are flaky at best. See Chapter 15 for more SCSI advice.

Finally, external drives will probably have a pair of audio-out jacks. These allow you to connect your CD-ROM drive to a stereo system amplifier and play your audio CDs at head-banger volume, if you choose. Internal drives won't have them—everything is fed through your Mac.

Once you've located all the various doo-dads you need to connect and control your drive (and looked up the ones you had trouble finding in your manual), you're ready to start hooking it up.

Plugging Right Along

The first thing you should do is turn off your Mac and all of your peripherals (printers, external hard drives, and so on). You should *never* connect or disconnect any cable while there is power running through your Mac. It could damage the Mac, the device (whatever it might be), you, or all of the above.

If you're hooking up an external drive, proceed to the next section; if you're hooking up an internal drive, skip the next section and go to the section called "Internalizing Your CD-ROM Drive."

An External Hook-Up

Everything turned off? Good. Next, dig out the actual SCSI cable you'll use to connect your drive to your Mac. The cable will be two or three feet long and about half an inch in diameter. At each end, there will be a *male* connector to connect it to the *female* ports on the back of the drive and your Mac (or an external SCSI device).

On the back of your CD-ROM drive, you'll plug one end of the cable into one of the two SCSI ports. The other end will plug into the SCSI port on the back of your Mac.

Many newer model CD-ROM drives make use of the more compact SCSI 2 connectors and cables. Don't be alarmed if you've got a drive that does—you can use the cable regardless of whether you've got a SCSI 2 adapter or not. You will,

Male The business end of a cable (or a port) that's got an arrangement of pins (usually 25 or 50 for a SCSI cable) that plug into a female connector or port of similar configuration.

Female The business end of a cable (or a port) that has an arrangement of holes that match up with the arrangement of pins in a male connector (or port).

however, need to be careful to get the proper type of cable (with a SCSI 2 connector at one end and a 50-pin connector at the other) if you want to use the drive in the middle of a SCSI chain. Chapter 15 covers SCSI chains in more detail.

Don't worry about plugging in the connectors wrong—you really can't. If you look closely at one of the connectors, you'll see that the pins are shielded with a (sort of) rectangular cowl of metal that's wider along one side than the other. The SCSI port on the back of your Mac (or other SCSI device) is the same lopsided shape, making it nearly impossible to plug things in the wrong way.

Before You Plug

With some CD-ROM drives (and other SCSI devices), it doesn't matter which of its two SCSI ports you use. With others, it does. Check your drive's manual to see if you should use a particular SCSI port for your initial connection.

If you're chaining two or more SCSI devices together, you can also plug the other end of the CD-ROM drive's cable into the second SCSI port on an external SCSI device. You may need an additional cable or an adapter.

Most Macintosh SCSI device manufacturers assume that you're going to be connecting their device directly to your Mac (which has a 25-pin SCSI port), not to another SCSI device (most of which have 50-pin SCSI ports). So they give you a cable with a 25-pin connector on one end and a 50-pin connector on the other. You can't plug a 25-pin connector into a 50-pin port, so you need another short length of cable that lets you plug in the 25-pin connector and gives you the appropriate 50-pin connector to plug into the SCSI device. Of course, you could just buy a new cable with 50-pin connectors on both ends.

Be sure the connections are tight at either end. Most SCSI ports have clips that snap onto the business end of the cable to hold it in place. If your CD-ROM has a detachable power cable, now would be a good time to attach it to your drive. Then plug the prong (male) end into an appropriate power outlet.

Your drive is officially connected, but you can't use it yet. You need to install the software that tells your Mac how to deal with the scads of information it'll be receiving from your new toy. That's covered in the "Soft Goods" section, coming up shortly.

Internalizing Your CD-ROM Drive

The majority of Mac users will probably go with an external drive, but just in case, here's the scoop. Installing an internal CD-ROM drive (or anything) in your Mac is a lot like playing *Operation*. It takes steady hands and the patience of, well, a surgeon. It's probably easier than you think, but it can be nerve-wracking the first time you try it. If your Mac is still under warranty, installing anything (including an internal CD-ROM drive) yourself will void what's left of the warranty. Be warned.

If you don't think your nerves or skills are up to the challenge, there is no shame in paying to have your CD-ROM drive installed by a trained professional. *Debt before dishonor*, that's my motto. If you're going to proceed on your own, here's help.

First, you need to pop the hood on your Mac. This procedure varies from model to model (usually, it's via a screw or two in the back), so check your manual for details.

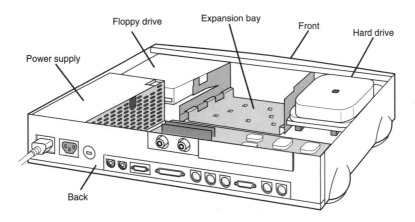

A topless Mac.

When your Mac is opened and you've steadied your nerves, the first thing you need to do is touch something metal to discharge any static electricity on you before you touch any of the delicate components inside your Mac. The metal cover on your Mac's power supply (shown in the preceding figure) is a good thing to touch because it's metal and it's grounded.

Next, locate the *expansion bay*, where you're going to install the drive. It'll be at the front of the machine, close to the floppy drive.

You can pop off the face plate where the drive will go—they're usually just held in place with clips. Removing it will let you slide the drive in so that it's level with the *front* of your Mac.

With some Mac models, you may need to install a support frame to hold your drive. Generally, you attach the frame to your drive, then the whole thing snaps or screws into place. Support frames also vary, so check your manual.

Try fitting the drive in place, but before you fasten it permanently inside your Mac, make sure you can get at the drive's SCSI and power connections. If you can, fine. If not, make your cable connections before you screw or snap the drive in place.

The first connection you should make is the power connection. You'll find a power cable coming from the Mac's power supply. It'll look something like the one in the following figure. Plug it into the power socket on the CD-ROM drive.

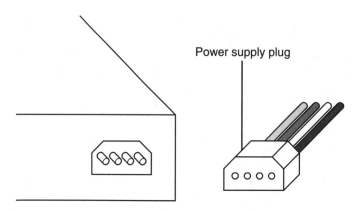

Power supply plug

Plugging in the power supply is a no-brainer. It fits only one way.

Next, find the SCSI cable: it will be about 2–3 feet long, gray, and flat like a ribbon— that's why it's called a (duh) *ribbon cable*. Depending on which Mac you have, it may be in your Mac or part of the drive's interface kit. Before you attach the ribbon cable to the SCSI port on the drive, make sure you check the drive's manual to find out where *pin 1* is located on the drive's port. It's usually described in relation to the power socket (the end closest to the power socket, or farthest away from it).

This is important. With some connectors, it's possible to plug it in incorrectly, and the drive won't do anything. Your Mac won't even know it's there.

First Pin Babble

Here's why pin 1 is important. When your computer receives and sends information to your CD-ROM drive, it always sends and receives it in the same order. The first bit shoots out along pin 1, the next bit along pin 2, and so on. If pin 1 is accidentally connected to, say, pin 50 of the cable, you're completely inverting the information being sent along the cable. Talk about bass-ackwards! Neither your CD-ROM drive nor your computer will be able to figure out what the other is talking about. They'll just ignore each other.

128

When you locate pin 1 on the drive, look at the ribbon cable; it looks like a bunch of really thin wires that someone poured a plastic coating over. That's because it's a bunch of really thin wires that someone poured a plastic coating over. One side of the ribbon cable (as in the figure) will have fine print running down it, or a red stripe. The wire that's under that line and/or fine print is the one that should be connected to pin 1 on the CD-ROM drive. Think of it as wire 1 if that helps.

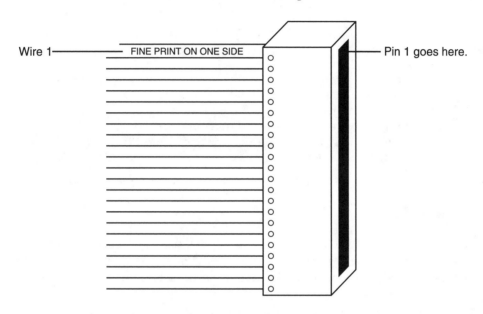

Wire 1 ——————————— FINE PRINT ON ONE SIDE ——————— Pin 1 goes here.

A ribbon cable resembles, not surprisingly, ribbon.

Make sure the printing runs down the same side of the cable where pin 1 is located. You may have to turn (or gently twist) the cable to make the connection, but that's okay. That's why the cable is as thin and flexible as it is.

In most Mac installations, the cable you connect to your CD-ROM drive will be a continuation of your hard drive's SCSI ribbon cable. You'll need to find the unused connector and plug that into your CD-ROM. The pin 1 rule applies here, as well.

Finally, you'll need to make an audio connection between the CD-ROM and your Mac's motherboard to get sound from the drive to your Mac's built-in audio system. This will vary a little from drive to drive and Mac to Mac, so check your CD-ROM drive's manual for details.

When that's done, everything is (or should be) connected. If you haven't done so yet, you can screw or snap the drive into place. Now would be the time to fire up your Mac and install the driver software. You may want to install the software with the hood still off of your Mac, just in case you need to troubleshoot or otherwise mess around with it again.

Don't Set Yourself Up for a Bad Hair Day

If you do power up with the top off your computer, make sure you've removed all of your tools (especially metal ones) from inside, and make *extra* sure you don't reach inside and touch anything while power is running through your system. You could fry your computer. Worse, you could fry yourself. Neither is a very pleasant prospect, and Don King's hair isn't really very attractive, now is it?

Soft Goods

If you haven't already done so, locate the 3.5-inch disk(s) of software that came with your CD-ROM drive. To be absolutely safe, you should make a backup copy of the disk(s) and put the original(s) in a safe place. Work only with the backup copy.

No Excuses!

If you don't know how to copy disks, you can look it up in your Mac's manual or your copy of *The Complete Idiot's Guide to the Mac*. It's very easy. So easy, in fact, you have no excuse not to do it.

Insert the disk (or the first disk) in your Mac's floppy drive and double-click on its icon to open it. The window that opens will look something like the figure here. It shows the software that comes with an NEC CD-ROM drive; if you don't have an NEC drive, your software will probably be a little different. As always, check with your manual for the specific installation instructions for your drive.

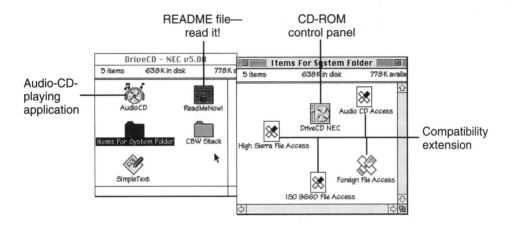

Here are the contents of the disk that came with my drive.

Installing with an Installer

Some software is installed with a little program called (duh) *Installer*. Double-clicking on the **Installer** icon will launch a program that walks you through the installation procedure. Just follow the on-screen directions; you won't need the step-by-step stuff coming up.

You'll have a driver for your particular model of CD-ROM drive, several extensions to allow your Mac to access the various CD-ROM disk formats, and (if your drive can handle them) an application for controlling your drive while it plays audio CDs.

Get ready to install. With the CD-ROM's driver disk in your floppy drive and its window open on your desktop:

1. **Double-click** on your hard drive's icon to open it.

2. Position your hard drive's window (by **click-dragging** on its **title bar**) so you can see the driver software's window.

3. Locate your **System folder icon** in your hard drive's window.

Driver A small bit of software that tells your Mac how to deal with a new piece of hardware.

Extension A small bit of software that adds extra capabilities (like using a CD-ROM drive) to your Mac. They go in the Extensions folder inside your System folder on your hard drive.

4. Holding down your **Shift** key, **click** on the icons of the driver software and extensions you need to install (these vary from drive to drive, so check your manual for details). That will select them.

5. **Drag and drop** the icons on top of your System folder icon.

6. Your Mac will give you a message saying Extensions need to be stored in the Extensions folder (or something similar). Click on **OK** (or press **Enter**), and your Mac will copy the software into the Extensions folder.

7. If you have an audio-CD-playing application (like the *Audio CD* application shown in the last figure), **click-drag** its icon and drop it wherever you like: in your hard drive's window, right on the desktop, even in the Apple Menu Items folder in your System folder (that will put it in your   menu for speedy access). System 7.5 users can also put it in their Launcher Items Folder in your System folder (that will put it in your Launcher).

8. You'll need to **Restart** your Mac (by selecting **Restart** from the **Special menu**) before your Mac can make use of the new software to access your CD-ROM drive.

You should now be ready to pop in a CD-ROM disc and lose yourself in a game, amuse yourself with information, or educate yourself with an informative game.

If things aren't working properly, you need to backtrack through the installation procedure and see where things went wrong. Odds are (50-50, at least) that it's some sort of SCSI problem. Check out Chapter 15 for the skinny on SCSI. You may also want to consult the troubleshooting chapter (Chapter 30) of this book and the troubleshooting section in your drive's manual.

If you're ready, why don't you skip ahead to Chapter 16, "Fire It Up!" and I'll help you get started. In the meantime, here's the least you need to remember from this chapter.

The Least You Need to Know

➤ When in doubt, check the manual.

➤ Never plug anything into your Mac (or unplug anything from it) while it's turned on. Shut down everything before you start to play with cables.

➤ Your CD-ROM drive must have a different SCSI ID number from any other SCSI device attached to your Mac.

➤ If your CD-ROM drive is the last device in a SCSI chain, it must be terminated. If it's in the middle of a SCSI chain, it should not be terminated. Check your manual to see how to turn your CD-ROM's termination on and off.

➤ For internal drives, make sure you remember the rule about pin 1 for your SCSI cable.

➤ You must install your driver software before your Mac can do anything with your new drive.

➤ Turn on your CD-ROM (and any other external SCSI devices you have) before you turn on your Mac. Internal devices turn themselves on when you power up.

Chapter 15

SCSI, IRQs, DMA, and Other Annoying Initials

In This Chapter

➤ General scuzziness

➤ IRQsome details

➤ DMA: more than just an anagram for MAD

➤ If at first you don't succeed...

Let me apologize up front. I figure if you're reading this, you've had some sort of trouble getting your computer to recognize your CD-ROM drive. The most likely culprit is a controller problem—whether SCSI (Macs and some PCs) or some other method of controlling the drive (through a sound card, IDE controller, or something else entirely). If this stuff doesn't straighten it out, Chapter 30 offers help with troubleshooting and other potential hassles.

SCSI Is as SCSI Does

I can't believe I just made a *Gump* joke. I apologize.

This particular section is about SCSI cards and devices. Mac owners can read it, and so can PC owners whose CD-ROM drives use a SCSI controller. The rest of you may talk quietly amongst yourselves.

As an extra special added bonus, this SCSI information applies to *any* SCSI device you may want to add to your computer, not just your CD-ROM drive. All you have to do is substitute the name of the other SCSI device wherever it says *CD-ROM drive* in the text.

Back to SCSI Basics

First, so you don't have to go flipping around trying to dig up the basic SCSI information already discussed, a little review. (Don't worry, there won't be a quiz after.)

SCSI, pronounced "*scuzzy*," stands for *Small Computer System Interface*. It's a standard for connecting certain devices (like CD-ROM drives, scanners, hard drives, and so on) to a computer. Right now, there are two kinds of SCSI setups available. One is just plain old *SCSI*. It's the first, the original, and is still pretty good. You can use plain old SCSI on any computer. The second kind is called (I bet they stayed up late thinking this up) *SCSI-2*.

If You Do Have a SCSI-2 Device... If you have a SCSI-2 device anywhere in the chain, you *must* have SCSI-2-compatible cables. If you don't, one or more items in your chain may not work properly (and the symptoms will be hard to diagnose). You usually can't tell if it's a SCSI-2 cable, except by looking on the packaging before you purchase the cable (or in the manual, if the cable comes with something you bought).

SCSI-2 moves information more quickly from the device to your computer (and back again) than SCSI. Faster is almost always better—it's also, usually, more expensive. SCSI-2 is relatively new (only a couple of years old); it hasn't replaced the original SCSI yet. Therefore, not every SCSI device you can buy can make use of SCSI-2's faster transfer rates.

Nor can every computer's SCSI adapter (either built-in or added as a card) make use of the extra speed. Buying a SCSI-2 add-in (like a hard drive) without an adequate controller is a waste of money. The drive can churn out information at the higher rate, but your controller (and your computer) can't do diddly-squat with it until it gets *sslloowwed* down to the regular SCSI rate.

You can, however, connect a regular SCSI device to a SCSI-2 controller/adapter. You won't get the speed burst from the regular SCSI device, but any other peripherals you may have that are SCSI-2-compatible should be just fine.

Who Goes There?

You can connect up to seven SCSI devices to a PC (*six* on a Macintosh because the Mac's internal hard drive counts as one SCSI device). To keep your computer from getting confused over which SCSI device is which, SCSI devices have to be identified with a SCSI ID number.

SCSI ID numbers are generally set with a push-button, a wheel, or a set of tiny switches (consult your manual for specifics on how your device's SCSI ID number is set). Whatever gadget you use to choose the ID number, you can choose a number from 0 to 7.

The ID number for a bootable device—one with the startup information (MS-DOS or a Macintosh System folder) necessary for running your computer—should be set to 0, 1, or 2. CD-ROM drives are too slow to be practical as startup drives, except in an emergency. Use the higher numbers if they're available. PC users need only worry about this if their hard drive is a SCSI device—and most aren't.

Mac users should only select ID numbers from 1 to 6. The numbers 0 and 7 are used to identify your Mac and its internal hard drive in the SCSI chain. PC users generally may use 0 to 6; 7 is usually the ID number assigned to the SCSI adapter card.

There is no other rhyme or reason to assigning ID numbers, except that each device in the SCSI chain has to have a different ID number. Otherwise, your computer will freak out trying to figure out which device is supposed to be doing what.

An easy way to remember how ID numbers work is to think of assigning ID numbers as if you're naming six or seven rambunctious dogs. It doesn't really matter what you name them, as long as they know what their names are, and stop piddling on the carpet when you yell at them.

The Terminator

Did you know that originally, Ethel Merman was supposed to star in that movie instead of Arnold Schwartzenegger? It was to be about a fading Broadway star who wanted to off all her critics so she could still play the ingenue. They were going to call it *The Mermanator*. Really. I swear I'm not making this up.

As far as SCSI devices go, the *terminator* is something else entirely. It's an electronic device that stops the data signal from moving eternally back and forth through the SCSI chain.

Sometimes the *termination* is on the outside of the device: a set of DIP switches, an on/off switch, or a terminating cap that fits into the second SCSI port on a device. These are, by far, the simplest forms of termination to add and remove.

Other devices are terminated internally—that is, with a resistor that must be removed from a circuit board inside the device in question. These are a pain in the butt, but thankfully they're rarely used anymore. You'll probably only need to worry about it if you buy a used hard drive that's three or more years old.

To keep the data from bouncing back and forth eternally through your SCSI chain, the first and last devices in the chain *must be terminated.* Check your manual to see what sort of termination your CD-ROM drive uses and if it needs to be terminated.

If you have one *internal* SCSI device, like a CD-ROM or hard drive, the internal device is terminated as the first item in the chain.

Am I SCSI Already?

For Macintosh users, your internal hard drive is a SCSI device. From the beginning, Macs were designed to make use of SCSI's capability to connect several devices along a single chain.

For DOS PC users, your internal hard drive may or may not be a SCSI device. Mainly, PCs start out with a disk controller card (like an IDE card) that controls one or two hard drives, one or two floppy drives, and may provide serial, parallel, and game ports. These disk controller cards are often called *super controllers* because they do everything, except they are *not* SCSI adapters. If your internal hard drive is connected to such a card, it isn't a SCSI device.

If you have no internal SCSI devices, the SCSI adapter card itself is considered the first device in the SCSI chain and must be terminated. Check your card's documentation to see whether it's terminated and how to change its termination if the need arises.

The last item in the SCSI chain must also be terminated, "last" meaning the one furthest from your computer and the last one connected to the chain. It has nothing to do with the ID numbers—that would make too much sense.

If you only have one SCSI device attached, that's the one that must be terminated. Check the manual to see how and where you can change its termination.

If you have two or more SCSI devices attached, then the last item in the chain (that is, farthest from the computer) should have its termination on. The others should not be terminated.

Stringing Them Along

When in Doubt, Look An easy way to spot which SCSI device in a chain is the last one is to look at its SCSI ports. The ports in the middle of the chain will have both SCSI ports occupied with cables.

The last port will have either one of the two SCSI ports open, and the second port may have a terminator cap plugged in it, or the device may have only one SCSI port.(External SCSI devices with only one port *have* to go last because you can't chain anything else to them—there's nowhere to plug anything else in. It doesn't much matter for internal SCSI stuff.)

All this SCSI talk can be a tad confusing. There's no way around it, really, because that's the nature of the rules. To make it easier to absorb and understand, let's play pretend.

Let's pretend that you're fabulously wealthy, and you just bought three (count 'em, three) CD-ROM drives to attach to your computer. You're going to make yourself the multimedia mogul of the world.

Because you don't have a lot of desk space, one of the drives you bought is an internal drive. That's the first one you install (as we discussed back in Chapter 13 or 14, depending on your computer).

Because it's an internal drive, it will be the first item in your daisy chain. It should have (what, class?) a SCSI ID number different from the rest (because it's first, let's make it "1"), and it should be terminated.

Mac owners: Your internal hard drive will *always* be the first item in your SCSI chain, and it is already terminated. If you install another internal SCSI device (say, in that big fat Quadra of yours), it should not be terminated.

(I'm trying like crazy here not to confuse you with this terminated/not terminated blather.) Remember the rule: THE FIRST AND LAST ITEMS IN A SCSI CHAIN MUST BE TERMINATED. An internal device, like a CD-ROM drive, would be considered the first device and should be terminated.

In this fantasy scenario, because we're installing a couple of external devices, too, one of those will be the *last* item in the chain. It will also be terminated.

Everything else in between (including a PC's SCSI adapter card) will *not* be terminated. Am I beating a dead horse here? Or should I say, a dead SCSI?

PC Adapter Card Blather

A SCSI adapter card in a PC is often terminated by changing settings with a set of DIP switches that look like a bank of teeny-tiny light switches. Consult your manual for the proper settings to turn the termination on or off, as you need.

If you have both internal and external SCSI devices, the card should *not* be terminated.

If you have only *external* (or only *internal*) SCSI devices, the card itself *should* be terminated.

The second drive you connect to your computer (an external model, cabled from its primary SCSI port to the computer's SCSI port) should have a different SCSI ID number (say, "2") and should *not* be terminated.

The third and final drive will be cabled from its primary SCSI port to the open port on the last drive you connected. It will have a SCSI ID number different from all the others (maybe "3"), and this drive (because it's the last and the ultimate CD-ROM reader) will be terminated.

With all that done and good, you should be able to fire up each of those drives, and then your computer, and just blow yourself away with digitized sights and sounds, right?

Well, yes. In theory.

In practice, however, sometimes no matter how closely you follow the scuzzy rules of SCSI, it just won't work. That's when you drag out that saying you probably learned when you were six or seven years old…

Rules Were Made to Be Broken

When I hooked up my new CD-ROM drive, I was daisy-chaining it to an external 160MB hard drive. I had everything all hooked up and ready to go when I thought, "Oh, @#$!%—I have to remove the termination from the hard drive." Then I swore some more because I couldn't remember how this hard drive's termination was set. That meant undoing all the cabling I'd done, pulling the drive out of its bat-cave of junk (did I mention I'm a slob?), and looking to see what I had to do.

Well, the bugger has internal termination—the kind that you have to remove resistors from a circuit board inside the drive housing. Oh, ack! And after all the people I warned against buying a hard drive like that, too. What a @#%*!!

140

To make a long story short, I couldn't find the resistors I needed to remove, and I was too chicken to just remove them blindly.

No one's ever accused me of having too much sense. I put the hard drive back in its housing and hooked the cables back up. I said to myself, the worst that can happen is nothing, and I fired that bad boy up.

It worked fine. It worked fine with everything in my SCSI chain terminated (my internal hard drive, the external one, and the CD-ROM drive).

The point is that dealing with SCSI chains is like Wednesday on the old *Mickey Mouse Club*: It's Anything-Can-Happen Day. If you carefully followed the SCSI rules outlined earlier and ruled out any other problems (like loose connections, no power, no driver software, and so on) and your CD-ROM drive still won't work, then ignore the SCSI termination rules. Try any combination of termination on and off you can think of—but be careful because you could lose your stored data.

In your rush to get things working, don't go changing any SCSI ID numbers. That is a hard-and-fast rule. Every SCSI device must have its own, unique ID number, or digital high jinks will ensue.

When it comes to breaking the rules, there's very little advice I can give you, except for two things:

➤ Don't panic. This happens to everybody at one point or another. It's just your turn.

➤ Before you go crazy breaking the SCSI rules, make sure you followed them to the letter the first time through. Don't assume that because it didn't work right the first time, it's become a no-holds-barred battle to the death. Double- and triple-check your work first.

Three! Except for three things! (I didn't expect the Spanish Inquisition...)

➤ Be methodical. Don't randomly start switching things around. Change only one thing at a time. Write down in detail each thing you try. If it fails, you won't try it again. If it works, you'll know what you did should you ever need to reproduce it.

Should you need help, there's always technical support. There's also Chapter 30, devoted to troubleshooting the other things that could possibly go wrong.

Other Controllers

If you're installing a CD-ROM drive on or in a PC-compatible, you may not be dealing with SCSI. You may have a sound card that doubles as the drive controller. You may have a CD-ROM controller card that only works with the drive you purchased. You may have an IDE controller card (like the one that controls your floppy and hard drives already) to control your CD-ROM.

Each kind of controller has its own advantages and disadvantages. I'm going to use the dreaded phrase: "I'm not one of Dionne Warwick's Psychic Friends, so I can't tell what you have. You're going to have to read your manual carefully." I can however, give you a few pointers to help you out.

One Is the Loneliest Number

If your new controller is your only add-on, other than the typical IDE controller and video card, chances are you won't have to fiddle with this stuff too much.

However, expansion cards can conflict in two common ways: IRQ and DMA settings.

I Am Soooo IRQed!

A card's IRQ settings give the card a particular way to interrupt whatever your PC is doing so you can get information sent from the CD-ROM drive. *IRQ* stands for *Interrupt ReQuest*. No two cards installed in your computer should have the IRQ settings; otherwise, the cards may collide and quibble over who gets to interrupt first, and your computer will crash.

Most computers have 16 IRQ addresses/numbers you can assign. Cards use some of them. Your computer uses others. How do you know what your IRQ settings are? Well, there are two ways. You can look in the manuals from any other cards you have installed and check to see what IRQ settings they had when you bought the card. If you didn't change the settings, that's your answer. Just make sure your new controller card doesn't use the same setting.

If you can't find the manual or can't recall if you changed the settings, you can use a system utility like *Microsoft Diagnostics* (*MSD* for short) that is included with later versions of MS-DOS and Windows 3.1 and later. You can also use any utility that gives you detailed system information, like *Norton Utilities* or *PC Tools Deluxe*. If your controller card has an install program, it may also be able to tell you what IRQs are in use in your system.

To use MSD, at your command prompt type

CD DOS

and press **Enter**, which will change you to your DOS directory (this assumes that your DOS directory is actually named DOS). The command prompt will change to C:\DOS>. Then type **MSD** and press **Enter**, which will start up MSD. It looks a little like the following figure.

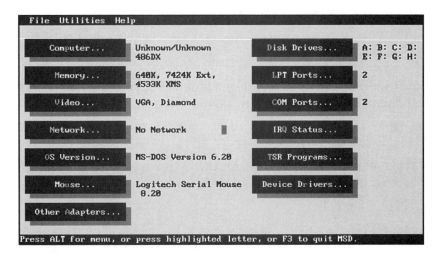

Microsoft Diagnostics, but you can call it MSD.

When it's running, click on the button that says **IRQ status**, or press **Q**. You will get a listing of all the devices in your computer that use interrupts, what they are, where they are, and what their IRQ numbers are. Jot them down. Assign an unused IRQ to your CD-ROM's controller. Check the card's manual for specific instructions on how to do that.

DMA It All!

DMA stands for *Direct Memory Access*. An expansion card with DMA is assigned a particular path for funnelling information directly to your computer's RAM. As with IRQ settings, no two cards should have the same DMA setting.

If two devices fight over a DMA number, one of them will lose and won't work; however, your system won't usually crash.

Most computers have eight DMA paths, or channels. In typical PCs, most of these settings are unused, so you may not have to tinker with them.

If your CD-ROM's controller card won't work, or an older card that always worked before (like your video card) stops working with the new controller installed, DMA settings are probably the culprit.

Again, a good installation program will tell you which DMA settings are in use so you can adjust your new card accordingly. Check your controller card's manual for details.

The Least You Need to Know

➤ Every SCSI device must have its own, individual SCSI ID number.

➤ The first and last devices in a SCSI chain should be terminated.

➤ If the termination rules don't work for you, don't panic. Methodically try to change the termination scheme until it works for you.

➤ *IRQ* stands for *Interrupt Request*. In a PC, cards you install should have different IRQ settings from those already in use.

➤ *DMA* stands for *Direct Memory Access*. Like IRQs, no two cards in your computer should use the same DMA setting.

➤ Did I say, "Don't panic?"

➤ Did I mention checking the manual for specific details about *your* controller card?

Fire It Up!

If you're like me (and you know you are), you didn't even take the time to wipe the sweat from your fevered brow after setting up your drive. You want to use it, and you want to use it now.

I don't blame you in the least, but (psst) wipe the sweat off of your forehead first. Catch your breath. The drive is yours, you know—you own it. It will wait for five minutes while you chill out enough to savor the experience. Round up the kids, your friends, cats and/or dogs, and show off your drive in style.

On second thought, maybe you better fire it up before you wake the neighbors. We don't want any humiliating fizzles in case something's hooked up wrong. That would just be too embarrassing. You can always shut it down again and then call everybody, and pretend you're seeing it for the first time, too.

Thank You, Mr. Murphy

You know Murphy's Law: Anything that can go wrong will go wrong, and at the worst possible moment. To help sidestep that cranky Mr. Murphy, do a final check of the most obvious things you can think of before you turn on your new drive. It's the obvious things that get you—well, that get me—every time.

Here are a couple of things to check before you power up for the first time:

➤ Is the drive plugged into a power outlet or internal power supply that works?

➤ For external and internal drives: Are the connections tight at both ends of the cable between the drive and your computer or controller card?

➤ Is the volume turned up to an audible level on your sound card (or your Mac's Sound Control Panel)?

➤ Are your speakers (if you have them) properly connected to your sound card and the drive? These connections vary depending on the type of speakers you have. You might want to check the manual, or skim through Chapter 6 again.

➤ Do you have a software or audio CD handy and (if appropriate) in a caddy?

If you can answer "yes" to all these questions, you're in good shape. The really obvious problems have been eliminated. On to Step Two.

You Turn Me On

When turning on peripheral devices, it's important to remember a simple rule of thumb: Turn on everything else before you turn on your computer.

Shocking!

When you send power through (that is, turn it on) a peripheral that's plugged into your computer, it can send a little jolt of power through your computer, as well. It isn't exactly harmful, but it can be a source of wear and tear on electronic components. Who needs the extra stress? Certainly not you or your computer.

Additionally, with SCSI devices, if they aren't powered up and running before you turn on your computer, your computer may not recognize that they are attached.

When your system starts up, it's like a mother duck: When it wakes up, the first thing it does is make sure all the ducklings are around. Similarly, your computer polls the system to see what is attached. If your computer can't see your CD-ROM drive at startup, it won't be able to access it.

At worst, you may get a cranky error message saying "no SCSI device located." At best, you'll have to reboot your computer—with all the SCSI peripherals turned on—so momma duck can see her ducklings.

Booting Me Softly...

If you do forget to turn on your CD-ROM drive before you turn on your computer and you need to reboot, be sure to use a soft boot. It's easier on your computer than the "hard boot" described in the "Shocking" sidebar.

PC users can use the Ctrl+Alt+Del key combination. Mac users can select Restart from the Special menu. Soft booting is a good idea whenever you need to restart your system.

If things start up normally, you should pat yourself on the back. You can move on. If your system hangs, freezes, or otherwise goes all weird on you, you should recheck the obvious. If that doesn't straighten things out, try Chapter 30, "Troubleshooting" or the troubleshooting section of your CD-ROM drive's manual.

Pop Quiz

"This is a test. This is only a test." Before you do anything else, you might want to put the CD-ROM drive through its paces, just to be sure there's nothing physically wrong with the drive itself.

Some CD-ROM drives come with a built-in diagnostic (a self-test) or have a diagnostic program as part of their software set. Check your drive's manual to find out what, if anything, you have available and how to use it.

For my drive, the self-test is accomplished by inserting a CD, turning off the drive, then turning it back on while holding down the Play/Pause control on the front of the drive. Doing this puts the drive in "diagnostic mode." The drive's diagnostics check up on every little bit of the drive's hardware to be sure everything's in working order. If everything is not working correctly, a message appears on the drive's message display telling you so. To end diagnostic mode, I turn the drive off and back on again.

Naturally, you may have a different drive than mine, so your drive's diagnostic routine (if it even has one) may be different. Again, check your manual.

Hey, Where'd It Go?

Turning your CD-ROM drive off and then back on again (while the computer is turned on) may confuse the heck out of your computer. If, after running the self-test on the drive, your computer cannot find (or refuses to acknowledge the presence of) a CD in the drive, simply do a soft boot to restart your computer. That should straighten it out.

If everything checks out, you should be ready to load a disc. If not, check whatever error messages you received from the self-test against the manual and see if you can figure out what's happening there. If that fails, call the drive manufacturer's technical-support line. (For more tips on troubleshooting and dealing with technical support, take a look at Chapter 30.)

Let Me Drive

After you know that everything is kosher inside your drive, and everything is powered up and running (including your computer), you can pop in a CD-ROM or audio disc and fire that up, too.

My Heart Belongs to Caddy

For many CD-ROM models, inserting a disc means first popping the disc into a caddy like the one shown here.

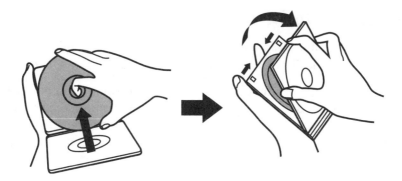

Inserting a disk into a caddy.

As you can see in the illustration, you should handle the disc by the edges only. Put the disc into the caddy with the label (or printed) side *up*.

After the disc is loaded into the caddy, you can slip the caddy into your CD-ROM drive. Most CD-ROM drives won't let you insert a caddy in any way but the correct way. For the sake of thoroughness, however, insert the caddy with the clear side facing up (you should be able to see the CD's label through it) and with the metal shutter-end of the caddy going into the drive first.

For the directionally impaired, there's usually a big ol' arrow embossed on that end, too, as well as the words **This side faces forward**, just in case you have any doubts.

Naked Launch

If you have a portable CD-ROM drive, or a model that doesn't use caddies, you just pop that naked ol' disc right into the slide-out tray. You still need to put it in label side up, and you still need to avoid touching everything but the disc's edges.

If your drive is the kind with a disc slot, just slide the CD in as you would a floppy disk. Some CD-ROM drives, like some audio CD players, have a tray that pops out when you push the eject button (usually right near the tray). You drop the disc in the tray (label side up, still), push the button again, and the tray carries the disk inside the drive.

If your drive has a lid that you need to open (like the one on a portable audio-CD player), you'll need to open it (duh) and then put the disc onto the hub in the center of the disc compartment. Press down gently until the disc clicks into place and lies flat in the compartment. Close the lid.

Will It Go 'Round in Circles?

When you push the caddy/disc in and/or close the lid, the disc should spin quietly for a second or two while the drive figures out what kind of disc it is (audio or CD-ROM).

If your drive has some kind of information display (many don't), it will then display either the number of audio tracks and the total amount of music time on an audio CD, or it will display some oblique and cryptic message saying it's ready to read your CD-ROM disc. Check your manual for a guide to translating your drive's set of cryptic-and-oblique messages.

You're ready to launch your first CD application or listen to your first desktop audio CD.

Let's Do Launch

Just *how* you launch your CD software varies from system to system, and can even vary from disc to disc. The following sections discuss some common ways you'll launch your CD-based programs, but you should always refer to the manual that comes with each disc to see how that particular program needs to be started.

On the whole, though, you can rest assured that launching software from a CD is pretty similar to launching software from any other kind of storage medium—it really is just a another kind of disk, after all.

Which One Do I Click?

Some CD software will come with multiple versions of the software on one CD, so that disc can be used on a Mac, a PC with DOS, or even a PC running Windows.

Always be sure to check the manual to see which files you need to use to launch the application on your system. I think the worst that can happen is an error message, or maybe your system will freeze up trying to read the data, but still—who needs the hassle?

For the Mac

When you insert a CD in your drive, its icon should appear on your Mac's desktop, just like your hard drive's icon or any floppy disk. To see what's on the CD-ROM disc, just double-click on the disc's icon; by doing this, you open a window, also like any other disk's window.

Read any "Read Me" files you might find, especially if you're the type to avoid manuals. Some CD-based software requires that you install special fonts, or even part of the application, on your hard drive before you can use the disc. Just follow the directions.

When you've taken care of any installation-type business, locate the application icon (check your manual if you're not sure which one it is—you may have to root around in a folder or two) and double-click on that icon, too. After the CD spins a little in the drive, the application should start right up.

Prepare to "*Oooh*" and "*Ahhh.*"

Curiosity and the Cat

Because I know how incredibly curious you can be: Yes. You *can* double-click on the icon of an audio CD. You'll get a standard Mac window with little icons for each song track on the CD.

However, all you get when you double-click on a song track is one of those annoying *Document cannot be opened—application missing* messages. For this I interrupted Aretha Franklin?

For DOS

Launching an application from a CD-ROM disc is much like launching any application from any disk.

One part of the driver software you installed is MSCDEX, which loads automatically when you start your system. It tells your system where your CD-ROM driver software is located, specifies how many memory buffers to assign to it, and assigns the CD-ROM drive the next available drive letter.

If you have A, B, and C drives, your CD-ROM will be drive D. If there's already a D drive, the CD-ROM will be drive E.

To start a CD application for DOS:

➤ At the C\: prompt, type *the appropriate drive letter*: (for example, **D:**), and press **Enter**.

➤ When the prompt changes to the CD-ROM's drive letter, you can type **DIR** to get a directory of the disc.

➤ Find the executable file with the .EXE, .BAT, or .COM extension after its name (you may have to root around in subdirectories). Your manual will say which it is.

➤ Type the executable file's name at the prompt (for example, **CD_DODO.EXE**) and press **Enter**.

The application should start right up, but (as always) you should read the manual specific to the application you're trying to launch.

For Windows

Launching CD software from Windows is much the same as launching any application under Windows—you probably need to install the software first. Here's a typical installation:

➤ From the Program Manager's File menu, select **Run**.

➤ Type: **D:** (or whatever your drive letter is)**\SETUP.EXE**.

➤ Press **Enter**.

The setup application should start. You may be asked a question or two in the process, so stick around and read the directions on-screen.

When the setup is finished, you'll probably have a new program group in your Program Manager. To start the application, just double-click on its icon in the Program Group window. Of course, you should always read the installation instructions in the manual first.

One in Every Crowd

Yes, truly, there *is* one in every crowd. In this case, it's a CD-ROM disk that takes special handling to start up.

RTFM Means Read the—uh, Fabulous, yeah—Fabulous Manual

This is yet another reason you should always at least *look* at the startup directions in your software's manual, even if you never look at anything else in it. It will spare you so many headaches and so much confusion.

Generally, you'll find many CD applications that involve heavy-duty graphics require you to copy a portion of the program to your hard drive. This is because your computer can access data from your hard drive faster than it can from your CD-ROM reader—the graphics (or animation, or movie) run more smoothly.

Often, in cases like these, you'll insert the disc into your CD, but you'll launch the application from the file(s) you copied to your hard drive, using the method appropriate to your computer and operating system (or shell program).

Also generally speaking, this copying of stuff to your hard drive is taken care of when you setup a Windows application. For plain DOS, and Macs, you may have to deal with an installer application or copy the files manually. Your CD-ROM disc's manual will give you the details.

If Music Be the Food of Love, Play On...

In order to use your computer to control audio CDs in your new drive, you'll need to launch the appropriate application from the CD-ROM's driver software.

Buttony-Button

If your drive has audio controls on the front, running control software from your computer will probably disable them. On the other hand, if you launch the control software while an audio CD is playing, using the drive's manual controls will confuse the heck out of your computer.

(You knew this was coming, didn't you?) Check your drive's manual for specifics on how to launch and use the software that came with your drive.

One of the popular programs, often included with drives, is called *Music Box*. It puts a set of CD controls up on your monitor. If you work in an environment (like Windows or Macintosh System 7) that lets you run more than one application at a time, you can control your music while doing something else on your computer. That's how I can be listening to Aretha while writing this ("Spanish Harlem," thanks for asking).

The Music Box controls look something like those in the figure (this is the Mac version; the DOS version looks slightly different). There's nothing to panic over here. If you can work a cassette player or audio CD player, you can deal with programs like Music Box.

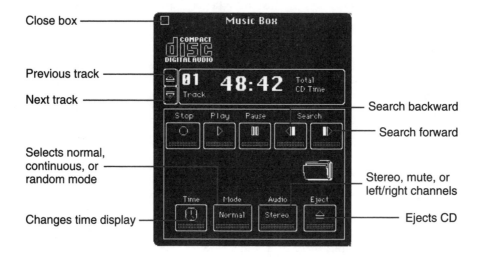

The Music Box desk accessory (Macintosh version).

I don't know about you, but I get a lot more work done with musical accompaniment (maybe it's all those years of doing musical theater). Admittedly, it is very hard to type while chair-dancing along with Aretha. Too many typos. Hazard of the job, I guess.

The Least You Need to Know

➤ Power up your CD-ROM drive (or *any* external SCSI peripheral) before you power up your computer, or the computer won't be able to locate it.

➤ Run your drive's self-test or diagnostic software (if you've got either one) before you launch your first CD application. That way, if something goes screwy later, you'll know it's the disc or something you're doing instead of a problem with the drive.

➤ There are a number of ways to launch CD applications. Be sure to read the manual that came with the disc before you try to launch a new program.

➤ If you want to control audio CDs with your computer, you'll need to launch the control program that came with your drive.

➤ Enjoy yourself... *let the games begin!*

Part 3
So? What Do I Do with It Now?

Very often, people buy a new piece of computer hardware (sometimes even whole computer systems) just to accomplish one particular thing. Once that's done, they often throw their hands up in despair and go, "Oh, great! So now what do I do with it?" Enter Part 3. Here you'll find a very broad overview of the different kinds of CD-ROM titles available to you in categories like:

➤ *Games*

➤ *Entertainment CDs (fun, but not games)*

➤ *Edu- or Info-tainment titles (fun, but educational)*

➤ *And bizarre stuff that doesn't fit into any category.*

LOUISIANA CD-ROM FIGHTS

Chapter 17

CD-ROM Accessory Software

In addition to the mountains of stuff you can find to use *with* your CD-ROM drive, there's a growing amount of software you can use *on* your CD-ROM drive. This software will make working with your CD-ROM drive simpler, faster, and easier for finding stuff you need from a disc.

Hurry Up!

If you're like me, you sometimes find yourself standing in front of the microwave yelling "Hurry up!" at your food. We're spoiled. We want what we want, and we want it *now*.

To folks in a hurry, waiting for a CD-ROM disc to load, display a window full of files to select, or get to the next level of a juicy game can just be too much to bear.

To help remedy that situation, clever software companies have come out with a variety of accessory software to help speed things along. Generally speaking, CD-ROM accessories fall into two categories: *alternate drivers* and *CD catalogers*.

Choose a Designated Driver

With Macs (alternate CD-ROM drivers are much more plentiful for Macs at the moment), a typical CD-ROM driver is a handful of extensions (or INITs, as we old-timers call them).

Control panel
A bit of software that lets you customize its behavior (and, therefore, your computer's behavior) to some extent.

Drivers tell your Mac how to deal with your new CD-ROM drive, but that's about it. The rest of the time, they just sit there.

The new breed of drivers are usually *control panels* that not only tell your Mac how to cope with CDs, but let you fiddle with *how* they cope. If you look at the following two figures, you'll see what I mean.

Casa Blanca Works' DriveCD.

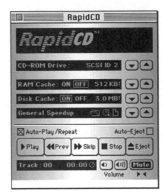

Insignia Solutions' RapidCD.

Casa Blanca Works' *DriveCD* not only functions as your driver software, it also acts as a SCSI utility (checking to see what SCSI devices are attached to your Mac), and lets you set up a RAM cache to give your Mac more elbow room to deal with data from big fat CD-ROM discs.

Giving your computer a RAM cache helps it retrieve and deliver information from a CD more efficiently and, therefore, more quickly to you with fewer waiting periods as data gets read from a disc. Very cool.

On the other hand, Insignia Solutions' *RapidCD* doesn't give you some of the SCSI features of *DriveCD*, but it does give you more cache functions. *RapidCD* gives you RAM cache and *disk cache* options. A disk cache behaves like a RAM cache, but instead of storing data in memory (RAM), it writes it temporarily to your hard disk. It's a good option for folks with limited amounts of RAM and an abundance (well, 3MB) of clear hard disk space.

RapidCD also doubles as an audio CD controller, replacing whatever player utility came with your drive (like *Music Box*, or one of the many others).

RAM cache
A bit of your computer's RAM set aside for a specific function. Not to be confused with a CD-ROM drive's built-in cache (discussed in Chapter 4), even though they are similar. A drive's cache is a permanent thing and part of the CD-ROM drive. A RAM cache is temporary and is created in your computer's RAM. There are caching programs for all types of computers.

161

PC Users...

While there aren't many alternate drivers for PC CD-ROM drives at the moment, there *are* utilities that give you a similar suite of cache options. If you're interested, you might want to check out Blitz 'n' Software's *CD-Blitz* and look for new titles. There are also caching utilities as part of many general utility packages. I'm sure there will be more shortly.

The benefits of replacing your one-trick CD-ROM driver include faster/better access of CD information, potentially smoother playing of audio and video clips, and an easy way to customize your drive's performance.

Do they work? Sure they do. As a matter of fact, NEC has started using a scaled-down, NEC-specific version of *DriveCD* with their CD-ROM drives. If you're considering buying an alternate driver package, double-check compatibility (usually listed on the box) before you buy. These drivers are compatible with most drives—just make sure you don't own one of the unlucky few that aren't compatible. Better safe than sorry.

You can find these and other alternate CD-ROM drivers from under $40 to as much as $50 by mail order.

Direct Me...

Another real time-consumer when working with CD-ROM discs is the amount of time it takes just to look for stuff. Imagine having to look for one specific photograph or bit of text on a CD that contains thousands of files. *Yikes!*

Depending on your needs, your wallet, and what you find yourself searching for, there are two general solutions available to you: *CD catalogers* and *image browsers*.

These are handy utilities, but you probably won't really need one until you've amassed a collection of a dozen or so CDs that need looking after.

Catalog This!

One of the problems with looking for just one tiny, little file on a CD is the amount of time it takes for your computer to read and display the disc's catalog of information. First, the catalogs are much bigger than the average floppy disk or hard drive's catalog. Second, CD-ROM drives are much slower at accessing that information than a floppy or hard drive.

Cataloging software sidesteps the issue by moving a copy of a CD's directory to your hard drive. Here the directory can be searched or read as quickly as the directory from your hard drive, speeding up the search process.

One such utility is Insignia Solutions' *CD Directory* (shown in the following figure). It includes a control panel and a small application that lets you tinker with your catalog files. Here's how it works.

Insignia Solutions' CD Directory.

After you've set up *CD Directory* (with the control panel shown above), every time you insert a new CD-ROM disc in your drive, *CD Directory* will read the disc's entire directory and store a copy in the CD Library folder it created on your desktop. You can go about your business.

At a later date, when you want to find something from that disk, you can open and browse through the copy of the catalog on your hard drive, find the file you want, and open it by double-clicking on it. You'll then be asked to insert the CD-ROM disc that holds that file, and you're on your way.

The advantage of a cataloger is that you can search through your collection of CDs without having to pop each disc in to search. The disadvantage is that these catalogs take up hard disk space, which may already be at a premium for you. (I can sympathize. I just had to shell out for a new external hard drive.) The *CD Directory* application lets you adjust how information is stored and displayed to help minimize catalog size—but still, you're cataloging up to 600MB of stuff. It will take up room.

You can find *CD Directory* (available for Macs only right now) for about $40 by mail order. Version 1.0 was a little cranky when I tried it out, but there should be a version 1.1 or higher out by the time you read this. There are similar utilities for the PC.

Browse Me, Baby

Image browsers are like catalogers, except they actually let you get a look at image files and video clips *before* you open them from the CD. That's a big help because most image files have names like "11014.TIF," which is not really handy if you're trying to figure out what the picture is. Instead, you get a display like the one shown here.

Aldus' Fetch, *image browsing utility.*

The figure is of the *Fetch* catalog from Apple's QuickTime QuickClips CD and shows half a dozen clips (from over 300) featuring one of my favorite computer divas (I wouldn't dare call her a geek), Laurie Anderson.

You can browse through the disc's contents and when you find something you want to look at, just double-click on it. It loads right up, and you can play the clip (if the appropriate CD is in your drive—otherwise, *Fetch* will ask for it).

Many browsers are able to display photographic images and even perform some minor editing (like cropping the image). Many browsers can also play audio and video clips.

Browsers are very helpful if you use a lot of CD-based photo or video files—they're *so* handy, in fact, that most discs come with some scaled-down version of a browser to make dealing with the disc easier. For average users, that may be enough.

If you find yourself with a lot of video and photo discs, and you're wasting a lot of time looking for a particular image, it may be worth the money to buy a full-featured image browser that will let you skim through your entire CD collection without having to pop a single disc in the drive.

There are a number of similar packages that vary as widely in capabilities as they do in price. Some names to look for include: Kudo Lite for Windows, Fetch, Image Commander. Most cost in the vicinity of $100, even by mail order, but you can often find limited editions on CD collections (Image Commander Lite, for example, comes on CompuWorks' *Color Clips* CD-ROM collection). You may also be able to buy a full-powered browser at a deep discount—like $15 for a $100 product—when you buy a CD of photographic images, for example, or a high-end presentation package (see Chapter 27).

As always, Mr. Phelps, you should shop to meet your budget and needs, and *always* try to find the best bargain you can. If you or any member of your CD shopping force gets caught, the secretary will disavow any knowledge of your actions.

The Least You Need to Know

➤ Mac users can speed up their CD-ROM drives by replacing their original driver software with a more flexible and powerful driver.

➤ PC users can get some of the same benefits by adding CD cache software to their computers.

➤ Catalogers are useful if you deal with lots of CDs that contain lots of files (or if your memory is shaky, like mine).

➤ Image browsers are like catalog utilities, except they usually deal with picture files of some type (photo, drawing, or video) and often contain minimal image viewing and editing power.

Chapter 18

Fun and Games

Okay. Confession time: I'm not that much of a computer gamester. I spend, pretty much, all the doo-dah day in front of one computer or another. When the shackles are unlocked, I tend to run away. I run away to a good book, a good movie, or just about anything you can do outside (like sitting under a tree and reading a good book). There's a book by Kurt Vonnegut calling my name right now. When I do toy around with computer games, they tend to be of the very simple variety: solitaire, puzzle sort of things, sometimes chess. Games where you spend the entire time looking down the barrel of a digital gun, killing things, well—they hold no appeal for me. I just thought you should know that up front.

What Do You Like?

Gaming is a very personal experience. Folks who are "into" particular kinds of games tend to be fanatical about them (to some extent). They're fiercely devoted to the games they love, and just as fiercely critical of the ones they dislike. Because that's the case with gaming, this chapter is more about the kinds of games that are available on CD-ROM, rather than any kind of recommendation of any particular product. You know what you like, right?

Beam Me Up, Scotty...

One of the cooler-looking products around these days is the *Star Trek: The Next Generation Interactive Technical Manual* from Simon & Schuster Interactive. It isn't a "game" per se, but more of a virtual-reality experience. It's the first product created with Apple Computer's QuickTime VR (for virtual reality), and that's what makes it so cool. In most CD-ROM stuff, you usually get what amounts to a collection of video clips or photographs in a slide show. You can't really stop the presentation and get a good, up-close-and-personal look at any particular item. You have to look at what the disc's designers want you to see.

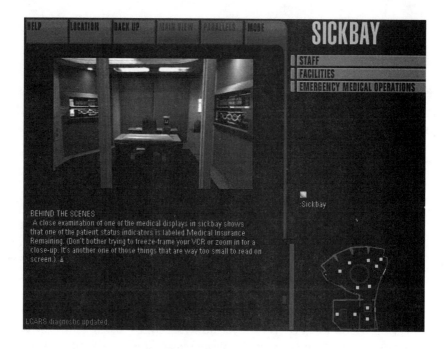

STNG Interactive Tech Manual.

Not so with the STNG technical manual (yeah, I'm a Trekker—but in my day, we were Trekkies—I haven't figured out what the difference is). Have a look at the figure above. It's one of the informational screens about the sickbay aboard the U.S.S. Enterprise.

The picture of Dr. Crusher's office in the figure isn't as still and boring as it looks on the printed page. It's dynamic—it changes. With your mouse, you can turn a full 360 degrees and look at everything in the room, as if you were standing in it (that's what makes it virtually reality). You can zoom in and get a closer look (and additional information) on a lot of the hardware in there. With some hardware, like the medical tricorder, you can actually "pick it up" and turn it around and look at it from every angle. Virtually real, even. Very wild.

Additionally, you can get some interesting (and pretty darn funny) behind-the-scenes information. There's an example of it in the figure above, if you can make it out. It says: "A close examination of one of the medical displays in sickbay shows that one of the patient status indicators is labeled Medical Insurance Remaining." I howled!

As I mentioned, *Star Trek: The Next Generation Interactive Technical Manual* is a Mac-only product right now, but there's probably a fleet of programmers hopped up on caffeine and candy bars trying to get a Windows version together. A Windows version should be available by the time you read this. It lists for about $70, but you can find it for about $45. After other developers get their hands on QuickTime VR, you can expect a number of products that will actually put you in a scene where you can control what you're looking at.

Mind Games

No, not the sort played by George and Martha in *Who's Afraid of Virginia Woolf?*, but games that require a certain level of brain activity on the part of the player(s). I like this sort of game where you need to figure things out to win, rather than simply blowing things up. (Again, this is just what appeals to me. You like what you like, and I won't say "boo" about it. Okay?)

One of the games that I've played (and finished, thanks for asking) is Myst from Broderbund. It's a time/dimension-traveling adventure where you have to solve a range of puzzles to move from one age to another and piece together the story. It's been going strong for over a year now, which is practically forever in terms of how long most games remain popular. In the following figure, you can see a shot of the strange and surreal landscape. The grayscale image really doesn't do it justice. It's beautiful.

An enigmatic set of gears from Broderbund's Myst.

Myst requires that you figure out what's going on (with the help of some subtle and not so subtle clues), how to make things work, how to move between the various ages, and whose side you're on in that age-old battle of good versus evil. I got through it in a couple of weeks, but I freely admit I couldn't have done it without some of the tips and tricks posted on some of the computer services (mainly America Online and CompuServe).

Myst is available for Mac and Windows. It lists for about $85, but you can find it for under $50 if you shop well (and shopping well is half the battle). Keep an eye out for Myst II in the near future. I will, too.

We're All Doom-ed

Another game that's raging out of control is Doom from id Software. If you're a PC owner, Doom could very well be the reason you're contemplating a CD-ROM drive in the first place. It's so popular, in fact, I couldn't even drum up a copy of it to check out for this section. I apologize. It's an adventure game where you try and blast demons to...well, hell. I can hear it now: Well, there's another fine demon all shot to hell.

Doom is an action/adventure game, intense and fast-paced, and you get to blow stuff up, shoot it, and watch oogy stuff leak out. The game has taken on a life of its own. It has turned into an entire software cottage industry. In addition to the original game, there's now a sequel (the cleverly titled Doom II: Hell on Earth), there are companion CDs (that contain tips, maps of all the levels, and various accessories), expansion CDs (that add levels and weapons to either Doom or Doom II), and even Lost Episode discs. I thought only TV shows had lost episodes. For Doom devotees, it's not just a game, it's an intense, all-consuming way of life. Who knew?

At the moment, all this Doom stuff is DOS-only and on floppies as well as CD. There's a Mac version in the works, but its release date keeps being pushed back. You can find Doom and Doom II (if you can find them at all) for under $50 street price. The accessory software covers a range of prices from $5–$10 to almost as much as the original game ($50).

Simple Mind, Simple Diversions

If you're like me (please, let there be somebody like me out there), all you really want is a simple little game to break up the monotony of your day at the computer. You rarely find "simple" little games on CD-ROM, though, since the medium lends itself more to huge, complicated extravaganzas. You can find some, however—games like WizardWorks Windows Fun Pack, which puts three sets of games, 21 games in all, at your disposal. In one, aptly called Squash! (shown below) you have to swat as many flies as possible in a short time. That gives you an idea of the sort of games you get: simple, distracting games that you can play for five or ten minutes while you stop obsessing about that report that's due, then get on with your life. With Squash! you won't be kept awake struggling to get through, but you will be amused for a few minutes. You can also play Pac-Man-like games, Battleship-like games, and similar variations on other popular computer and arcade-type games.

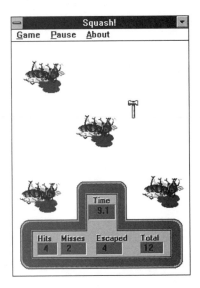

Squashed! This is about as bloody as I care to get in a game.

This is one of those CDs where you can't run the games from the disc, but you have to install them all on your hard drive to use them. There are a number of similar packages available. This one is for Windows, and you can find it for under $30. There are also sets for Mac and DOS, and they tend to all run in the $20–$30 range.

Running the Gamut from A–Z

It seems like there's a bazillion different kinds of games around. Here are a few broad categories:

➤ Simulations, where you fly bomber planes, play sports, you name it.

➤ Mystery games, where you're the gumshoe in charge of a (insert crime here) investigation.

➤ Shoot 'em-ups, where you can kill stuff on earth, in space, on other planets, in other dimensions.

➤ Strategy games, like chess, where it's advantageous to think and plan in advance.

➤ Puzzle-type games, where you need to figure out mazes and math problems to win.

➤ Role-playing games, where you (and usually a hearty band of adventurers) assume the roles of historical, mythological, or fictional heroes and launch yourself on a quest. Think The Holy Grail and The Lord of the Rings.

Chapter 19

Entertainment

In This Chapter

➤ Movie dish

➤ Musical diversions

➤ Gossip, gossip, gossip

➤ Hobbies galore

Entertainment is a big ol' broad category that gets lumbered with a lot of CD-ROM titles that have no other homes (see Chapter 26 for some examples).

I've chosen, instead, to look at some strictly entertainment-related CD-ROM titles, to allude to some other types, and to ignore some others—the category's just too large to cover in any kind of detail.

As always, you should view this as an introduction to the category, not an exhaustive study. As usual, I try to limit myself to titles that are available for Windows and Mac systems, sometimes DOS, and prices are rounded, approximated, and subject to change without notice.

Movie Madness

There's a very interesting trend developing, where you can find many of your favorite movies on CD-ROM—either the whole film or a catalog of films and film information.

You Provide the Popcorn

In the "whole film" category, there's The Beatles' *A Hard Day's Night* (shown below) from Voyager. This amazing CD-ROM not only contains the entire 90-minute movie, but it also has the theatrical trailer (you know, those "Coming soon to a theater near you!" clips), the prologue that was added to the 1982 theatrical re-release, plus a copy of the script that you can read along with the film.

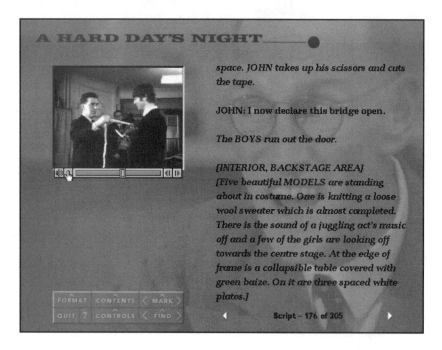

A scene and the accompanying script from The Beatles' film debut, A Hard Day's Night.

It's a great film, if you've never seen it. The film and its director, Richard Lester, are credited with the invention of the music video. It's also a *very* cool learning tool for anyone interested in script writing and movie making.

The companion script shows which bits of dialog were written for the movie, which scenes and lines were later cut from the film, and which bits of dialog and business The Beatles made up as they went along.

There are also interviews, essays, and clips from Richard Lester's early directing work. There are powerful searching tools to help you navigate through all the video and text information. Oh, yeah. The music's good, too.

A Hard Day's Night is available for Mac and Windows (it's QuickTime-based) and lists for about $40. You can usually find it for $30 or less.

And the Summary, Please...

Sorry, the Academy Awards were just on, and I'm all caught up in Oscar Fever.

The movie information type CD-ROM discs cover a number of bases. *Criterion Goes to the Movies* (covered in more detail in Chapter 25) not only gives you the scoop on over a hundred movies, but it also gives you the chance to order the laser disc version.

Microsoft's *Cinemania '95*, shown below, crams four film critics into your computer: Roger Ebert (of *Siskel and Ebert* fame), Ephraim Katz (author of *The Film Encyclopedia*), Pauline Kael (former critic for *The New Yorker* magazine), and Leonard Maltin (who turns up on *Good Morning America* all the time). You not only get the critics but their reviews of literally *thousands* of movies. Selections from Katz's *Film Encyclopedia* explain what oblique filmmaking terms (like "best boy" and "gaffer") mean.

Cinemania's take on one of my favorite films of 1994, Four Weddings and a Funeral.

In addition to information about the films, you can see photo portraits of your favorite actors, read biographical information, listen to movie music, clips of dialog, and watch video clips.

If you're in one of those "I want to rent a movie, but I don't know what I want" moods (I hate it when I get like that), you can use *Cinemania Suggests* to play wheel of movies. Vanna White is not involved.

Cinemania is available for Mac and Windows, is updated annually, and lists for about $60. You can find it for a smidgen less by mail order.

Music, Music, Music

Naturally, with most CD-ROM players, you can listen to audio CDs while you're working at your computer—I'm doing it right now, as a matter of fact (R.E.M.'s *Green*).

Additionally, there are a number of CD-ROM discs around that will fill you in on the ins and outs of classical music. Microsoft's *Multimedia Beethoven* (below), for example, is one of the many classical music CD-ROMs that helps you learn about the classics. In this case, it's Beethoven's 9th Symphony.

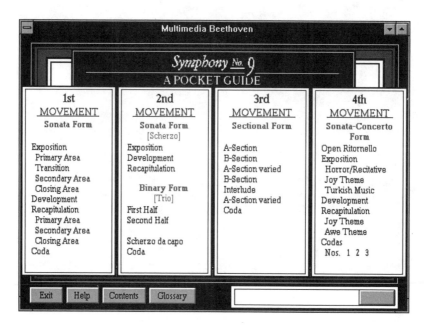

Microsoft's Multimedia Beethoven—*the composer, not the St. Bernard from the movies.*

As you can see in the previous figure, you can listen to (and learn about) the 9th by each movement, with explanations and access to a glossary of terms.

There's also biographical information about the composer and his life, and what was happening in Beethoven's world while he was composing the symphony.

Microsoft's music series, (*Multimedia Beethoven, Mozart, Straus, Stravinsky, and Shubert*) are only available for Windows PCs and list for about $60 each.

Mac users, there are a number of similar packages available for Macintosh if you're interested. If your taste runs to more contemporary music, you can check out CD-ROM titles by the likes of Peter Gabriel (*Xplora 1*), David Bowie (*Jump*), The Residents (*Freak Show* and *Gingerbread Man*), and the artist formerly known as Prince (*That Symbol Thingy Interactive*). Cutting edge musicians are pushing the envelope of performance with some really wild stuff. Of course, most of these are Windows-compatible, too.

Hollywood's Buzzing

If movies and music aren't your thing, perhaps you're more captivated by the private lives of the celebrities. You can indulge yourself with a CD-ROM like Voyager's *People Weekly: 20 Amazing Years of Pop Culture.*

People's 20 Years of Pop gossip... I mean Culture, yeah, that's the ticket, Culture.

The CD includes 20 years of *People* covers and cover stories. Listen to Princess Di babble on the phone. Watch Michael Jackson's face morph through it's various surgical incarnations, and watch Liz Taylor morph through diets and husbands.

If you're into such things, you can also see 20 years worth of Best and Worst Dressed photos and catty commentary about cleavage, plastic surgery, and underage dating. Me, I really don't care for it, but you might.

People Weekly is available for both Mac and Windows computers. It lists for about $35, but you can find it for under $25.

The Sporting Life

Let's see: so far we've had hockey and baseball strikes. Maybe it'd be better if we all just curled up with a sporting CD-ROM disc. There are a number available, including two from Microsoft: *Complete Baseball* and *Complete NBA Basketball*.

The CDs include the standard assortment of things you'd expect: photos and video clips of your favorite players, statistics out the wazoo, trivia, audio clips of commentary and the roar of the crowd.

The cooler aspect is that with either CD, and a modem for your computer, you can subscribe (yes, it costs extra) to an online service (*Basketball* or *Baseball Daily*, depending on the CD-ROM you have) to get news, player and team statistics and standings, all from the comfort of your home.

It's cool for two reasons: If you're a sports nut, it's like an IV information feed right into your brain. If you're a computer geek, you can sniff out the beginning of Microsoft's long-awaited foray into the world on online services. (*This* is the kind of gossip I do get into—and don't let anyone tell you differently: *men do gossip*.)

Both of Microsoft's sports CDs mentioned here are available for Windows only, and list for about $50. There are, however, *tons* of sports CDs available for Mac, DOS, and Windows. Check your favorite catalog or retail store.

The Complete Hobbyist

Whatever your interests, there's probably *one* CD-ROM title that covers your favorite obsession. Science fiction fans, there are a number of SF-related CD-ROMs around. Comedy fans can find titles devoted to *Saturday Night Live* and *Monty Python's Flying*

Circus, among others. Chefs can find cookbooks. Computer geeks, and geek wannabes, can find CDs that show you how your computer works in minute detail. Wine connoisseurs can check out Multicom Publishing's *Wines of the World* CD, shown below. Me, I'm a wine kinda-sewer.

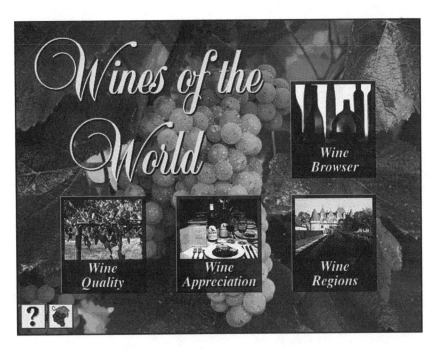

Multicom's Wines of the World *teaches you everything you ever wanted to know about wine but were afraid to ask.*

The point is that no matter where your interests lie, there's probably a CD-ROM title that will appeal to you. If there isn't right now, there soon will be.

Adults Only

It was the strangest thing when I was at Macworld Expo this year—for the first time, ever I think, there were vendors peddling decidedly *adult* CD-ROMs. And they were doing a *brisk* business.

Penthouse magazine was there, among others, doing the whole multimedia *shtick*, with their own slant: photos, movie clips, interactive games. The subjects were women, the customers were men. (I can hear the women readers now, *"Oh, sure. Typical."*)

I promised myself I wouldn't give it any serious coverage until there were CD-ROM discs full of men, too, to avoid being called any sort of sexist. Only one vendor I checked with had a CD of men in the works, but it probably won't be available until Fall '95, so this is all I have to say on the subject: If you're into it, it's out there.

The Least You Need to Know

➤ The Entertainment category of CD-ROM titles is huge, and this in no way does it justice.

➤ If you have an interest or hobby, you can probably find a CD-ROM that relates in some way.

➤ In my opinion, putting films on CD is the coolest trend in entertainment, not so much for the movies (that's what VCRs are for) but for the background information and behind-the-scenes details.

Chapter 20

Educational Entertainment

In This Chapter

➤ Building a green-eyed monster

➤ Brain building

➤ For the artistically inclined

Man, kids have it *sooo* great. There are hundreds and hundreds of really cool CD-based games and learning tools designed especially for them. What was the coolest thing I had to play with when I was a kid? A Batman utility belt. Plastic. I lost the Bat-a-rang. I'm so jealous.

But as the saying goes, what comes around goes around. Now I get to play with *all* of this stuff and, best of all, it's my *job*.

What you'll find in this chapter is a mere handful of the CD-ROM titles available for kids. There are literally *tons* of them—way too many to cover in-depth here. Use this as a short "get acquainted" chapter, just to familiarize yourself with the broadstrokes of children's CD titles. Then take your favorite kid CD-ROM shopping. There *must* be a child-spoiling holiday or event coming up. Isn't there always?

Rainy Day Kids

If you've read any of my other books, you know that I have a pile of nephews and godsons I like to spoil rotten. One of the biggest joys has been finding stuff to keep them entertained and informed on days that they can't go out and terrify the neighborhood like they usually do.

Better Homes and Gardens magazine to the rescue with their *Cool Crafts* CD-ROM (from Multicom Publishing). *Cool Crafts* (shown below) is a collection of 101 things to do and projects you can create with your kids (or kids you've borrowed for the occasion) ages 3–12. Craft-type things include toys, decorations, snacks, and just bizarre things like the Ugwuzz shown in the figure. An Ugwuzz is a monster puppet made from a foam burger box, a bendy straw, and (can you believe it) dryer lint.

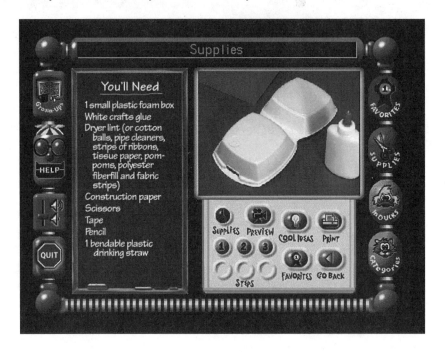

Multicom's Better Homes and Gardens Cool Crafts.
Things to make with dryer lint.

Cool Crafts gives you a video preview of the completed project, lists of supplies you'll need (shown in the figure above), and step-by-step directions. You can also print out essential information so you aren't chained to the computer while working with scissors and glue.

There are tips and information for parents, teachers, and for folks who want to use the projects as party activities. *Cool Crafts* is available for both Macs and Windows machines and lists for about $40, but you can find it for $30 by mail order.

What Was That Word Again?

Even if you have a CD-ROM encyclopedia or dictionary, like those discussed in Chapter 23, some kids might be put off by their grown-up attitude and interface. Why not find a dictionary for the kids in your life?

One such dictionary is the *Macmillan Dictionary for Children* (shown below) from Simon & Schuster Interactive. It gives you a pretty good dictionary with audio pronunciations, photographs, and an assortment of word games. Kids can keep their own lists of words to learn and can play the word games (Hangman and Words Within Words) from their list for drill and practice. Kids can even have their own spelling bee.

A is for Alpaca.

Each word in the dictionary is defined and pronounced. Challenging words in each definition are linked to their definitions, too. So all the child has to do is click on the word, and she's taken right to its entry.

You can search through the dictionary with a search utility, or you can just browse through. The *Macmillan Dictionary for Children* is available for Windows and Macintosh, and it lists for about $30. You can find it for about $20 by mail order.

Learning to Read, Reading to Learn

The hands-down winner in the "helping kids learn to read" category is still the *Living Books* series from (oddly enough) Living Books.

Living Books are full books that will read themselves to your child, along with amusing animation; or your child can read by himself (getting help with a word or line whenever he needs it, just by clicking on it). After the page is read, kids can explore the page by clicking on different parts of the picture, and fun and goofy stuff happens. In the figure below (which is a much simpler book than most of the *Living Books*), clicking on the boy provokes a giggle and a wave. Clicking on his shadow makes the shadow caper and dance.

Living Books The New Kid on the Block *CD—a collection of silly poems by Jack Prelutsky.*

There's a whole series of *Living Books*. The one in the figure is *The New Kid on the Block*, a collection of wacky poems. There's also *Little Monster at School* and *Just Grandma and Me* (from the Mercer Mayer stories), *Arthur's Teacher Trouble* and *Arthur's Birthday* (from stories by Marc Brown).

Living Books are available for Macintosh and Windows, and list for about $40. Most are for children aged 6–12, with some for as young as 3 years old. You can usually find them for a little less by mail order.

Logic Builders

Please, no Mr. Spock jokes. Thank you.

I think one of the best skills you can give a child is the ability to reason things out—figure out how they work. Analytical thinking is one of those things that will *always* be useful.

One of the many CD-ROM packages that do just that is *Thinkin' Things* from Edmark, for kids ages 4–8 years old. *Thinkin' Things* gives kids a set of mental challenges where they have to compare attributes, complete analogies (what comes next sort of things), and remember and repeat patterns. It sounds tedious put into technical terms, but it's actually a lot of fun, as you can see in the figure below.

The Fripple Shop *from* Thinkin' Things Collection 1. *Kids have to figure out which Fripple meets their customer's needs by comparing and contrasting Fripples.*

In the *Fripple Shop*, shown previously, kids take orders for colorful little creatures called Fripples, either from people at the door (who speak), by telephone, or from the fax machine. Kids then have to figure out which one of the Fripples in the shop meets the order's requirement. In the figure, that would be a Fripple with straight hair and any color except green. Don't hurt your brain—it's impossible to figure it out in black-and-white.

Other challenging games include: repeating musical patterns played on a xylophone (by a duck, no less); creating the next part of an analogy; and creating and playing with combinations of shapes, sounds, colors, and music.

All in all, a lot of thought-provoking fun. *Thinkin' Things Collection 1* (there's a *Collection 2* for older kids 6–12) is available for Macintosh, Windows, and DOS computers. You can find it for about $40 by mail order.

Edmark also has a series of similar titles geared toward early learning in specific subjects: *Millie's Math House*, for math; *Bailey's Book House*, for reading; *Sammy's Science House*, for science.

Math Builders

Speaking as a math-o-phobe, I wish I had had some of these math-related titles when I was growing up. I'd probably know *all* of my multiplication tables right now, instead of being completely dependent upon computers and calculators. Kids: Don't let this happen to you.

You can help your children improve their math skills no matter what level they're at. There's a wide range of software available from basic math to advanced algebra.

The leader of the math pack is Davidson and Associates, who produce the *Math Blaster* series for folks ages 6–adult.

Math Blaster: Episode 1 (shown next) covers basic math skills.

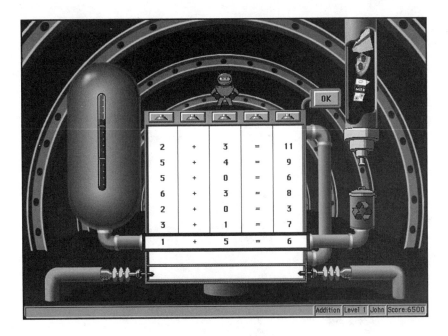

Recycling space junk in Math Blaster: Episode 1, In Search of Spot.

Kids help our intrepid space explorer, Blasternaut, recover his beloved friend Spot. They do this by solving math problems to power a tractor beam (to retrieve space garbage that is recycled for fuel), do math on the fly to navigate through a perilous series of caves, and finally solve equations to rescue Spot from the clutches of the Trash Alien. Very exciting.

Math Blaster titles are available for Windows and Macintosh. They list for about $60, but you can generally find them for about $35 by mail order.

Creativity Tools

Competition is fierce in the creativity department. Everybody wants to help the kid in their life paint a painting, tell a story, or compose a multimedia masterpiece.

Kid Pix Studio

In the multimedia department, there's Broderbund's *Kid Pix Studio* (shown below). Based on the award-winning *Kid Pix* (with impressive painting and drawing tools), the Studio version also has the capability to add animation, video clips, music, and sounds to any picture or slide show production.

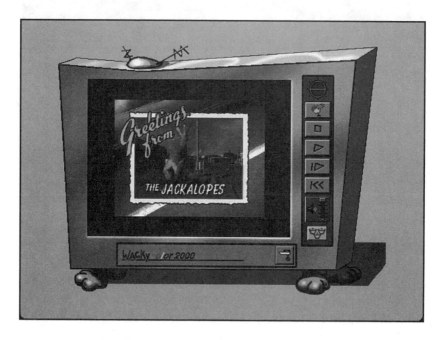

Movie Tools from Kid Pix Studio.

Kid Pix Studio is available for Mac and Windows, and you can find it for a little under $50 by mail order.

Imagination Express

Edmark's *Imagination Express* is an interactive storybook maker where kids can take theme elements (the neighborhood, a castle, and so on) and assemble a story of their own. In the next figure, I'm building a neighborhood story.

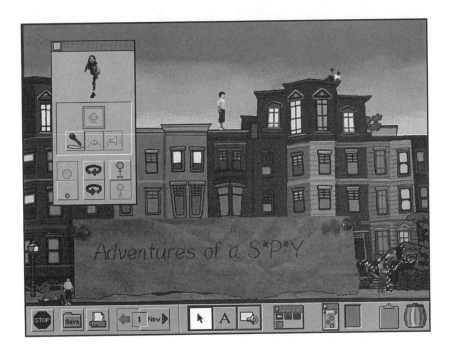

Tales of the neighborhood, with Imagination Express.

You can build on several backdrops, add a variety of inhabitants (in the figure, I'm going to add a voice to one of the characters), create titles and text, and build a story from preassembled parts. There's even a fact book for fun information and a collection of story ideas to help your kids get started.

You'll also be able to add more theme packs shortly. Right now, the neighborhood and the castle packs are the only ones available, and they come with *Imagination Express*. *Imagination Express* is available for Macs and Windows computers, and you can find it for about $40 at mail-order pricing.

Creative Writer and Fine Artist

Never one to leave a market share unturned, Microsoft has entered the kid-market with two impressive products: *Creative Writer* and *Fine Artist*, which (if you didn't guess) give your kids the tools necessary to write a story and create a picture.

Microsoft Fine Artist *and a picture of my cat. Sad, isn't it? I have no artistic skills whatsoever.*

Aimed at children ages 8 and up, these are kid-sized word processing and painting packages, with kid tools and wacky characters that pop up to help. *Creative Writer* helps kids write their own stories, newsletters, banners, and cards. *Fine Artist* (shown above) has all the tools they need to animate pictures, make posters, create comic strips, and more.

Kids can work from scratch or (as I did in the figure) start with prepared backgrounds and stickers, and just assemble and paint them. Both products are available for Windows and Macintosh for about $40 each by mail order.

Gobs More Stuff

We've barely scratched the surface here. Let's not forget about cool stuff like:

➤ *Carmen Sandiego* in all of her various incarnations. Kids love her, I love her, and she's *everywhere*. There's even a brand-new Junior Detective Edition for kids 5–8, from Broderbund.

➤ Cool encyclopedia kinds of stuff, like Microsoft *Dinosaurs* and *Dangerous Creatures*.

➤ Fascinating and informative stuff, like Simon & Schuster Interactive's *Firefighter!*, where kids can see what it's like to be a firefighter for real.

One Size Doesn't Fit All

Remember that when shopping for CD-ROMs or *any* software for the children in your life, many of these packages are age and/or skill-level dependent. Buy software that's appropriate to the child you're giving it to. Pre-algebra stuff doesn't really go over well with most 6-year-olds. Interactive monster stuff aimed at 2–6-year-olds will not please an 11-year-old at all.

Think before you buy. When in doubt, ask—ask a parent, teacher, guardian, another parent, or an experienced sales clerk. Get a second or third opinion.

The Least You Need to Know

➤ Kids get all the really cool CD-ROM software.

➤ This barely scratched the surface of all the kinds of CD software available for kids. Check out your favorite store, mail-order catalog, or magazine review section for the latest scoop.

➤ Shop carefully with the needs and abilities of the child in mind.

➤ Don't be jealous. You can play with this cool stuff when the kids are asleep. I won't tell.

Chapter 21

Continuing Education

In This Chapter

➤ Making history

➤ Going ape

➤ Iambs and trochees

➤ Talk with your hands

Maybe I'm just a victim of my environment—my parents and grandparents were always saying stuff like "Learn a new thing every day" when I was growing up—now I'm always looking for new and interesting information. It's turned me into a PBS junkie, a voracious reader, and an all-around information sponge. And I *still* can't get on *Jeopardy!*

New CD-ROM titles also fuel my info-addiction. You'll find tons of diverse, interesting, and informative titles available in the CD-ROM section of your favorite store, or in the pages of your favorite mail-order catalog. What's covered in this chapter is really just a quick look at a handful of titles that struck my fancy. Your fancy might fancy some other titles.

While this chapter's name "Continuing Education" implies that these titles are all aimed at adults, I think they're appropriate for anyone high-school age and up, as high as you can count. Do your brain a favor and check out some brain food.

A Sense of History

Growing up in the '60s as I did, one of my earliest recollections is of the Apollo 11 astronauts walking on the moon for the very first time. I remember watching it on my parent's big ol' black-and-white television. I remember my brother quizzing me on what all the acronyms stood for—like LEM (Lunar Exploration Module), EVA (Extra Vehicular Activity), and LOX (not smoked salmon, but Liquid OXygen).

Today we're spoiled. The space shuttle goes up and we're all so blasé about it. We forget that NASA was only created a little over 30 years ago. They put a man on the moon in under a decade. The mind boggles.

Folks who were there, watching breathlessly as we started exploring the final frontier, will be left equally breathless by Voyager's *For All Mankind*. You pups who think of trips to the moon in the same way you think of wagon trains west will learn something.

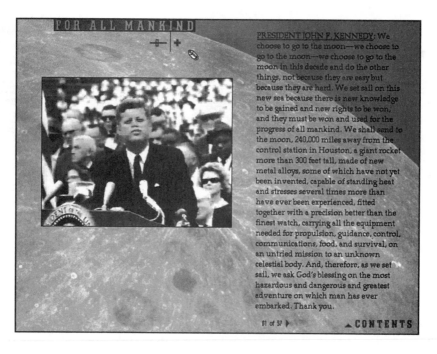

President John F. Kennedy announcing the formation of NASA and the goal of putting a man on the moon before the end of the '60s.

For All Mankind, like many of the titles from Voyager, is built around a documentary film of the same name (an Academy Award nominee, no less) by Al Reinert. It covers

NASA and the Apollo program from their inception through the landings of 24 astronauts on another world.

You can watch the film while reading a transcript of it (as shown in the figure). At the same time, you can click on an underlined name (like Kennedy's in the figure) to get more information about the major players in the drama.

You can also get information about each of the Apollo missions, including the crews, the nicknames of the command and lunar modules, mission dates and duration, photographs, and engaging essays about the missions with behind-the-scenes information from the participants.

I don't often have trouble disengaging myself from a CD when I'm under a deadline, but I found it really hard to stop watching the film and poking around through the related information. Info-junkie—I told you.

For All Mankind lists for about $40, but you can usually find it for $30 or less by mail order. It's available for both Windows and Macintosh computers.

Obligatory Disclaimer

As always, prices mentioned are "rounded and abouted." They're current as of this writing, but who knows what tomorrow will bring.

A Sense of Mystery

There are a lot of mysteries in the world beyond the *whodunit* variety. Mysteries like: What really happened to the dinosaurs? Why did a lot of animals lose their thumbs while humans kept theirs? Why can't you ever get away from Muzak?

Scientist/naturalist/biologist Stephen Jay Gould lives to explain it all to you—well, except for that last one.

I was first exposed to Gould's work in college when I had to read his book, *The Mismeasure of Man*, for a course. It's a series of essays about the historical misuse of intelligence testing to show that non-Caucasian people are somehow inferior. I fell in love with his work and have read several of his other books since.

Voyager (again) has put together *Stephen Jay Gould: On Evolution* as part of their *First Person* series. It includes a 60-minute video lecture by the man himself (don't roll your eyes at the word "lecture," please—he's a very engaging speaker) on three puzzling riddles about Darwin and evolutionary theory.

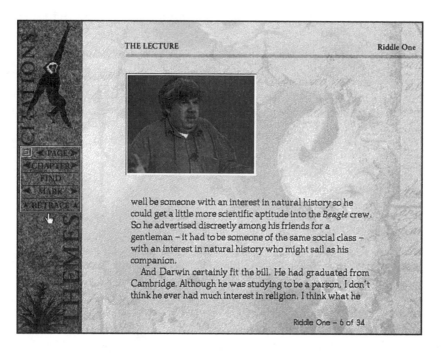

THE LECTURE   Riddle One

well be someone with an interest in natural history so he could get a little more scientific aptitude into the *Beagle* crew. So he advertised discreetly among his friends for a gentleman – it had to be someone of the same social class – with an interest in natural history who might sail as his companion.

And Darwin certainly fit the bill. He had graduated from Cambridge. Although he was studying to be a parson, I don't think he ever had much interest in religion. I think what he

Riddle One – 6 of 34

Stephen Jay Gould explains it all for you.

If You're Interested...

In addition to the *Stephen Jay Gould: On Evolution* title, the *First Person* series currently includes two other titles: *Donald Norman: Defending Human Attributes in the Age of the Machine* and *Marvin Minsky: The Society of Mind*. Check 'em out.

Supplementing the video lecture (which was co-produced by PBS giant Thirteen/WNET) are complete texts of Gould's *Bully for Brontosaurus* and Darwin's *The Origin of the Species*. There are also writings by other scientists, illustrations, and historical documents.

Now, no one has ever accused me of having a scientific mind (bloody few people have accused me of having a *mind*, period), but I found *Stephen Jay Gould: On Evolution* thoroughly enjoyable, easy to follow, and informative. Granted, I'm predisposed to like this guy, being a fan, but you may be, too. It could be genetic. It could be his next book.

Voyager's *First Person* series is currently available only for Macintosh. The titles list for $50 each, but you can find them for about $35 in mail-order catalogs.

A Sense of Rhythm

(This is starting to read like *True Confessions*, but I want you to understand why these CDs appeal to me.)

I love words—written, spoken, sung, and toyed with. I'd be in a pretty crappy profession if I didn't. In one area, I've always felt a little cheated; I've only gotten into a very limited number of poets. T.S. Eliot, W.H. Auden, Maya Angelou, and a few others are the poets I reach for when I feel like I need a quick fix.

Voyager's *Poetry in Motion* CD has broadened that list to include 24 of today's top poets. Among those poets are such luminaries as Alan Ginsberg, Ntozake Shange, William S. Burroughs, and Tom Waits.

Built around Ron Mann's documentary film of the same name, *Poetry in Motion* not only gives you the opportunity to read some great poetry, but also the chance to see and hear the works performed by the people who wrote them—a *completely* different experience from merely reading a poem.

As you can see in the following figure, the works are presented in video clips from the documentary. You can follow along with two text versions of a poem (if available), either "as performed" or "as published." The two versions often vary widely because poetry often translates differently from the written to the spoken word.

Additionally, many of the authors were interviewed for the film, talking about their lives, works, and inspirations, and those video clips are also available to you.

Whether through their performances or interviews, you get to see the beliefs and passions that drive these creative minds. The most striking, for me, was Tom Waits' "Smuggler's Waltz," which, when you simply read it, is rather grim and depressing ("Daggers of moonlight/Murder the sheets/in the stink of a four-dollar room") but becomes somehow pretty, if melancholy, when performed by Waits as a lullaby.

Amiri Baraka's "Wailers" from Poetry in Motion.

The effect of joining the written and spoken words and your own interpretation with the author's makes *Poetry in Motion* a compelling experience. You don't even have to be a poetry nut.

Poetry in Motion runs on both Macs and Windows PCs. It lists for $30, but you can find it for about $20 through mail-order companies.

Voyager CDs for the Financially Squeamish

Sure, I really like (and babble on) about Voyager's way-cool line of CD-ROM products, and it's very simple for me to say, "Hey, check it out"—but you might be hesitant to drop between $20 and $50 to see if you like something. There's a cheap alternative. If you think you might be interested in some of Voyager's stuff, you can call 1-800-446-2001. For $10, they'll send you a demo CD that includes short clips and explanations of 45 of their current line of products. It's practically free, and you get the chance to try before you buy—and that's always a smart thing to do.

Speaking in Tongues (and Fingers)

One of the first uses for CD-ROM discs was to help people learn another language. The ability to combine spoken examples, written explanations, and video supplements made CDs an ideal way to teach language. It's like having a teacher on call.

I think everyone should know more than one language. You can find language CDs galore, even from the world-famous Berlitz school of language, covering German, French, Spanish, Italian, and Japanese. They'd be a great help to anyone (student or traveller) who needs to brush up or learn a whole new language. Most CDs list for between $100 and $200, but you're usually getting 3 or more CDs in the set.

For most languages, video clips aren't an essential item. You don't really see, say, Japanese at work any differently in video than you do with the written word. However, there *is* a language where the video portion is not only helpful, it's essential.

American Sign Language, or ASL, is the language used by many hearing- and speech-impaired people to communicate through standardized gestures. To learn the language, it really helps to see it.

Previously, sign language dictionaries and guides relied on a series of illustrations (which weren't always easy to follow or reproduce). Now, HarperCollins Interactive has come out with *The American Sign Language Dictionary on CD-ROM*, which not only includes the traditional illustrations, but further demonstrates the signs you're trying to learn with video clips of people using the sign being described (shown in the following figure).

When I first learned to sign, I had it easy. I had deaf friends and hearing friends to teach me and keep me current. Signing is one of those things that, if you don't practice or use it regularly, you forget a lot. I've forgotten a lot of it (except for some of the naughtier signs—funny how those stick) because I haven't had anyone to practice with.

The CD-ROM dictionary gives you multiple learning opportunities. You can skim through the dictionary by category or by one sign at a time. You can study basic techniques, go through memorization drills, and even play a "Concentration-type" game where you have to match signs with their verbal equivalents.

You can set the dictionary up to keep track of different users so it knows what you've studied already and what you've yet to learn. That way it can compile appropriate reviews for your level of learning.

After a basic brushup (the alphabet, pronouns, and phrases like "My name is," and such), the first phrase I put together from the dictionary was: I am very rusty, please sign slowly.

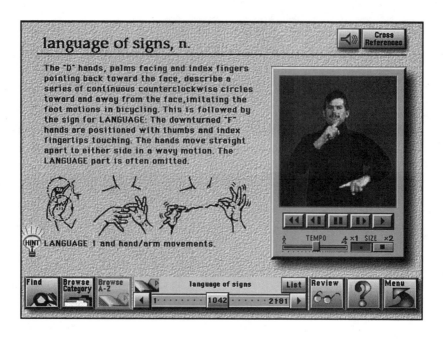

How to say "the language of signs" in the language of signs.

Of course, you still need someone to practice with (because recognizing and using signs is much faster in actual conversation), but *The American Sign Language Dictionary on CD-ROM* is an excellent way to learn a new language.

The dictionary is available for Windows and Macintosh, and you'll also find it in bookstores. It lists for about $70 for the CD alone and $80 for the CD and a supplemental book. Some bookstores discount 10%–15%, so get the bargain if you can.

The Least You Need to Know

➤ Contrary to popular opinion, you *can* teach an old dog new tricks. Some old dogs can even teach themselves.

➤ There's a wide variety of informative and entertaining CD-ROM titles that will appeal to open minds of all ages. Those mentioned here are just a small sample.

➤ The best advice I can give you is pick a subject that interests you and then see what's available on CD-ROM. There's so much stuff available now that there may be a few titles that will spark your curiosity and fire your imagination.

Chapter 22

Being Productive

In This Chapter

➤ Software favorites on CD

➤ Avoiding the floppy shuffle

➤ Run 'em from the disc

One of the growing trends in regular, productivity-type software (word processors and the like) is to distribute it on CD-ROM discs. It benefits the software companies because those ten or more disks of program and accessory files can fit on one CD, with room left over for extra things that increase the value of their product. You and I look at the extra stuff (like Microsoft Bookshelf, discussed in Chapter 23) and say to ourselves, "What a bargain!" and snap it right up. Plus, one CD costs less to manufacture, ship, and store than half a dozen floppy disks—which is another bonus for the software companies.

Regardless of whether you feel that's a good thing, a bad thing, or a real yawn, the trend is here to stay. So let's take a look at some of your options when buying traditionally disk-based software on CD-ROM.

Diskless Wonders

Some of the first folks (to my knowledge, anyhow) to jump on the CD bandwagon were the people at Microsoft, who leapt at the chance to replace the 50 or so floppy disks that made up the suite of applications called *Microsoft Office* (*Word*, *Excel*, *PowerPoint*, and *Mail*). They were quickly followed by Apple Computer, who distributed the latest version of the Mac OS (System 7.5) on either floppy disks or a CD.

Microsoft Office

Microsoft Office includes a word processor (Word), spreadsheet (Excel), a presentation package (PowerPoint), and a network e-mail utility (Mail). The Windows Professional version also includes a database program (Access). That's a *ton* of software, measured in floppy disks.

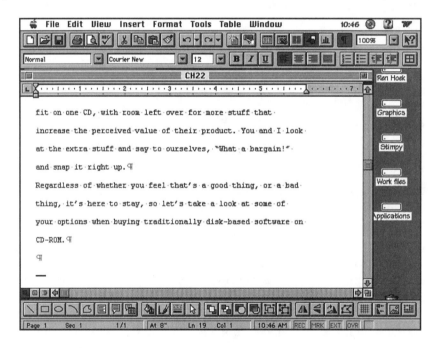

A draft of this chapter in Microsoft Word, Mac version, part of Microsoft Office.

The advantage of getting the CD version of the software is that there's only one disk to install from—you don't have to spend hours feeding your computer floppy hors d'oeuvres. You also don't have to find a place to store dozens of floppy disks after it's installed. That's about it for the benefits. You still have to install the software on your computer to use it, so you don't conserve any of your valuable hard drive space. It's still business as usual.

The Microsoft Office CD is available for Windows and Macintosh. It can be found for about $450 by mail order, which is about $150 less than you'd pay for Word and Excel if you bought them individually—another benefit. The Professional version is available for Windows only, and you can find it for about $560 by mail order.

Macintosh System 7.5

Operating systems (like the Mac OS and MS-DOS) keep getting bigger and bigger. For the Mac, it's mainly because multiple versions of the operating system (OS) are included to keep folks from having to buy the Power Mac or regular Mac versions of the same thing.

Additionally, you get extra goodies (QuickTime video clips, a movie player, demo versions of software, and so on) and copies of the disk-sized versions of the OS—just in case you want to have an emergency copy of the OS on floppies ready to install in a crisis.

As with Microsoft Office, the CD version of the Mac OS won't do anything for you if you don't install it on your Mac's hard drive. It will also set you back about $100. Windows, if you didn't get it free with your PC, is also available on CD.

Photogenic Software: Photoshop

Adobe *Photoshop* has become pretty much the industry standard for image editing and enhancement, for professionals and amateurs alike. As shown in the following figure (using one of the photographic images from the CD at the back of this book—*ooh, pretty!*), Photoshop lets you tinker with images on your computer. In minutes, you can accomplish what used to take days in a photo lab to accomplish.

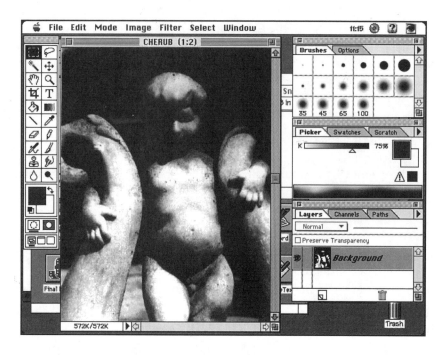

Adobe Photoshop 3.0 (Mac version) looking cherubic.

Like the software discussed earlier, you can't run Photoshop from the CD—you must install it on your computer first. However, the CD version of Photoshop is chock-full of extra goodies for you to have and hold: an interactive demonstration of the software, some photographic images to play with, an art show of what some professionals have done with Photoshop, and demo versions of other software you can use with Photoshop. You also get a *free* (one of my favorite words) copy of the Adobe Type On Call CD (covered in Chapter 24).

Photoshop is available for Macintosh and Windows for about $560.

Print Shop Deluxe

Broderbund's *The Print Shop* is a program I have owned and used with every computer I've ever had. I bought it for my Apple IIe, my first Mac, and even for my PC. It's one of those applications you never really appreciate how much you use it until you don't have access to it.

Making a birthday card with The Print Shop Deluxe CD Ensemble.

As you can see in the figure, it's a program that lets you create greeting cards—but you can also use it to create flyers, banners, business cards, calendars, and more, quickly and easily.

This program's been around for *years*. In the past, you had to buy The Print Shop, The Print Shop Companion, and then add collections of clip art and fonts to use with it. It could get pretty pricey. Now, with the introduction of The Print Shop Deluxe CD Ensemble, you get it all (well, *most* of it) on one CD. The added attraction is that you can choose to either install the whole thing to your hard drive (taking up megabyte after megabyte of space—about 16MB altogether) or do a *minimum* installation, which takes up practically no space at all (about 5MB for the fonts and a couple of folders).

Now the bonuses not only include having just *one* disc to store, but also the added benefit of being able to conserve your valuable hard drive space for other uses.

The Print Shop Deluxe CD Ensemble is available for both Mac and Windows machines, and can be had for about $80 at mail-order pricing. I can't live without it—I am forever whipping out custom birthday cards and other cards at a moment's notice. And people don't think, "Oh, he waited 'til the last minute again." They think, "Oh, wow! He *made* me a card."

So? Why Bother?

This isn't a development that rates a sleepless night or a lot of pages here. It is, however, a trend that will continue as CD-ROM drives become more of a basic equipment item and less of a novelty.

When shopping for software, keep an eye out for CD versions of your favorite stuff. CD versions tend to be easier to install (no floppy shuffling) and to store (one CD versus dozens of floppies), and the few applications that can be run from CD will conserve space on your crowded hard drive. While not horribly exciting, these things can simplify your computing life, and that's always a good thing.

The Least You Need to Know

➤ More and more productivity-oriented software will be released on CD-ROM.

➤ You often get extra free goodies on software CDs to increase the value and fill up some of that otherwise wasted space.

➤ Most CD-ROM software of this type still needs to be installed on your hard drive, save for rare titles like The Print Shop Deluxe CD, where you can get away with a minimal installation.

Chapter 23

References Available upon Request

In This Chapter

➤ Shoveling... ummm... *stuff*

➤ Aardvark to Xylophone: multimedia encyclopedias

➤ Hooked on classics

➤ I've got your number

Because CD-ROM disks can hold so much information, they're ideal for putting together big, fat collections of stuff on one disc.

One of the first things that made the leap, for example, from the printed to the digital page were encyclopedias. Speaking as someone who had to carefully choose his report topics in grade- and high-school (so I didn't get one that fell in a volume we didn't get, or get *yet* from the supermarket), I can't tell you what a *relief* it is to have a full encyclopedia all in one place, on one disc. It's a pleasure.

An encyclopedia is only one example of the kinds of voluminous information you can find on CD-ROM. Let's look at some.

A Word About Shovel-Ware

Some of the first CD-ROM discs that were sold (for lack of a decent way to present the material) were pretty much a huge gob of formless information—some useless and outdated—with no way to search it. There's still some of it around. It's called *shovel-ware* because the discs seem like someone just shoveled a pile of random stuff on a disc and called it "interactive."

It isn't necessarily a *bad* thing, but I'd hesitate to call it a *good* thing, either. Some of the collections of classic literature aren't pretty but serve their purpose.

In other cases, you get the impression (from the packaging) that you've got your hands on a really whiz-bang bit of multimedia information, and it turns out you've got 400MB of lifeless text files and a couple of pictures. That's misrepresentation and reprehensible (can you tell I've been poking around in a CD-based thesaurus?).

You shouldn't get all paranoid worrying about it, but you should scrutinize CD-ROM packaging carefully.

Encyclopedic Knowledge

There are a number of multimedia encyclopedias around: Microsoft *Encarta*, Grolier's, and some lesser-known titles. Essentially, with an encyclopedia, you'll find all the things you expect to find in their paper cousins (essays and other text, photographs, and illustrations), but you'll also find sound, video clips, and animation, all to better illustrate the concepts being explained in the text.

With Microsoft *Encarta*, for example, you can search through the disc's contents for a particular word or phrase, browse through the list of categories, or look for items that relate to a particular time or place. Additionally, you can look through all of the media files (photos, video clips, and so on), all 7,173 of them, by themselves. *Encarta's* Media Gallery is shown in the following figure.

208

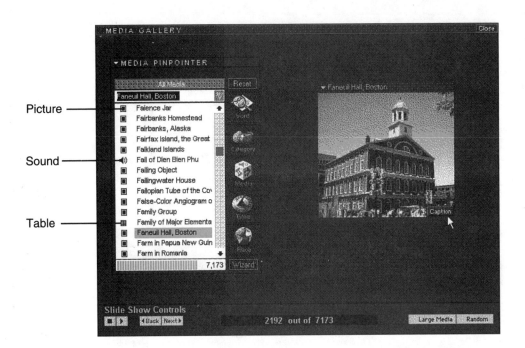

Picture

Sound

Table

Microsoft Encarta '95, *Windows version. Now showing: Faneuil Hall, Boston, a great place to visit.*

Searching through *Encarta*, you'll find that much of the information is linked. Reading through the article on, say, David Letterman (only because I just got tickets to his show, after waiting about a year), you can click on words and phrases in the text that appear in red (television; Indianapolis, Indiana; Los Angeles) and jump automatically to those related topics for more information—all without having to *shlep* back to the library shelf for another volume.

Multimedia encyclopedias are great for anyone who needs to do research from time to time, especially students.

Encarta comes out annually and is available for both Windows and Macintosh computers. You can generally find it for about $85 by mail order, which is about the same as Grolier's, too.

What Was That Word Again?

I just got this today, and I'm working the heck out of it: Microsoft *Bookshelf* (shown below).

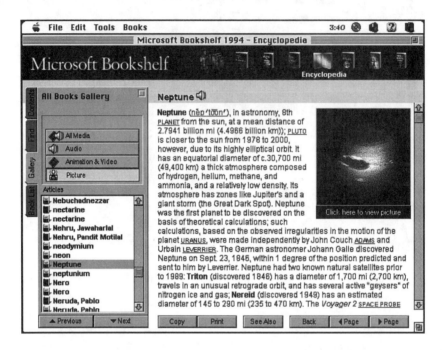

A desktop reference library on CD-ROM: Microsoft Bookshelf *'94 (Mac version).*

When word processors and other applications started coming with built-in spelling checkers, I was briefly in hog heaven. The problem for me has always been that sometimes I *know* I don't know how to spell a word, and when I type *my* version of the spelling and ask the word processor to figure it out, it usually can't. I still wind up thumbing through my dog-eared paperback dictionary.

Microsoft *Bookshelf* gives me a dictionary I can browse through on my computer and just copy and paste the correct spelling (even the whole definition, if I want) into my word processing document.

Additionally, *Bookshelf* provides you with a thesaurus, small-scale encyclopedia, book of quotations, an atlas, a timeline of history, and an almanac for looking up fiddly bits of knowledge like the population of Indiana (5,544,159 in 1990).

Obligingly, installing *Bookshelf* also adds an easy-access item in your menu, called *QuickShelf*. It lets you access *Bookshelf* from within most any application, which makes it very handy, indeed. Already, working on just this chapter, I've used it three times. Once for spelling, once for a thesaurus word, and once for the population of Indiana. I have a feeling this is a disc I'll be popping into my CD-ROM drive on a regular basis.

Bookshelf is available in Mac and Windows versions. You can find it for about $70 mail order; but wait, you can also find it bundled for *free* with several other Microsoft CD-ROM products, like the multimedia version of Microsoft *Works* and Microsoft *Office* (see Chapter 22). If you're considering one of the other products anyway, why not look for one that gives you *Bookshelf*, too? The student, writer, or spelling-impaired person in your home will thank you.

What's Cooking?

If you don't find yourself chained to a computer for eight or more hours a day, and reference works aren't your thing, maybe you're a fan of the culinary arts—that is to say, cooking.

Books On Disk offers the *Digital Gourmet Deluxe CD*, a collection of just about every type of cooking you can imagine—African, French, Italian, Kosher, and lots more.

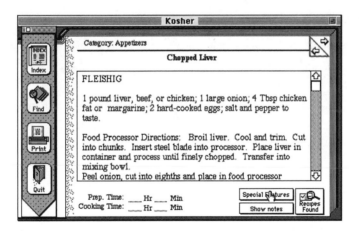

The Digital Gourmet Deluxe, *Mac version. What am I? Chopped Liver?*

If you're into cooking (or eating, as I am), you'll get hungry just looking through the *Digital Gourmet*. In addition to the recipes, you can have the Gourmet assemble an entire menu for a dinner or party, have it do the math to turn a recipe that serves 6 into a recipe that serves 16, *and* generate a shopping list that you can print out and take to the store with you. You can, of course, also print out the recipes, which is much easier than hauling your computer into the kitchen.

The shopping list is very handy. I know that when I'm getting ready to throw a party, I always forget to get *something* essential to what I'm making and have to go back to the store two or more times.

Health conscious chefs will appreciate the automatic nutrition calculator that tells you how good, or bad, a planned meal is for you. There are also photos to show you what some of the final products look like, with tips on presentation. You also get tips on choosing and handling meats and seafood.

Additionally, you can add recipes of your own to the *Gourmet* (in a file that gets saved to your hard drive, not the CD), which makes it easy to print out a copy when your friends squeal, "Darling! It's *fabulous*! You *must* give me the recipe!"

The *Digital Gourmet Deluxe CD* is available for both Macintosh and Windows computers. You can find it for about $90 by mail order.

But Wait, There's More!

The CD that gives you the *Digital Gourmet Deluxe* also contains a couple of other reference works: the *Complete Works of Shakespeare*; *5000 Quotes*; and a digital version of the *King James Bible*.

Each title can be unlocked from the CD by calling Books On Disk at an 800 number and paying $19.95 for each reference book you want unlocked—what a bargain.

All three titles use the same interface as the cookbook (of course, without the nutritional and recipe-doubling features). None of the three is as elegant in execution as Microsoft *Bookshelf*, but you can search for text, print out what you find, and copy and paste sections into your own documents.

I wish I had a complete Shakespeare (or just Bill, as I call him) on CD when I was in college—it would have saved me a lot of squinting and retyping as I threw relevant quotations into a report or paper. *C'est la vie.*

A Crash Course in Literature

You'll find a lot of CD-ROM discs that claim to be "all of the world's great literature!" and such—most of them are shovel-ware, as discussed at the top of the chapter. Just so you know what one looks like, have a gander at the following figure.

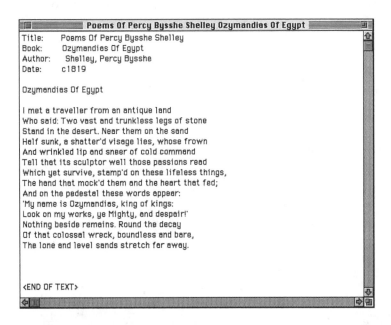

Bureau Development's Great Literature *CD-ROM.*

The figure shows a poem (Shelley's "Ozymandias") from the *Great Literature* CD. As you can see, it's pretty much a no-frills affair, just the text of the poem and some basic information.

To be fair, as far as shovel-ware goes, this is pretty good. It's got a good search routine, which lets you browse through both images and text. There are images, by the way, and music, and even some narrated versions of the texts by George Kennedy and Bob Saget.

What makes it shovel-ware is that the selection of the literature is pretty spotty (there's some Aristophanes, but no Euripides; John Jay's *Federalist Papers*, but nothing by Thomas Jefferson, among other odd choices—that's the English major in me getting cranky); there's no annotation to explain antique words (what *is* an "oeliade" exactly?); and there's little integration between the elements. You can't really do more than one thing at a time.

Yet, you get what you pay for; this and similar titles (generally available for Mac, DOS, and Windows, often on the same disc) only cost between $15–$20. A single paperback anthology of any one of the authors would cost you that much.

They're out there, they're available, and you know about them. Nothing horribly exciting, unless you're turned on by the thought of having a copy of Kant's *Metaphysics of Morals* on CD-ROM.

One Ringy-Dingy

(Insert appropriate Ernestine snorts here, and I apologize to Lily Tomlin for the abuse.)

In both editions of this book, I asked the musical question, "Which would you rather carry around: a dozen phone books from big cities, or a couple of CD-ROM discs?" Now it's more than just a rhetorical question to make a point. You *can* carry around a couple of CD-ROM discs, rather than dozens of phone books. Meet *Select Phone*.

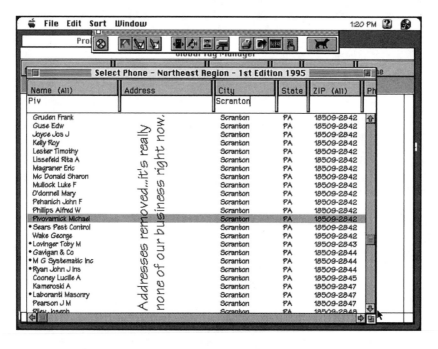

Select Phone 1995, *where I found my parents' phone number, and all of their neighbors', too.*

214

Select Phone, from ProPhone, is a set of five regional CD-ROM discs that contain over 83 *million* yellow and white page listings, including name, address, telephone, ZIP+4 ZIP codes, and the date of publication (so you know how current the information is).

You can search by any one of the information fields, which give you the very cool ability to be able to key in a phone number and find out who it belongs to—just like they do in detective stories. As in the figure, you can also find the person or company you want, then click on a button, and you get all of their neighbors, as well—in order by address.

After you find a set of phone numbers, you can save them to your hard drive or export them to your favorite address book or database programs for future reference.

Select Phone is very cool, lots of fun, and intriguing to play around with. I lost two hours searching the country for Pivovarnicks (there are more of us than you think), but I can't imagine many average home users needing it—especially at $150 mail-order pricing. It's more suited to business-types who need fast contact information.

However, there are smaller, less expensive versions available: *FreePhone*, which gives you access to AT&T's toll-free number directory (at only $30); and *HomePhone*, which gives you access to over 72 million residential phone numbers.

All the *Phone* CD-ROMs have powerful searching tools and run on Macs, Windows, and plain DOS machines. Oh, and if a famous person had the foresight to get an unlisted telephone number, it won't be listed on the CD-ROM, either. I know, I tried. No midnight calls to Stephen King from me.

The Least You Need to Know

➤ The enormous capacity of CD-ROM discs make them ideal for storing huge reference works like those discussed here.

➤ A multimedia encyclopedia would be an excellent investment for anyone with students.

➤ Likewise, a multimedia set of standard reference books couldn't hurt, either.

➤ There are lots more titles to choose from than those listed here. Shop for what you need and can use.

Chapter 24

Exciting Sights and Sounds

In This Chapter

➤ Therapy for the font addict

➤ Clip art without scissors

➤ Photos and movie clips galore

➤ Rude noises

I was going to try and fob this off on you as a chapter about increasing your productivity. My intrepid editor wouldn't let me lie to you like that. She likes to keep me honest, even if she can't completely curb my basically evil nature.

So the truth. The truth is that CD-ROM offers a lot of diversions and distractions, which are also perfectly legitimate business investments (I say that for the benefit of any IRS agents who might be reading this): cool sights, fabulous sounds, and all manner of artistic Tinker Toys that, in the long run, can help you produce better, um, *stuff* (whatever it is you personally produce with your computer).

Unfortunately, they are (for me, at least) too much fun to be actually called productivity boosters (although there is a legitimate chapter on productivity-boosting software—Chapter 22). If you've ever wasted an hour (as I have) seeing what a memo will look like in combinations of all the different fonts you own, you know what I mean.

Here's a quick overview of some very fun, professional stuff. If you aren't a so-called "professional," I won't tell if you want to get some of this just for the fun part.

As always in this software section, I've chosen to talk about packages that are available in at least both Windows- and Macintosh-compatible formats, so you can use these products no matter what system you own. In instances where a product is available for only one platform, I'll say so.

Of course, you should always do your homework and check compatibility with your computer system before you buy CD-ROM discs.

Font Junkies

I (or someone) should start an Alcoholics Anonymous-type twelve-step group for the font-dependent.

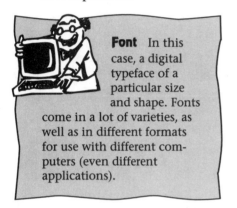

Font In this case, a digital typeface of a particular size and shape. Fonts come in a lot of varieties, as well as in different formats for use with different computers (even different applications).

Step One would be something like: I admit that I am powerless over typography and that my fonts have become unmanageable. (Those of you who have read the font chapter of *The Complete Idiot's Guide to the Mac* know this is true of me.) I love fonts, but I hate it when I'm working on a project and discover I'd really like to use a particular font that (*gasp!*) I don't own. That means running out to the all-night font shop or calling a mail-order place and sitting on my hands for 24 hours while I wait for the font to be delivered.

The wonderful world of CD-ROM has relieved me of that burden. You can now purchase CDs with a company's complete font library stored on it ("Happy-happy, joy-joy!").

Font Libraries on CD-ROM

Fonts are my idea of heaven. They're the different styles of alphabets you can use to give your documents (letters, reports, flyers, and such) a look and feel all their own—stodgy and businesslike, wild and woolly, or anything in-between. The fonts you use for, say, a report can affect the reader's perception of your report almost as much as the report itself.

Because there are so many fonts available to computer users (of all stripes), I'm not going to get into the picayune details of fonts and their various uses—that would be a book all its own. Check your Mac's manual, your Windows manual, or your DOS-software manuals for details on the kinds of fonts you can and cannot use with your system and/or application software.

Suffice it to say that a font library on CD-ROM will give you more fonts (hundreds and hundreds) than you could possibly use in a lifetime—though I'd like to try. The libraries are usually in Adobe PostScript Type 1 and/or TrueType (either Macintosh or Windows) formats; check to see whether you can use either before you get too excited at the prospect.

How They Work

When you buy a company's font library on CD-ROM, it usually comes with several fonts you can use immediately, so you can feel like you actually bought something. The rest of the fonts are locked. You can't do anything with them until you call the company and pay a fee (which varies from font to font). The company then gives you the magic word that unlocks the font, and *voilà*! That font is in your personal library for you to use and abuse as you see fit. Of course, some font CDs don't come locked at all. Read the box before you buy.

Adobe's Type On Call 4.0. *I'm in font heaven, here.*

In the complete-font-library range, there are several competitors. Two of the heavy-weights are *Type On Call* from Adobe Systems (the creators of PostScript) and Agfa's *AgfaType* CD-ROM. *Type On Call* is shown in the figure above. Both provide over a thousand different fonts, plus other goodies thrown in for free and/or cheap. Both allow you to unlock individual fonts or entire sets with a phone call (and a credit card). They also

Shareware Software (in this case, fonts) that you can try before you pay for it. If you like the software, you pay a fee to the software's author. You can find shareware in some software catalogs, most online services (such as CompuServe and America Online), and user groups. It is very, very tacky to keep and use shareware without paying the fee.

Freeware Software that you can just have and use, and it doesn't cost you much of anything (maybe the price of a disk). The authors, in their beneficence, give a little gift to the computing world. You can find freeware in most of the same places as shareware.

both list for about $100, but you can find them for about $60 (just remember: you have to pay an additional fee for each font you unlock from the disc later on). Adobe is fairly liberal in just giving away copies of *Type On Call* when you purchase some of their more expensive software (like *Photoshop*).

In addition to these (and dozens of other) professional font packages, you can also find collections of *shareware* and *freeware* fonts on CD and regular floppy disks. These collections are generally less expensive than commercial packages; however, the quality can be uneven. I scoured the computing universe for the lovely shareware fonts that are on the CD in the back of this book. See Chapter 28 for details.

Remember, when shopping for fonts, it is vital that you buy the correct kind of font for your system or applications. Macs using System 7 and later can use TrueType fonts and also PostScript Type 1 fonts with the addition of Adobe Type Manager (ATM). System 7.5 users with QuickDraw GX can use both of those, plus specific GX fonts. Windows users can choose from Windows' version of the same fonts (you also need to add ATM to use PostScript Type 1 fonts). DOS users are saddled with finding fonts that work with particular applications (check your manuals for more information). Happy fonting!

What a Clip Joint!

The concept of clip art has been around for a very long time—practically as long as the printing press. Once upon a time, you bought a book of funny little pictures, boxes, and decorative borders, literally cut them out of the book, and pasted them onto the document you were creating. It's also the origin of the phrase "cut and paste."

In this digital "information age," the concept of "clips" has been expanded to include lots of different categories besides art: video clips, sound clips, music clips. You name it—if you can clip it, there's probably a CD-ROM disc full of it.

Art the Artless (and Lazy)

A CD clip art library is full of cool things that you'd like to incorporate into your own projects but don't have the time (or talent, or equipment) to create for yourself.

Me, I can't draw. I rely on clip art to add some artistic merit to documents I create. I also don't have the time (or budget) to take photographs and convert them to digital format, much less movies or music. You may have no patience with feeding sounds into your computer (through a sound card or other sound-input device). Well, there are CDs just chock-full of things you and I don't have the time or inclination to make. They're aimed at design and production professionals (and can be expensive), but they won't explode if a mere amateur gets ahold of one.

Beware the Hidden Expenses Some clip libraries (whether they're collections of art, photos, sounds, or anything) will charge you—in addition to the cost of the CD-ROM disc—an additional fee (a royalty) for each clip you use. Using a clip without paying the royalty is illegal. If you don't want to hassle with the fees, make sure the disc you want is "royalty free" or comes with "full reproduction rights."

How You Can Use CD Clips

Clip collections save you time and effort. If you use your computer and CD-ROM drive to create flyers, brochures, newsletters, ads, presentations—anything that can be jazzed up with art, photographs, video, or sound—you can find a CD-ROM disc with just the jazzy element you need. You can then incorporate that element (say, a photographic image of a Hawaiian sunset) into the flyer promoting your club's "Win a Hula in Hawaii" contest.

Like any other computer documents, clip libraries on CD-ROM come in a wide range of file formats (like PICT and TIFF for graphics—I won't bore you with the technical specifications). In order to use them in a document, the program you are using has to be able to cope with the format of the element you want to use. If your desktop publishing program (for example) can't use a TIFF file, you'll be wasting your money buying a CD full of TIFF images for desktop publishing. As always, check the manuals of your favorite software for information on file-format compatibility before you buy any clip media (on CD or just plain old floppy disks).

Speaking of Graphics File Formats...

TIFF is a **bit-mapped graphics format**, as are Paint (Mac) and BMP (Windows) formats (among others). That means that to your computer and software, the "picture" is actually just a map to where all the dots (bits) go, thus, "bit-mapped." If you take a bit-mapped graphic and make it larger, it can get all blocky and chunky-looking as the dots get bigger.

Graphics that need to look good no matter how big or small you make them come in what are referred to as "scalable" or "vector" formats. Instead of a collection of strategically placed dots, each shape in a scalable graphic is represented (to your computer) mathematically. When you scale such a graphic, the math gets fiddled with, so the end result looks as close to the original as (in)humanly possible. Vector/scalable formats include CGM (popular for IBM-compatibles) and EPS (popular for Macs).

Graphics formats can be very confusing to the uninitiated, so always check before you buy.

57 Varieties—Okay, Four Varieties

This will give you just the barest glimpse at all the various kinds of clip collections out there. If you like the idea of having clips like these on hand, you can try some out (there's a small, but terribly classy, assortment on the CD-ROM at the back of the book for you to play around with). See Chapter 28 for details and directions.

Clip Art Packages

In the category of clip art, there are collections like CompuWorks *Color Clips* CD-ROM. *Color Clips* ($50 list) comes with over 3,000 color drawings for use in your documents and presentations. It also comes with *ImageCommander Lite*, an image file management program for Windows.

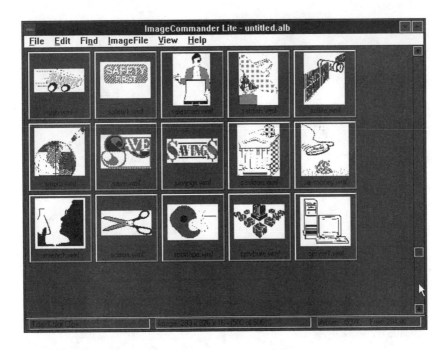

CompuWorks Color Clips, *previewed with* ImageCommander Lite.

Yes, *Color Clips* is for PC users, but it's just one of the hundreds of clip art collections flying around in this big, wide, wonderful digital world we live in. Check the shelves of your favorite software store or the pages of your favorite mail-order catalog.

Photographic Image Packs

For photographic images, you can get simple background patterns and textures to spice up boring text: photographs of fireworks, stone textures, wood grain, ice crystals, misty mountains, moss, leaves—texture, you get the idea.

Photo-quality images tend to be large (visually) and therefore take up a lot of disc space. Where you might get a collection of thousands of drawn images, most photo discs will have merely hundreds of images.

One such collection, out of the thousands available, is PhotoDisc's library of Fabulous '50s *Retro Americana* images (shown on the following page), which you can use for multimedia presentations and desktop publishing. PhotoDisc's full line is very nice, but the retro images are *outrageous*.

PhotoDisc's Retro Americana Collection. *Did people ever really look like this?*

Individual PhotoDisc collections (there are over 20) will set you back about $280 by mail order and include over 300 high-resolution images. The more frugal can get a *Starter Kit* (which includes a complete catalog of all the other libraries) for about $30. It comes with 25 high-resolution images.

Most photo collections are collections of nouns (you know, "people, places, and things") and have a particular theme. For beginners, a general assortment of image types might be most helpful. There are bazillions of photographic image collections available on CD, both in PhotoCD and other formats. Shop carefully; there are some pretty tired collections out there, too.

Is Your Computer Up to Photography?

Photo-quality images can be quite demanding of your computer system. Make sure it's up to snuff before you shell out big bucks for CD-ROM images. PC owners should have at least a VGA card and monitor capable of displaying 256 or more colors. Mac users need a color monitor capable of displaying 256 or more colors. You also need a substantial amount of RAM (4MB at least) to open some of these suckers. You can check out the PhotoCD section of Chapter 5 for what Kodak suggests you have to deal with PhotoCD images. You can also practice with the photographic images on the CD in the back of this book.

Of course, if you need images of particular kinds of things (and if you are, or know, a passable photographer), you can always take your own photos, have them developed onto a Kodak PhotoCD (see Chapter 5), and save yourself some major bucks.

Zounds! Sounds!

You can find all sorts of sounds on CD-ROM discs: sound effects (like breaking glass, cash registers ringing, funny voices) or bits of dialog from your favorite movies and TV shows (my all-time favorite remains Pee Wee Herman's famous "Duh!" sound). You can incorporate them into your multimedia presentations or use them as alert sounds on your Mac or with Windows. Educorp's *Sound Machine* disc ($49.95, not discounted) comes with 450 sound bites.

If you need more than a simple sound for your multimedia extravaganzas, you can also get clips of music.

Hi Rez Audio has a CD of over 40 minutes of high-quality (and royalty-free) music and sounds you can use in a variety of sound formats. The *Hi Rez Audio Volume 1* lists for $150, with a street price of $100.

Of course, you can save yourself the bucks and record music and sound snippets from audio CDs to your computer. Too cool! Chapter 6 has the details. There are also some sound files and utilities on the CD-ROM disc (where, class?) at the back of the book.

Video Killed the Radio Star

If music clips exist, can video clips be far behind—music videos, even? No, they can't. You can find them in both QuickTime and Video for Windows formats.

While there are many makers of CD-ROM video clips, some of the strangest I've ever seen are on Apple Computer's *QuickTime Starter Kit* CD ($109, rarely discounted to less than $99). Like the clip of the two older women in Fabulous '50s pink-and-black outfits (the Brown twins, shown here) who squeal and say things like, "I think we got ahold of some bad RAM." (Where'd they get those hats?! But that's Apple—they pride themselves on cool products and strange attitude.)

The Brown Sisters, from Apple's QuickClips *CD. I actually saw these ladies waiting for a cable car in San Francisco—and was I impressed.*

QuickTime movies on CD can be run from either Macs or Windows PCs with QuickTime software installed. *Video for Windows* (duh) is just for Windows. Check Chapter 5 for system requirements for using video on your computer.

For people with more pedestrian taste, there's Wayzata's *QuickToons* CDs: a collection of classic cartoons from the '30s and '40s. It includes Porky Pig, Daffy Duck, and the ol' "boop-boop-a-doop" girl herself, Betty Boop. (She looks good for, what? 70? 80?) They list for $20–$25, but you can find them for about $15 each by mail order. If it's ever been videotaped, you can probably find a clip library of it.

The Least You Need to Know

➤ Font libraries on CD guarantee you'll have access to just the right font when you need it.

➤ Clip-media CDs (art, photos, sounds, music, and video) save you the time and expense of creating them yourself—a great boon if you're artistically impaired, like me.

➤ Be aware that clip media can really put your computer through its paces. Make sure that your computer is up to the task before springing for expensive (hey, even cheap) CD-ROM libraries.

➤ Remember that it is illegal to use copyrighted material (like clips from audio CDs) for anything other than personal use, without permission. I don't want to have to visit you in jail.

➤ Have fun with all the sample stuff on the CD that comes with this book. Chapter 28 tells you all about it.

When the Going Gets Tough... the Tough Go Shopping

Whether you love to shop or hate to shop, we all shop. You may have noticed, unless you've been living under a rock somewhere, that shopping has changed a little over the last couple of decades. Malls, mail order, and television shopping have all changed the way we shop.

While we all sit around and wait for the promised information superhighway that will let us order groceries and pizzas from our television sets, we can practice by shopping with our computers and CD-ROM drives.

Yes, CD-ROM has combined the best features of all the current shopping trends into one tidy, little package.

Three Steps Forward, Two Steps Back

If you read the last chapter, you already know you can buy fonts from a CD (Adobe's Type On Call CD, among others). If you read the first edition of this book, you might recall a flirtation with selling complete software packages by the same method. You'd scan the CD for software, try a demo version, and then call an 800 number with your credit card, and you'd buy a code that would unlock the full version of the software from the CD.

At the time, it sounded like a great idea—but I looked at those software discs, said "Cool idea," and put them aside never to look at them again. Apparently, I wasn't the only one because the Mac Zone has discontinued their "Instant Access" program, and Apple Computer seems to have discontinued "Software Dispatch."

There will probably be a period of head scratching while they figure out why people stayed away in droves. Then similar CD-ROM discs may reappear in a different format—after all, it *was* a good idea, it just didn't catch on. Two of the few other survivors of the foray into CD-based shopping come from Magellan Systems: *The Merchant* and *The Traveler*. A third survivor is *Criterion Goes to the Movies* from Voyager.

The Merchant

The Merchant is a Windows- and Macintosh-compatible CD-ROM disk that brings you catalogs from 23 popular merchants, including JC Penney, Spiegel, LL Bean, and Target, to name a few.

Here's how it works: You pop in the CD, launch the software by the method appropriate to your system (Windows or Macintosh), and you get an index of catalogs like the one shown in the following figure. You click on the vendor whose wares you want to browse, and you can see product photos, descriptions, and (in some cases) video clip demonstrations with music and sound.

The Merchant*'s collection of catalogs—just click to browse.*

I got this copy of *The Merchant* just in time for Christmas shopping and wound up ordering my Christmas and Chanukah cards from Greet Street Greeting Cards' catalog on the CD (shown here).

The Merchant*'s Greet Street catalog.*

Why did I wind up ordering from the CD? Because I'd delayed picking out cards in a store too long, because it was there, and most importantly, there were cards that met—and even exceeded, if you can imagine—my own twisted sense of humor.

Ordering was fairly simple: Click on the check mark beside the item(s) you want to order. When you're done shopping, click on the **Orders** button to see everything you've marked. Then you have the option of calling or faxing in your order (have your credit card handy) for speedy delivery.

All in all, it was pretty painless, and I got a lot of those "*Where* did you find this card, you demented pup?" phone calls after I mailed them out.

You can get a copy of *The Merchant* CD by calling 1-800-561-3114. It was free when I got mine, but there may be a shipping and handling charge added by the time you read this.

See the World: The Traveler

The other surviving CD-shopping venue is *The Traveler*, brought to you again by Magellan Systems. *The Traveler* is a travel agent on disc, with information provided by airlines (Air France), adventure companies (Mountain Travel-Sobek), as well as national and regional tourism bureaus from around the world (California, Canada, Switzerland, and Australia).

When you fire up *The Traveler*, you can start with a map of the world (shown here) with areas marked where there's tourist information. Click where it interests you, and you zoom in closer.

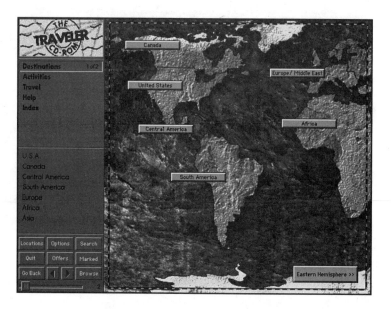

The world on The Traveler.

232

Because I've always wanted to go there, and because a friend of mine just came back from there, I clicked on Africa. I got a closer view of the areas I could travel and then clicked on Zimbabwe (because that's where my friend went, and I wanted to wallow in jealousy). That brought up the screen you see in the following figure.

Adventures in Zimbabwe.

The screen provides a few pages of information about Zimbabwe and the things you can do (canoe down the Zambezi River, explore wild game parks, visit Victoria Falls, and a host of other exciting activities).

If you're more interested in what you do instead of where you do them, you can search through *The Traveler* by activity rather than destination. Watch video clips of hang gliders, check out hotel and restaurant information, and generally just drool over fabulous-looking vacation spots.

If you can actually take one of the package vacations, all the better. Me, I just get jealous and bitter.

The Traveler, like *The Merchant*, works for Macintosh and Windows machines. You can get a copy by calling 1-800-561-3114 (again, be prepared to pay a small shipping and handling fee, just in case). If you wind up taking a trip, send me a post card. Or, better yet, take me with you.

Laser Disc Movies

The final CD-ROM shopping available to you comes from Voyager. *Criterion Goes to the Movies* is a CD-ROM-based catalog of more than 140 movies available on laser disc you can order from Criterion.

As you can see in the following figure, you can watch clips from the movies, read the cast list and credits for each film, get information about special features of a laser disc (like the inclusion of scenes cut from the original film), and even read essays about some of the important films in the collection. The one in the figure, *Invasion of the Body Snatchers*, is one of my all-time favorites.

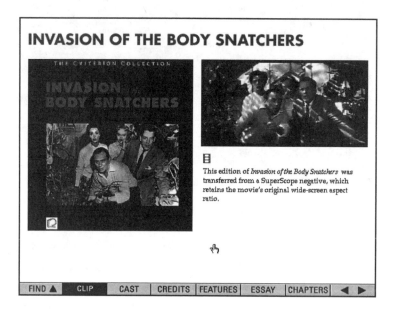

Criterion *gets invaded by the body snatchers.*

By clicking on the **Find** button, you can search the collection by a number of criteria: by director, actors, and Academy Award winners.

Even if you don't have a laser disc player (which are making a comeback in spite of the trouncing they took from VCRs early on), the information about the movies is fascinating to movie buffs. You can watch a clip of Katharine Hepburn wandering the canals of Venice whenever you want to... *really*, you can.

Criterion Goes to the Movies is available in both Mac and Windows format. It lists for about $25, but you can usually find it for $20 or less by mail order. It comes with $125 worth of coupons for discounts on movie purchases.

Down the Road a Piece

If you'd asked me a year ago, I would have said be prepared to be swamped with CD-based catalogs and tours. The medium lends itself well to such things. However, with all the manufacturers and merchants running around trying to find their niche in the growing CD-ROM marketplace and the demise of some CD-ROM ventures and the growth of others, goodness knows what will happen next. That's the trouble with a developing technology. You kind of have to play along and see what develops.

Be ready for anything, that's my motto.

The Least You Need to Know

➤ Shopping by CD-ROM is in a transitional phase right now. It may blossom again in new and inventive ways, or it may peter out and disappear forever.

➤ The survivors of the shopping wars are Magellan Systems' *The Traveler* and *The Merchant* CDs. They still exist. I called today (1-800-561-3114).

➤ You can check out these CDs for free (or cheap), or you can just wait to see what other CD-based sales pitches other vendors come up with.

Chapter 26

None of the Above

In This Chapter

➤ CD software that's hard to classify

➤ CD software that's just plain odd

Sometimes I pity the folks who have to sort and categorize CD-ROM software, to pigeon-hole it nicely for a catalog, or find the appropriate spot on the shelf in the software store. Some of this stuff is hard to peg. (Some of it isn't, really, but falls into a category of its own. I've put those here so they'll have company.)

Snips and Snails: Compilation CDs

CD-ROM discs are a fabulous way to distribute tons of stuff. To that end, you'll often find CDs that are nothing but collections of odds and ends: freeware, shareware, information files.

Often they're put together with no fancy interface—you just browse through folders and directories looking for things that strike your fancy. You read them, play with them, try them out, then you move on.

This is a dangerous category of CD-ROM discs, not because they'll harm you, but because many folks who put them together are, shall we say, less than scrupulous (or more than scrofulous) about asking the authors of the stuff on the disc for permission to use it, or making sure they have the latest, greatest versions of whatever it is they're including on the disc.

One of the easiest and safest ways of acquiring a software-compilation CD is by ordering it from a *user group* appropriate to the kind of computer you use. There are a lot of user groups, many national and international, that offer CD and floppy-based collections of stuff for sale as part of their service to members and as a fund raiser because most are non-profit concerns.

User group
A group of computer users who share their computing insights and experiences with other members of the group. Groups come in different flavors: according to the computer (Mac, PC, or other) or for particular software (Windows); or a big general group with small **SIGs (special interest groups)** devoted to particular topics within the main group.

BMUG's PD-ROM of software, fonts, image files, and other stuff.

One of the biggest and best user groups around for Mac users is BMUG. Their motto: *We're in the business of giving away information—* and they do it really well. They offer the BMUG PD-ROM (about $40) shown previously, which contains over 600MB of stuff you can use. They also offer TV-ROM discs of QuickTime movies for your edification and enjoyment.

Comic Books

Sorry. I guess I should be politically correct and say "graphic novels," but they're all comic books to me, and there's no disrespect intended. I'll show you my autographed *X-Men* if you'll show me yours.

Two of the harder-to-categorize CDs, happily, deal with comic books. One CD shows how comic books got that "you'll rot your brain out" reputation, and the other CD shows how untrue that reputation is.

Comic Book Confidential

This one was hard to peg because it's first a documentary film on CD—which makes it entertainment, but also history (the history of comic books) and sociology (the craze to ban and/or clean up comics that were corrupting the youth of the day).

You Should Join a User Group Mac users interested in joining BMUG (individual memberships are $45 per year) can get information by calling or writing BMUG at:

BMUG, Inc.
1442A Walnut St. #62
Berkeley, CA USA
94709-1496
(510) 549-2684

PC users (Mac users, Windows users, and just about any other kind of user) might want to join The Boston Computer Society (individual memberships are $49 per year). You can get information by writing or calling:

The Boston Computer Society
101 First Avenue, Suite 2
Waltham, MA USA 02154
(617) 290-5700

Most user groups can net you discounts on software and hardware products, publish informative newsletters, and are just lots of fun. You don't even have to go to the meetings if you don't want to.

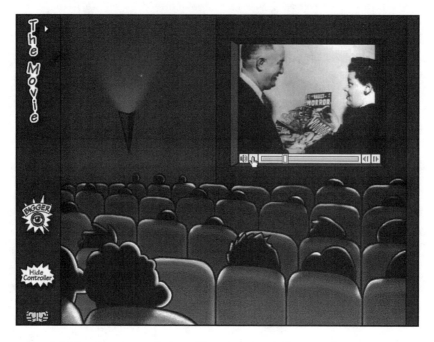

Making America safe from the corrupting influence of comic books.

Can you believe it? In the 1950s, there were actually Congressional hearings held to prove a link between comic books and juvenile delinquency. That sort of thing would *never* happen today. (Pardon me while I choke on my own sarcasm.)

Beyond Ron Mann's excellent documentary, *Comic Book Confidential* also provides 120 pages of work by artists (the likes of underground sensation R. Crumb and commercial comic book juggernaut William "What, me worry?" Gaines) featured in the film, with biographical data and commentary.

It's another excellent title from The Voyager Company. Friends have been slobbering over it since I got it, but this one's *mine*, kiddies. It's only available in Macintosh format, I'm sorry to report, and it lists for about $50 (but you can find it for about $35 by mail order).

The Complete Maus: A Survivor's Tale

If comic books are so bad for you, how come this one won the Pulitzer Prize, hmmm? *Maus* is the retelling of author Art Spiegelman's father's experiences during the Holocaust. Jews are recast as mice (*maus* is German for *mouse*). Collaborators are pigs, and Nazis are cats.

A page from Art Spiegelman's The Complete Maus.

The artwork, as shown above, is lush and evocative, and the story is touching. What makes *Maus* hard to pigeonhole is the availability of the actual recorded interviews with the senior Spiegelman upon which the work is based and Spiegelman's own thoughts on his relationship with his father and the story. There are also video clips of the younger Spiegelman's pilgrimage to visit the important sites of the story in Poland. For comic-philes, there are rough drafts and sketches of the work in progress.

All in all, a marvelous work available from The Voyager Company. It's also a Macintosh-only title, too, I'm afraid. *Maus* lists for about $50 (you can find it for $35 or so). If you haven't got access to a Mac with a CD-ROM drive, the original book version (two volumes) is still around and well worth a look.

Divine Divination

I feel like I should begin this section with one of those disclaimers they run in teeny-tiny print at the bottom of those Psychic Buddy phone line commercials: *The following CD is for entertainment purposes only and should not be construed as a belief in, or encouragement of belief in, astrology or other arcane practices.*

The Chart Room from Multicom's Astrology Source *CD-ROM.*

The *Astrology Source* CD-ROM is a complete information package about astrology and horoscopes. With it, you can peer into the personal Zodiac information of celebrities (the likes of Microsoft's Bill Gates, President and Mrs. Clinton, Marilyn Monroe, and others). You can see who, astrologically speaking, would be a good life-partner for you.

To cast a horoscope for yourself (or your friends), you enter the Chart Room, shown above), click on the great book of horoscopes, and enter the pertinent information (name, place, date, and time of birth), and *Astrology Source* will create an astrological chart for you. From the chart, you can have your (or your prospective partner's) personal traits explained in a multimedia presentation. You can also use the CD to do your own daily horoscope, like the one shown on the next page. You can print the charts and daily horoscopes so you can carry them with you to plan your day, or whatever.

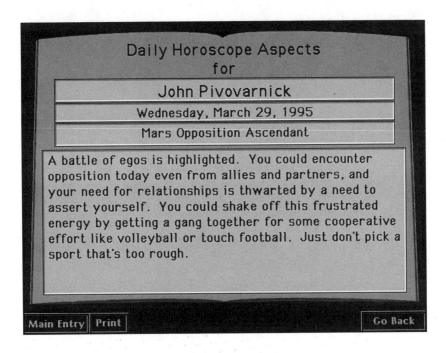

My horoscope for today. Ego? Moi??

The truth about the *Astrology Source* is this: Sure, I take horoscopes with a big, fat grain of salt-substitute; sure, I've seen prettier, more practical CD-ROM discs; sure, I've used less clumsy interfaces; however, the fact remains that (just for giggles and yucks, mind you) I've kept using this CD. It's fun. My friends all want their charts cast, *then* they want daily horoscopes.

The bottom line is, bogus or not (depending on how you feel about astrology in general), the disc is fun. It wows 'em at parties, and it's available for Macs and Windows computers. It lists for about $40, which (for a party, say) is a small investment in fun.

If astrology isn't your cup of tea leaves, you might want to check out *Virtual Tarot* from Virtual Media Works. I didn't preview it, so this is strictly hearsay, here. Instead of astrology, this CD does a tarot card reading for you. It's also available for Windows and Macintosh and can be found for $40 (though it lists for $70).

There are also CDs on palmistry, ghosts, UFOs, and other paranormal things that go bump in the computer.

The Least You Need to Know

➤ CD-ROM discs are a burgeoning field, and some of the newer titles defy easy definition.

➤ Because some of these CD-ROM discs are hard to place in standard software categories, be sure to look carefully in your favorite store or catalog for odd and interesting CD-ROM titles. A lot of the cooler/weirder titles get lumped together under headings like Entertainment or General Interest.

➤ Collection CDs, from a reputable source like a user group, are an excellent way to stockpile cool and unusual software for your computer.

➤ I'm not an occultist, but I *will* toy around with my horoscope, in spite of what it says about my ego.

Chapter 27

Roll Your Own Presentations

In This Chapter

➤ Presenting presentation software

➤ Cheap to expensive tools

➤ Video and animation tools

➤ PhotoCD-compatibility

Should the impressive array of CD-ROM multimedia software inspire you to dabble in multimedia yourself (or if you expressly bought a CD-ROM drive to help you create multimedia presentations), you should know that there's an equally impressive array of authoring software out there, too.

Déjà vu alert! Wherever possible, I've chosen to talk about packages that are available in DOS-, MPC-, and Macintosh-compatible formats, so you can use these products no matter what system you own. In instances where a product is available for only one platform, I'll say so.

Of course, you should always do your homework, shop well, and check any package's compatibility with your computer system before you buy it.

After you've put together your CD library of graphics, sounds, PhotoCD pictures, and video (whether you create them yourself or buy canned packages), all you need is the software to assemble them into your own multimedia extravaganza.

(insert your name here) Proudly Presents!

I know what you're thinking—you're thinking, "Hey, I'm not the CEO of a Fortune 500 company. Why in the world would I want to put a presentation of *any* kind together?"

I thought you might ask that, so here are some ideas for presentations you might want to consider:

➤ *Interactive homework.* You can assemble reports either for the classroom or a big event like a science fair. Very cool. Very impressive. (Did someone whisper, "Easy A."?)

➤ *Family newsletter.* Don't just write about baby's first steps, share them!

➤ *Self-promotion.* Send a presentation/résumé out to prospective employers showing your work and your creative nature.

➤ *Family history.* Throwing a surprise party for Aunt Mildred's 100th birthday? Don't just call Willard Scott. You might want to put together a "This is Your Life" presentation or document the whole celebration so everyone has a memento.

Read More About It

Presentations really are an art form unto themselves, involving art, design, photography, typography, psychology, and a few other disciplines, too. If you're completely new to the whole presentation game or just need to hone your skills, you might want to hightail it to your local library or favorite book store. There are at least a few good books out there on creating dazzling and effective presentations.

Regardless of how you convey your information (with handouts, slides and transparencies, or computer projection screens), there is software available to help you out.

The Right Tool for the Job

My father is fond of saying, "You have to have the right tool for the job." (Usually it's followed by, "So who stole my *%$&!@** ballpeen hammer?") In this case, *presentation software* is a set of tools that provides everything you'll need for the job of getting your information together (and prettied up) in short order.

Rather than having to rely on a set of stand-alone applications (a word processor, a page-layout program, graphic and photo-editing software, and so on), presentation software puts all the tools you'll need into one package for ease of use and smooth integration of the finished product.

A presentation package (a good one, at least) will provide you all the tools you need to create your presentation, from its inception to the finished product. Some even offer an outline feature, where you can enter ideas for the different parts, juggle them around so they make a coherent whole, and then flesh them out. The fleshing-out process may involve creating charts and graphs so the presentation package will have charting and graphing functions.

Because most presentations also rely on graphic and photographic images (often with text superimposed over them) for visual impact, there will be graphic editing tools. You should also be able to create graphic images from scratch. All the graphic and text functions will be available in color (because color livens things up). Some functions will also have sound capability for those who use a computer for their final presentation. Many packages will also generate both speaker's notes and audience handouts based on the presentation—saving you the trouble of re-creating the work in two more formats.

For that final presentation, the program will also offer a "slide-show" feature, where you organize your text, art, charts, and graphs into whatever order you choose; the program will display them one at a time. You can specify an amount of time for each "slide," or you can control the display manually.

More advanced packages also include video editing capability, and the whole presentation (including art and still images) can be strung together as a digital movie. The final movie can either be played on a computer or (with the proper video hardware) recorded to video tape for play in any VCR.

You don't, however, have to invest a fortune to create presentations. There are a wide range of options available to you.

Give 'em the Works

For presentations on a shoestring budget, you could probably get away with using an integrated "Works" package with color capability (such as Microsoft Works 4.0, shown below).

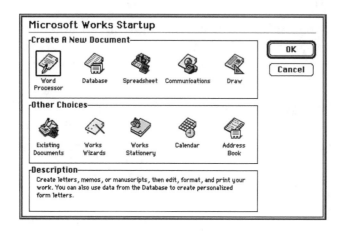

Microsoft Works, Multimedia Edition, Mac Version. The New File dialog box lets you choose between types of documents you can create.

While a Works package may have some of the specialized features needed to incorporate sound and video or to present your work as a slide show, they may not be the best choice for frequent or specialized presentation work, but would be an acceptable make-do for once-in-a-blue-moon use.

Works-type packages are available for all platforms, and most can be found by mail order for about $90. Many also get bundled with computer systems, so you may already own one.

Get All Hyper

Mac users can take advantage of two hypermedia products to help them assemble presentations with a minimum of fuss: *HyperCard* (from Apple) and *HyperStudio* (from Roger Wagner).

Integrated A single software package that includes a combination of word processor, database, spreadsheet, painting and/or drawing, outlining, charting, and telecommunications software. They're called "integrated" because you can use features of many of the different programs in one document. They're all called "something" Works because they come with the works.

248

PC Hypermedia Products

Don't get the idea that there are no hypermedia products for PC users out there. There are (like *HyperPad*, to name one), but they haven't caught on the way they have for the Mac (mostly because once upon a time, all Macs came with a free copy of *HyperCard*). As a result, PC hypermedia products are difficult to find, but you may get lucky if you keep your eyes peeled.

Media gets *hyper* when you can move through it any way you care to, instead of in a straight line. Elements are linked so that, say, a card about Africa will be linked to related cards about, oh, elephants, conservation, and other topics. Clicking on the relevant word or phrase on the first card (elephants) will take you right to the card that covers that topic specifically.

Apple's *HyperCard* (which you can find for about $90 by mail order) is the basis for many popular multimedia CD-ROM titles, including a lot of Voyager's products discussed in Chapter 21.

A sample presentation created with HyperStudio, *it includes a full-color QuickTime movie with sound.*

Roger Wagner's *HyperStudio* (shown above, about $120 by mail order) is actually a little more powerful (in some regards—like the use of color, QuickTime movies, and captured video) than *HyperCard*, and is firmly entrenched in classrooms. That makes it an ideal choice if your budding multimedia mogul is still in school.

Either product is easy enough for a child to use and learn, and both are powerful enough for professional-strength presentation work. *HyperCard* is the Macintosh standard.

More Power to You

There's a variety of full-featured, high-powered presentation applications on the market for Windows and Macintosh computers. Most are aimed at business professionals (and carry high-powered price tags), but if you have access to them, why not use them?

Aldus *Persuasion* ($500 list, $325 street) comes with an assortment of predefined presentation templates you can simply fill in with your own material—or you can build a whole new presentation from the ground up. *Persuasion* will not only generate speaker's notes and handout materials, it will format your speech to match the presentation and will include small "thumbnail" sketches of the slides in the speech (better than having to crane your neck to look at the screen).

Microsoft *PowerPoint* (also $500 list, $300 street) offers many of the same capabilities as Aldus *Persuasion*. It will also add thumbnail-sized images of your slides to your speech, but new versions of *PowerPoint* also offer QuickTime and MS-Video.

In addition to these, which are both available in Macintosh and Windows versions, there are presentation packages that are available for only one particular platform. Check your computer store or mail-order catalog for some of those titles.

In the video category, there's Adobe *Premiere* ($700 list, $450 street). *Premiere* gives you a mini-movie studio on your desktop, complete with special effects and transitions between scenes (fades and dissolves, just like the movies).

Macromedia Director ($1,200 list, $800 street), shown in the following figure, will create and sequence animation, graphics, text, and allow you to make your stand-alone presentation interactive—allowing the viewer(s) to control the course of the presentation.

In between the "make-do in a pinch" integrated packages and the high-end "Honey, I mortgaged the kids" packages, there's a wide range of presentation-authoring software that sells for $50–$200. Features and options vary, so you really need to shop for what you need.

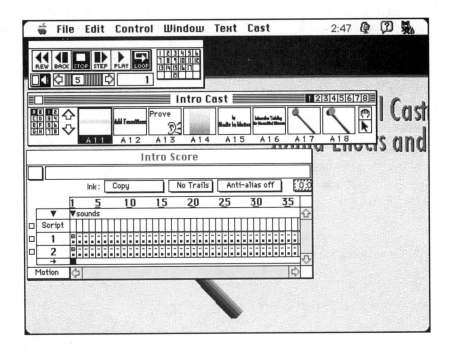

Macromedia Director (Macintosh version 3.11) sample screen.

Interesting Accessories

While you're in the mood to create, I thought I'd take a moment to let you know about some doodads and thingammys that, while not essential (or even necessarily related) to multimedia presentations, are interesting and kind of fun. And we could all use some more fun.

PhotoCD Goodies

If you want to use PhotoCD images (like those on the sample disc in the back of this book) in your multimedia productions or just want to look at them with your graphics applications, you'll need to make sure that the software in question can handle the PhotoCD format. Most of the current versions of graphics software (like Adobe Photoshop) are PhotoCD-compatible. You can use them to open, edit, print, and even export images to other applications (like page layout or presentation software).

You may want to check and see what applications you own (or consider buying) are PhotoCD-compatible.

Deep—Very Deep

Images on a computer screen have only two dimensions (height and width). With some applications, you can give the illusion that these 2-D images actually have the third dimension, depth.

Pixar Typestry ($300 list, $190 street) will turn your boring two-dimensional headlines into attention-grabbing 3-D wonders you can import into other applications to spice up presentations and printed documents. You won't even need those red-and-blue glasses to see it! You can also get 3-D rendering programs that let you create three-dimensional images. Very cool.

Export When one application saves your document in a format that can be used by another, different application, that's called **exporting**. When the second application uses that file, it **imports** it.

Hey, Render This, Pal...

Programs that render images in three dimensions take some heavy-duty computing power. Most require a high-end machine (like a 486 or Pentium PC, a Mac Quadra or Power Mac, with a math processor chip installed). Be sure you know that your machine is up to snuff before you spring for one of these puppies.

Pulling Back the Reins

Given the chance, I'll babble away about all the funky and different stuff you can con a computer into doing. I live for that kind of thing. You may not, so I won't bore you with more.

Let me just say this: After you get comfortable with your CD-ROM drive, don't get complacent, too. There are a lot of things to be done with this technology, so don't think there isn't room for growth. Every now and then, check out a software aisle other than those you normally browse. Pick up an interesting-looking box and read it. You might find things to make your computing life both easier and more interesting.

The Least You Need to Know

➤ You don't have to be CEO of a Fortune 500 company to benefit from presentation software. You don't even have to be a grownup.

➤ There are software packages designed to make creating business presentations less of a chore. They range in price from inexpensive Works-type programs to full-tilt $1,000+ production facilities.

➤ The moderately priced software packages, like *HyperCard* and *HyperStudio*, are often found in the education section of the store or catalog—but you can still use them for presentation and other multimedia work.

➤ If you want to use Kodak PhotoCD images in your work, you're going to need at least one application that is PhotoCD-compatible.

➤ Be open to new computing experiences.

Part 4
The Care and Feeding of Your CD-ROM Drive

I won't try and bamboozle you. CD-ROM drives can get a little cranky if you don't take care of them—of course, so do spouses, children, and pets. Part 4 gives you tips on how to painlessly maintain and care for both your drive and your CDs. In the "feeding" department, it also talks about all the stuff you'll find on the CD that came with this book. Consider the CD an appetizer, to whet your appetite for other CD titles.

You'll also find the standard assortment of Idiot's Guide *accessories:*

➤ *A chapter of troubleshooting tips*

➤ *Some information on more doo-dads you may want to add later*

➤ *And the ever-popular Speak Like A Geek glossary.*

Chapter 28

About That CD...

The disc that's pasted in the back of this book is just chock-full of fun, cool, and bizarre things you can use and abuse to your heart's content. Some of it is new, never-before-seen, original stuff that I hope you will find both attractive and useful.

Others are shareware fonts and applications that will be useful to many readers, and (if you decide to keep and use them) you'll need to register them with their authors and pay the requested fee. It's all detailed here and in the documentation for the software in question.

The CD-ROM disc is for both Windows and Mac users, and there is a comparable range of stuff for each platform. DOS users will be able to use some of the Windows stuff (the clip art and photo files, which really aren't Windows-specific).

As appropriate, there will be sections devoted to Mac-only/Windows-only items. Fire up your CD-ROM drive and computer, load up that CD. Look around, most of all, have *fun*.

PhotoCD Images

On the disc, there's a folder called **PHOTOCD**, and inside it is a folder called PHOTO_CD, and inside *that* folder is one called IMAGES (the path statement would be \PHOTOCD\PHOTO_CD\IMAGES). Oddly enough, the IMAGES folder contains over two dozen photographic images in Kodak's PhotoCD format (discussed in Chapter 5). These images were especially created for this book and (because I'm not much of a photographer) were created by the artist and theatrical designer T. Greenfield.

You'll find images of nature, artwork, textures, and scenes from around the world. You can see small, thumbnail versions of them below. They can be used as backgrounds for presentations, incorporated into reports and newsletters, and just about anything else you can think of.

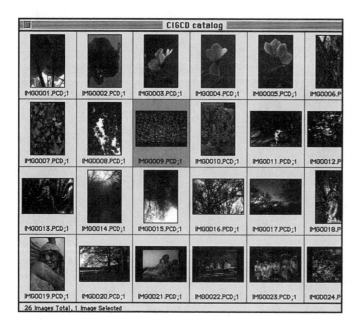

The PhotoCD images from the CD-ROM. If you squint, you can figure out what they are.

In order to use the PhotoCD images, you must have an application that is compatible with the format. Many of the popular graphics programs can, these days. If you don't have one that is, don't panic: there are PICT format versions, at various resolutions, in the folder called **Photos**. Almost *any* painting, drawing, or general graphics application can use PICT files.

Using the PhotoCD Images in Your Work

The PhotoCD images on the disc are yours to use however you see fit; however, they remain the property of Mr. Greenfield, so you cannot sell them or give copies to your friends. If you choose to incorporate them in a publication, presentation, or some other work, please give him the appropriate credit:

Photograph copyright ©1995 by T. Greenfield.

If someone asks where you get them, tell them to get a copy of this book. That's not much to ask, is it?

Scanned Reality

Additionally, there's a handful of scanned images on the CD (shown below). These are in Macintosh PICT, and DOS PCX formats, widely usable on their respective platforms. You'll find them inside the system-specific folders on the disc, in a folder called **Scans**. (For the truly anal-retentive, the path statements would be \WIN\CLIPS\SCANS or \MAC\CLIPS\SCANS, depending on your system.)

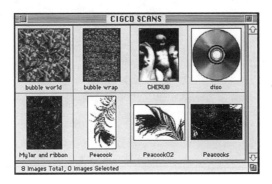

Scanned images from the CD, by yours truly.

There's one image of a cherub, that's a close-up, black-and-white photograph of a fountain here in Philadelphia—a favorite of mine for many years. The photo was taken by Langston Earley and hangs on my wall—I thought I'd share it with you.

The remaining scanned images are fairly bizarre—I think, anyhow. I had fun with three-dimensional objects, seeing what happens to them when they're scanned. I was especially curious about objects that are somewhat reflective because color scanners work by bouncing red, blue, and green light off of whatever is being scanned. It was a case of me thinking, "Well, if that's how *that* works, what happens if you scan *this*?" The peacock feathers and Mylar were the most fun—did I mention that I'm a toy-brain?

Babbling About Scanning

If you care, this is all the techno-babble about the scanning process. Feel free to yawn.

All the images on the disc (those covered in this section, and those in the "Clip Art" section coming up) were scanned using a Relysis Avec Colour 2400 flatbed scanner on a Macintosh Quadra 660AV. Photographic images were scanned into Adobe Photoshop 3.0.1. Clip art was scanned into Microfrontier's Color It! 3.0. PCX versions were also created in Photoshop.

All these items may look unusually large to you on your computer's screen. Most computers display stuff at 72 lines per inch. So they would print better, these images were scanned at *150* lines per inch. To get all that extra information on your screen (more than *twice* the information) your computer makes them seem twice the size. An image that *looks* like it's 9 × 12 inches on your screen will actually be 4.5 × 6 inches when you print it out on a laser, or other high-quality printer.

The images are also larger than you'll probably need because a big image made smaller (generally) looks better when printed than a small image made big. Just so you know.

The results are yours to do with as you please—all I ask is that you don't sell or give away copies of the scanned images. I don't need no stinkin' credit. Otherwise, go nuts with them.

Clip Art

Clip art, as you'll recall from Chapter 24, is art that somebody else prepared that you can cut and paste into your own documents to dress them up. The clip art files are in both Macintosh PICT and DOS PCX formats because most applications can deal with these formats. You'll find them inside the system-specific folders on the disc.

Christmas Clips

I do appreciate the fact that there are *other* holidays and other religions in the world. However, since this is a sampler affair (with Sebastian Cabot as Mr. French), I had a tough choice to make. I could include a dozen clips for, say, Christmas, or one each for Christmas, Chanukah, and Kwanza; one for President's day; one for the 4th of July; and so on through the calendar. I went with the easy, if culturally rude, choice. I apologize to readers who do not celebrate Christmas.

Clip art in a seasonal vein.

The Christmas clips (shown above) are variations on popular Christmas themes, adapted and drawn by *another* artist and theatrical designer friend, Teresa Fallon. Her caricatures and cartoon characters have always made me giggle. The drawing on the disc of the poor little guy in his chair made me laugh out loud—that's how *I've* spent many a Christmas.

For the hard-of-browsing among you, the path statements to the Christmas clips are MAC/CLIPS/CHRISTMA for the Mac and \WIN\CLIPS\XMSCLIPS for the PC.

Using the Christmas Clip Art in Your Work

The Christmas clips on the disc are yours to use however you see fit; however, they remain the property of Mrs. Fallon, so you cannot sell them or give copies to your friends. If you choose to incorporate them in work for general distribution, please give her the appropriate credit:

Artwork copyright © 1995 by Teresa Fallon.

It's only polite and—well—it's the *legal* thing to do, too.

Use them to dress up your holiday letters to your family and friends. Incorporate them in a church bulletin. Make greeting cards—I'm sure you'll think of something. Check your word processor, graphics program, or page layout application manual(s) for instructions on how to use graphics with your software.

Large Clip Art

The large bits of clip art cover a wide variety of themes and images. You'll find borders, boxes, cartoons, designs, and other pieces of art you can use in your personal creations. There are over 40 of them on the disc, and you can see a few samples below.

A sampling of the large clip art on the CD.

These are also original works, by the same fellow who did the PhotoCD images, T. Greenfield. As a matter of fact, as I'm writing this (on my PC) he's over on my Mac cleaning up the images so they're especially pretty for you. Every now and then, we swap computers, just to make things tougher. It's exactly like tag-team wrestling, but without the Spandex.

The clips are located inside each system folder, inside the Clips folder, in a folder called Large Clips. For the path statement dependent, that would be \MAC\CLIPS\LARGE_CL for the Mac and \WIN\CLIPS\LGCLIPS for the PC.

Using the Large Clip Art in Your Work

The large clip art files on the disc are yours to use however you see fit; however, they remain Mr. Greenfield's property, so you cannot sell them or give copies away. If you choose to incorporate them in a publication, presentation, or some other work, please give him the appropriate credit:

Artwork copyright © 1995 by T. Greenfield.

Most of the images are simple black-and-white line drawings. A few are done in 16 shades of gray, to get some of the cool effects (Border02 and Write02 are examples of what I mean, if you care to check them out).

A couple of the images are fairly simple outlined shapes, like the parrot, that are attractive as is, but you could open them with your favorite painting program and tinker. Add color, or patterned fills to the open areas, just like you'd color in the pictures in a coloring book. You'll need to use a graphics program to convert the black-and-white images into color or shades of gray first. Your graphics program manual will tell you how it's done.

You'll probably want to scale these images down (that is, make them smaller) for use in your documents. Most of them will pretty much fill a standard 8.5 × 11" page—which is too big to tuck into the corner of a newsletter. You can scale them with your graphics or page layout program as well.

Fonts for Days

Well, maybe not for days, but certainly for *hours*. There are three complete font families on the disc, more than a dozen fonts, by font designer Susan Townsend of Hot Metal Type. She does nice stuff, as you can see in the figure on the following page. The fonts are in TrueType format for both Windows and Macintosh. You'll find them in the Font folder, inside the folder for your specific computer (that's \MAC\FONTS or \WIN\FONTS, depending on your computer).

COJONES

JALAPENO

Rosabell Antique

Vintage Typewriter: Corona

Some examples of the fonts you've got on the CD.

These fonts are *shareware*, so if you like them and use them, you should send Ms. Townsend a check for each font set you want to register. Here's the scoop:

Cojones and Jalapeno are $10 for the set. The family of four Rosabel Antique fonts is $25. The six Vintage Typewriter fonts are $20. If you like and use them all, you should send a check or money order for a total of $55 to **Susan Townsend, 5662 Calle Real #146, Goleta, CA 93117.** You can also contact her on America Online, her screen name is **FredaPple.**

She also has a number of other lovely/bizarre fonts to offer—feel free to contact her for more information about them. (I, personally, ordered *all* her fonts—that's how much I like them.)

In order to use the fonts, you're going to need to install them. Here's how:

Installing Fonts on a Mac

If you're using a Mac, and running System 7.0 or later, all you need to do is open the folder that contains the Mac version of the fonts (which means of course that your Mac is on, and the CD-ROM disc is in the drive). Click or shift-click on each of the three font suitcases to select one or more of them, then drag and drop each (or all) of the suitcases onto your closed System folder.

Your Mac will say something to the effect of: "Fonts need to be stored in the Fonts folder... shall I put them there?" Click **OK**, and your Mac will do the rest.

When it's done copying the files to your Fonts folder, you need to restart your Mac to use the fonts. To do that select **Restart** from the Special menu. You'll be ready to roll.

If you're using a version of the Mac OS *earlier* than System 7.0, you need to use the **Font/DA Mover** that was included with your System software. Check your manual for details (don't sweat it, it's easy).

Installing Fonts with Windows

To install these fonts on a computer running Windows, make sure Windows is running and the CD is in your drive. Then do the following:

1. If it isn't already open, **double-click** on the **Main** program group icon to open it.

2. Then, **double-click** on the **Control Panel** icon to open *that.*

3. Next, **double-click** on the **Fonts** control panel icon to open *that.*

4. When the Fonts control panel opens, **click** the Add button. That will open the dialog box shown below.

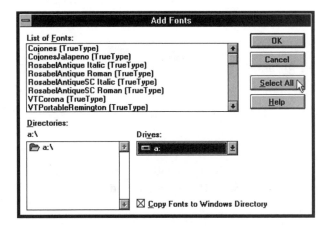

Adding fonts to Windows.

5. Use the pop-up Drives menu to select the CD as your source. (It's probably drive D: or E: depending on how your system is set up.)

6. Use the **Directories** list to navigate to the **Fonts** folder inside the **Win** folder, and **double-click** on it to open it.

7. All of the fonts should appear in the **List of Fonts** window. Make sure the box in front of **Copy Fonts to Windows Directory** is checked (as in the figure above).

8. **Click** Select All.

9. **Click OK.**

Windows will copy all of the fonts from the CD into your Windows directory. When it's done, close the Font control panel and you're ready to use your cool new fonts.

Stuff for Windows

You'll also find a number of freeware and shareware applications on the CD, they'll be in the folder named **Apps** inside the folder appropriate to Windows. Windows users get two spiffy applications: one that will let you play and control audio CDs; and one that will let you record and play a variety of sound file types through your PC's sound card. You also get a selection of sound files in Windows WAV format.

CD Wizzard

CD Wizzard is the audio CD player, written by Brett McDonald of BFM Software. It's very cool, as you will see. In order to use CD Wizzard you must have:

➤ 386 or higher processor

➤ Windows 3.1 or higher

➤ Mouse or other pointing device

➤ Color monitor, SVGA resolution recommended

➤ A CD-ROM drive that's audio-CD-capable

CD Wizzard isn't a freebie. If you like it and use it, you should register it. The registration fee is a measly $15.95. Details are included in the file CDWREAD.TXT in the CDW307 folder.

Installing CD Wizzard

To install CD Wizzard, all you need to do is copy the CDW307 folder from the CD-ROM disc to your hard drive (use Windows' File Manager for this).

Next, you need to set it up as a Windows application. To do that:

1. Open the **Main** program group and **double-click** on the **Windows Setup** icon.

2. From the Options menu, select **Setup Applications**.

3. You'll get a Setup Applications window asking if you want Setup to search for applications, or ask you to specify an application. **Click** on the radio button in front of the "Ask you to specify..." option and **click OK**.

4. Windows will next ask you to specify the application. If you know it, you may type in a path statement (like the one shown in the following figure) or, you can use the Browse option to navigate to where you've saved CDW307 on your hard drive. Either way, **CDW.EXE** is the file you want to set up.

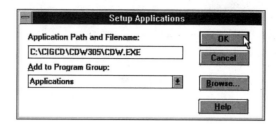

Setting up an application with Windows Setup.

5. If you care to, you can specify what program group CD Wizzard will land in. The default, as shown above, is Applications.

6. **Click OK**. Windows will add CD Wizzard to the program group you specified.

Using CD Wizzard

To use CD Wizzard, first launch it by double-clicking on its icon in the Applications (or whatever) program group window. CD Wizzard will launch, and it will look like the figure below (although you probably won't have "Sgt. Pepper" loaded in your CD-ROM drive—but you might).

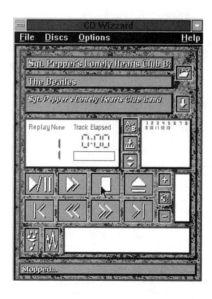

CD Wizzard is smashing, it's wizard, it's keen.

When you insert an audio CD in your drive for the first time, CD Wizzard will present you with an Edit Disc Data window where you can enter the name, artist, composer, classification, and other information about the disc.

If you want to (you only need to do it once for each audio CD), go ahead, then click Save when you're done. Or you can just click Cancel, and go right to the controls.

The controls function just the controls of any audio CD player you've ever encountered. You should have no trouble figuring those out.

Other features, however, are not as obvious: the disc database, sound mixer, and more. To learn more about the advanced features of CD Wizzard, you can use the online help (under the Help menu), which is very straightforward and, well, *helpful*.

Multimedia Sound Recorder

Sound Recorder is a VOC, WAV, and SND (which are all sound file formats) player, editor, and recorder for Windows. To use it, you need:

➤ A sound card (or Microsoft speaker driver)

➤ Microsoft Windows with Multimedia Extensions, or Windows 3.1

➤ A Microsoft-compatible mouse

➤ A microphone compatible with your sound card

If you've got all that, then you can install the Sound Recorder. Sound Recorder is free, by the good graces of its author, David Mullen. Use it well.

Installation and Setup

The steps for installing and setting up the Recorder are surprisingly similar to those for installing CD Wizzard from the last section. Just repeat those steps, but substitute **MSREC31** whenever you see **CDW307** in the instructions.

Using Multimedia Sound Recorder

To use the Sound Recorder, first launch it by double-clicking on its icon in the Applications (or whatever) program group window. Sound Recorder will launch, and it will look like the following figure.

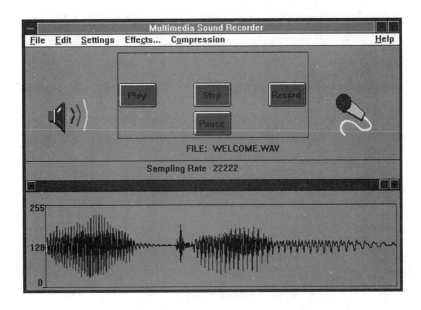

The Sound Recorder screen.

To play a prerecorded sound file, select **Open** from the File menu. Navigate to the sound file you want to play (there are some in the folder called WAV (path: \WIN\WAV) on the CD) and double-click on it. To play the sound, click the **Play** button.

The Stop and Pause buttons stop or pause whatever the Sound Recorder is doing when you click.

To record a sound, click the **Record** button. The display changes to give you a Start button at the top of the screen. Click **Start** to begin recording—make sure your microphone is plugged into your sound card for recording, or it will be a mighty quiet sound. When you're done, click **Stop**.

Enhancing, editing, and otherwise modifying sounds are the stuff of physics. To learn about Sound Recorder's more advanced functions, read the online help files available under the Help menu. You can also read the **MSREC.WRI** file—it's in the MSREC31 folder on the CD and/or your hard drive.

What You Didn't Get

Windows users, unlike Mac users, didn't get a QuickTime movie player on the CD. That's owing to the fact that every Mac owner with a current version of the Mac System software, or a CD-ROM disc that requires QuickTime has it.

Apple, on the other hand, keeps pretty strict control of QuickTime for Windows. To complicate things a little further, at the moment, Apple is suing Microsoft about QuickTime for Windows stuff with Video For Windows, and Microsoft is countersuing. The control and legal issues made it impossible to get a QuickTime player for you in time to meet the production deadlines. I'm sorry.

If you've got QuickTime 2.0 for Windows, and a player, you may be able use the QuickTime movie on the CD. If you don't have QuickTime, you may acquire it from Apple, if you care to, or simply purchase a CD-ROM disc that uses QuickTime. The QuickTime software normally comes on those CDs. You can turn up a video player on most online services and from Windows user groups.

Stuff for the Mac

Mac users get a couple of fun things: a simple audio CD controller that's brilliant in its simplicity; a sound recording and editing utility (and some sound files); a QuickTime movie player (and some goofy little video clips I made).

CD Menu

CD Menu is a shareware audio CD controller by Henrik Eliasson of Sweden. The software itself is a control panel that gives you some cool customizing options—but I prefer it in its plain vanilla mode. Whichever way you set it up, if you like it and continue to use it, the shareware fee is $10 (*cheap*). You can find out where to send the money by clicking on the About button on the CD Menu control panel.

CD menu works on just about any Mac (except the Plus, the SE and the PowerBook 100). It requires System 7.0, or later, and an Apple compatible CD-ROM drive with the appropriate audio CD driver software installed. It should have come with your CD-ROM drive.

Installing CD Menu

To install CD Menu, locate the application's icon in the CD Menu folder inside the APPS folder, which is inside the MAC folder on the CD.

Drag the CD Menu icon onto your closed System folder. Your Mac will say something like, "Control panels need to be installed in the control panels folder...okay if I do that?" Click **OK** and your Mac will drop the control panel there. When it's done, you'll need to restart your Mac. Use the Restart option on your Special menu.

Using CD Menu

When you've restarted your Mac, you'll notice you've got a new thingy in your menu bar —a thingy that looks like a CD. It *is* a CD—it's the CD Menu menu. When you click on the CD icon, a typical set of audio CD controls drops down from your menu bar (you can see it in the following figure).

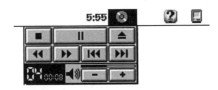

CD Menu gives you audio CD controls right from your menu.

These are standard audio CD controls, so you should have no trouble figuring them out.

The hardest part to get used to is that you have to hold your mouse button down while you slide the pointer arrow over the controls. You'll see the buttons push in as the pointer touches them. When you're pushing the button you want pushed, release the mouse button. The menu goes away, and CD Menu executes your command.

Pop in an audio CD and give it a shot. You'll get used to it in no time.

If you care to try some of the customizing options, the control panel and all of its features are fully explained in the Read Me file that accompanies CD Menu.

Color Tracks

If you've ever double-clicked on an audio CD's icon, just to see what happens, you've probably noticed that the icons for the audio tracks are in dull black-and-white. Boring— oh yawn.

You can fix that. Just locate the Color Tracks folder inside the APPS folder (which is inside the MAC folder). Drag the Color Tracks icon onto your closed System folder.

Your Mac will ask if it's OK to put the extension in the Extension Folder on your hard drive. Click **OK**. Your Mac will copy the file. Restart your Mac with the **Restart** command in the Special menu.

The next time you open an audio CD's file window, those tracks will be in glorious color.

Color Tracks is a freeware confection written by J. Andrew Schafer. It may not win the Nobel Prize, but it does its job and lends a little grace to the computing world.

Ultra Recorder

Ultra Recorder is a shareware sound recording utility ($10 if you choose to keep and use it), written by EJ Campbell. To use it, you need a Mac equipped with a microphone—most of the models released in the last three or four years have one.

To install Ultra Recorder, drag the Ultra Recorder folder from the CD (it's inside the APPS folder, inside the MAC folder), and drop it on your hard drive's icon. Your Mac will copy the folder and its contents to your hard drive.

Using Ultra Recorder

To launch Ultra Recorder, double-click on the Ultra Recorder folder on your hard drive to open it. Then double-click on the Ultra Recorder icon. Ultra Recorder will fire right up, and it will look just like it does in the following figure.

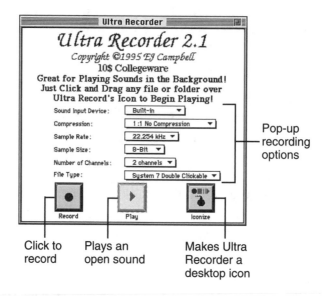

EJ Campbell's Ultra Recorder.

To record a sound, click the **Record** button. You'll get a Record/Pause/Play dialog similar to the one you may have used with the Mac's Sound control panel. Click **Record**.

Make a noise in the vicinity of the microphone, then click **Stop**. You can then play the sound to see if you like it (just click **Play**) or save it for you can have it forever (click **Save**).

If you'd rather, you can listen to the sound files from the CD, they're in a folder called SNDS, inside the MAC folder. To open one, use the **Open** command in the **File** menu, navigate to the SNDS folder, and double-click on a SND file. Then click **Play** and Ultra Recorder will play it for you.

There's more detailed instructions in the Read Me file that accompanies Ultra Recorder. For information about registering your copy, choose **About Ultra Recorder** from the   menu.

EasyPlay

EasyPlay is a very simple QuickTime movie player, written by Mike O'Connor of Leptonic Systems. It's shareware, which means that if you keep and use EasyPlay, you *will* send Mike a check for $20.

EasyPlay is a stand-alone application, so no special installation is required. Just drag the EZPLAYER folder (which is inside the APPS folder, inside the MAC folder) from the CD to your hard drive. Your Mac will then copy the folder and its contents to your hard drive.

To launch EasyPlay, double-click on the EasyPlay folder on your hard drive to open it. Then double-click on the EasyPlay 2.0 icon. EasyPlay starts right up.

It doesn't look like much when it starts. To get an idea of what it really looks like, you need to open a movie file. To do so, select **Open** from the **File** menu. You'll get a standard open dialog. Use it to navigate to the folder called Movies, on the CD-ROM disc. There are a couple of silly little things in there—don't get too excited, Cecil B. DeMille I'm not. Double-click on the name of the movie you want to see. It will open right up and start to play, like the one shown in the following figure.

These movies were made with Connectix QuickCam, discussed in Chapter 31. They aren't of the quality you might expect from movies made with a regular video camera and then converted to digital format. Plus, I'm not much of a movie maker, either. (Could I possibly apologize any *more* for these??)

To stop the movie, click the **Pause** button on the controller at the bottom of the screen (the arrow is pointing at it in the figure). On the right side of the movie controller are the frame forward and frame back buttons, so you can go through the film frame at a time (while it's on pause).

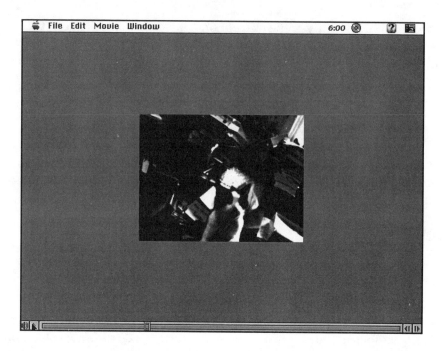

Me being annoyed by my cat in glorious black-and-white.

There are a number of other things you can do with EasyPlay, like looping a video clip so it plays forever. All that good information is available by selecting **About EasyPlay** from the menu.

The Least You Need to Know

➤ The CD at the back of the book is a sampler of the kinds of things you'll be able to find on CD-ROM discs. It's a jack of all trades, master of none.

➤ While there are few restrictions on what you do with the photos and clip art files (just don't sell them, or give copies away), when you use them, please give the artists appropriate credit.

➤ Some of the applications on the CD are shareware, which means you should send the author some money if you keep and use his or her software. Nothing here will break the bank. It's all from $10–$20.

➤ Comments, questions, and suggestions can be mailed to me care of the publisher. You can also e-mail me on America Online at the address **Piv**, or (from the Internet) to **piv@aol.com**. I'm pretty good about answering all of my mail, but e-mail gets a faster response.

Chapter 29

It's No Pain to Maintain (and More of a Pain If You Don't)

In This Chapter

➤ Handling discs

➤ Cleaning discs

➤ Caddy smarts

➤ Storage

➤ Drive safely

CD technology, because of the precision required to aim the laser and read those teeny-tiny bits of data from the discs, can get a little cranky if not properly cared for.

For that matter, so do I.

You don't want your CD-ROM drive to *ever* need internal maintenance because that will mean living without it while it is serviced somewhere. What a ghastly thought. To avoid that particular horror, I'm suddenly turning into Heloise (I read her column religiously) to provide you with handy-dandy maintenance tips that will reduce the chances of your drive getting boogered up.

You Can Look, but You Better Not Touch

Poison eyeeee-eye-vee...

Sorry. I forgot what I was doing for a second.

But, speaking of not touching things, there's a right way and a wrong way to handle the discs you put into your CD-ROM drive:

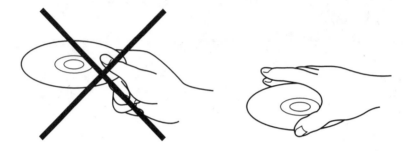

Choosing between right and wrong.

The correct way to handle a CD (any CD, not just those for your computer) is by the edges. That will reduce the amount of skin oils (the stuff that leaves fingerprints), sweat, chocolate, and whatever else you've been touching, to a minimum.

Not Clean Enough...

Don't think that if you just washed your hands, you're free of skin oil... chocolate, maybe, but not skin oil. If you washed your hands so often that they were free of natural oils, your hands would be so chapped and dry, you'd hardly be able to bend your fingers.

If you must touch one of the flat sides—for whatever reason—touch only the top, the side with the printing on it. Never touch the bottom, the silver side with the pretty rainbows glinting in the light. This is the data side of the disk. Fingerprints and chocolate smudges can interfere with the laser beam as your drive tries to read the disc.

If any crud deposited on the CD happens to get dislodged as it's spun around inside your drive, it could get flung off the disc and into the works. Bad news.

Dirt Happens

The proper handling of your discs is all well and good, but if you have children using your CD-ROM (or friends who aren't quite as conscientious as yourself), you could still wind up with dirty discs. Even if *everyone* who uses your computer is careful about handling your discs, dirt still happens. Dust collects on things. Stuff gets spilled. Cats and dogs shed in the strangest of places.

You can clean your discs by simply wiping them off with a clean, dry, soft cloth—preferably lint-free and all cotton. Fibers in other types of cloth could possibly scratch the CD-ROM's surface. Gently wipe the disc, starting near the center hole and wiping out to the edge of the disk. Wipe all of the way around, on both sides, and your disc will be squeaky clean.

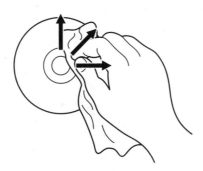

Cleaning a CD.

If something stickier than dust or fingerprints winds up on the disc, you can *wet* the cotton cloth with a little plain, lukewarm water. Make sure you dry the disc well before you use it. If water doesn't do the trick, try a gentle eyeglass cleaner or a drop of *denatured* alcohol.

More Cheap Tricks

Don't waste your money on expensive CD cleaning kits. The techniques discussed here work perfectly well, and if your drive has a built-in lens-cleaning brush (many do, check your manual), the residue from a commercial cleaner can build up on those brushes and reduce their effectiveness.

If you want to buy something to clean with, invest in a pack of dry, cotton lint-free wipes (available in most computer stores) or even a pad of good camera lens paper (available in your local camera shop). I just found a 12-pack of lint-free cotton wipes on sale for $1.99—more than $3 off! Such a bargain! I didn't even need them, but I bought them anyhow.

Never-Never Land

There are some things you should never, ever do to a CD-ROM disc. YOU SHOULD NEVER:

➤ Stick any kind of label on either side of a compact disc.

➤ Use anything stronger than water to clean a disc. Use eyeglass cleaner or denatured alcohol only as a last resort.

➤ Use a knife or other sharp object to scrape crud off of a disc.

➤ Expose a disc to high heat or direct sunlight.

➤ Expose a disc to extreme (sub-zero) cold.

Be Gentle with Me

While they look like some sort of space-age metal, CDs are actually coated in plastic. Plastic is fragile, and pits and scratches may render a disc unusable. Products like Windex, 409, and other cleaning sprays can (over time) damage the plastic coating, as can sharp objects and rough handling.

Pink Caddy-lac

As part of their crud-protection systems, many CD-ROM players will only accept a disc that's in a CD caddy.

If you look at one, you'll notice that it makes your CD look like a hyperthyroidal 3.5-inch disk. It's got a sliding shutter on the bottom that protects the data side of the disc until you insert it into a drive (then the shutter slides back, revealing the CD).

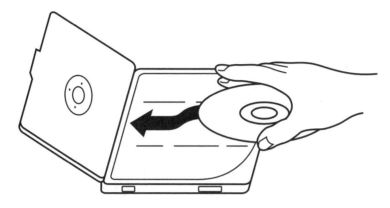

A typical CD caddy.

The caddy also gives you a place to stick a label, should you so choose, making it easy to pick the CD you want out of a line-up of caddies.

If You Need One, You've Got One

If your CD-ROM drive requires you to use a CD caddy, you should have gotten one with your drive. *Buy more.* It's really a pain in the tush to have to swap CDs in and out of a single caddy if you use more than one disc on a regular basis.

If youngsters have access to the CD-ROM drive, you should put their CDs in individual caddies and leave them there. It will reduce the chances of something bad happening to the expensive disc. Better to damage an $8–$9 caddy than a $30–$230 CD-ROM disc.

You can buy spare CD caddies by mail order. A three-pack will set you back about $25. A five-pack, $35.

The caddy does a couple of things for you. If there is any *shmutz* on your disc, the caddy will keep it from being flung all over the inside of your drive. It also relieves you of some of the careful handling discs require. You don't have to be as careful, but you should still be careful.

CDs go into the caddy with the label side (the side with the printing on it) facing up. Caddies can be cleaned the same as the CDs themselves, with a dry (or lightly damp) cloth. You still don't want to use anything stronger than water—not for fear of damaging the caddy but because the residue of the cleaner could build up on the dust brushes inside your CD-ROM drive.

You can store your frequently used CDs right in their caddies if you have enough (did I mention you should buy some extra caddies for convenience and safety's sake?). The caddies are the same size as the jewel boxes audio CDs come in, so they'll fit in a storage box just as well.

Speaking of storage...

To Store or Not to Store...

Storage of CDs is a ticklish issue, with me at least. I'm the guy with about 200 floppy disks tied up with rubber bands and stacked all over his desk, and all sorts of untidy habits running amok.

In terms of storage, the least you should do is store your CDs in their jewel boxes or caddies to protect the discs from accidental damage when they aren't in use. Even I do *that* much.

They should be kept away from extremes of heat and cold, and out of direct sunlight (my office is a dungeon, so this last one is not an issue for me). If you want to be cheap about it, you can put them all in a shoe box or something of similar size to keep the mountains of them from sliding all over the place. If you want to be a little more anal-retentive about it, you can buy a nice little rack or box to keep them in, with spines or labels showing (if your eyes can read that tiny print).

Still More Cheap Tricks

I haven't confirmed this yet, but I *suspect* you'll pay less for a CD rack if you go to a music or department store instead of a computer-supply store. Techno toys and their accessories are usually more expensive than run-of-the-mill toys and accessories that do the same thing. Just a hunch.

Or you can go whole-hog and buy a spiffy teak roll-top multimedia storage box with a lock and everything. It will certainly protect your CDs from sunlight (like they're vampires or something), and will keep them away from prying eyes and fingers if you have nosy kids or co-workers.

Drive Safely

In acknowledging the fact that CD-ROM drives are very susceptible to dust, manufacturers have implemented several standard features to help keep dust and other pollution out of your CD-ROM drive.

When coupled with the disc-handling and maintenance tips in this chapter, they can help keep your drive up and running for a long, long time. But you can do more.

Dust doors are meant to keep dust from getting into your drive. Don't defeat their purpose by leaving them open, or (worse) open with a disc poking out. Also, clean around the drive occasionally so the unit's fan won't suck dust inside. Wipe down the outside of the drive with a dry (or slightly damp) cloth.

Dampen, Not Soak-en

Always dampen the cloth, not the hardware. If you get the cloth too wet, you can always wring it out. It's hard to wring out hardware. Plus, cloth doesn't have a reputation for short-circuiting when you get it wet.

For the truly lazy (like my own self), you can buy a can of compressed air (without the ozone-killing CFCs, please and thank you) and blast the dust from around, under, or on your drive.

The Least You Need to Know

➤ Dust and crud is bad, bad news for your CD-ROM drive.

➤ Handle your CDs by the edges. Don't touch the flat sides, especially the shiny (data) side.

➤ Clean dusty discs with a soft, dry cloth. Wipe from the center hole out to the edge of the disc.

➤ Never use anything stronger than water on a disc—it might damage the plastic coating and ruin the disc.

➤ If your drive requires you to put your discs in caddies, maintain the caddies as you would the CDs themselves.

➤ Store your CDs in their jewel boxes or caddies, away from direct sunlight, extreme temperatures, and sources of dust (like an ashtray).

➤ Clean the outside and around your CD-ROM drive on a regular basis—dust can't get in it if there's none around it.

➤ Just doing some day-to-day simple things can spare you (and your drive) a carload of heartache down the road.

Chapter 30

Troubleshooting

In This Chapter

➤ Don't be an idiot—assume you've been an idiot

➤ Common CD-ROM woes—PC and Mac style

➤ Calling for help

"Troubleshooting" has a nice sound to it. It sounds like, when something is bothering you, you can hunt down the troublemakers and shoot them.

In one sense, it's true. "Troubleshooting," in this case, is a search-and-destroy mission for problems plaguing your computer and CD-ROM drive—fortunately, no guns involved. It's more likely you'll use your fingers, a screwdriver, maybe some tweezers (Hey, you got a license for them tweezers, pal?). Actual violence never solves anything, anyhow.

In Plain Sight

Whenever you add a new thingy to your computer system—either the CD-ROM I've been blathering about or some other widget—there's a chance that something will go wrong. That's a basic truth in this corner of the universe, one of the few that you can take to the bank with you. Get used to the idea.

Just as you were getting to the important bit of the installation, the dog jumped up on you, the kid cried, your lover wanted attention, you had to pee, whatever—you got distracted. You zigged when you should have zagged, and didn't notice. It could happen. When you think you're finished and you go to power up your new toy (*gasp!*), it doesn't work. (*Shriek!*)

Don't panic. Before you run screaming into the night or take your Walther PPK (one of the guns favored by Bond, James Bond) to your computer, take a couple of deep breaths, have a cookie—do *something*, anything else. Walk away for a minute and come back a little calmer.

It's a Math Thing—I Wouldn't Understand

There should be a mathematical formula for calculating the chance that a hardware problem is the result of an oversight caused by excitement. It'd be something like:

$$\%E = SCJ/(C/D)$$

%E is the possibility of making a really obvious mistake. SCJ is the Silly Childlike Joy you feel at the prospect of using a new toy. C/D is your level of Confidence divided by the Difficulty of the installation. Something like that—but I'm not a mathematician, so don't send me letters correcting my math theory. Thank you.

When you calm down, come back and check the obvious mistakes you could have made. The things that are *sooo* obvious they don't bear checking—check those *twice*. (Naturally, these first three don't apply to an internal drive.)

➤ Is the CD-ROM drive plugged in?

➤ Turned on?

➤ If it *is* turned on, did you turn it on before you turned on the computer?

➤ Is all the necessary driver software installed?

➤ Are all the connections right? Tight?

➤ Is the PC's controller card(s) seated properly in the slot?

➤ If you have multiple SCSI devices installed, is everything chained correctly, termination correct, different ID numbers assigned? (See Chapter 15 for more on the SCSI follies.)

➤ For an internal SCSI drive, does Pin One of the SCSI connector match up with Pin One on the cable? (See Chapter 17 for more scoop on internal drives.)

➤ For any other sort of controller, did you check to be sure you were using unique IRQ and DMA settings (that's in Chapter 15, too)?

➤ Is the internal drive connected to the power supply correctly?

➤ If the drive came on, but you can't access it—did you put in a CD?

➤ Is the CD in the drive correctly (label side up, in a caddy if appropriate)?

I won't be so presumptuous as to speak for you, but I know how loony I can get, excited at having a new toy. It makes me stupid. I remind myself to remember to do something, maybe a hundred times, then immediately forget to do it. I'm like that—not 33 years old, but like eleven 3-year-olds rolled into one. (I may get stupid, but I also enjoy myself.)

Before you get to pulling your hair out and waking the neighbors, check the obvious. If that doesn't fix it, read through your manual's installation procedure ONE STEP AT A TIME and make sure you did everything you were supposed to. In a moment of distraction, you may have skipped a step, or misread a step, or missed an important warning. I'd hazard a guess that about 85% to 90% of the time any problems can get resolved at this stage of the game, before they reach "calling technical support in a panic" or "bludgeoning the computer with whatever's handy."

If checking the obvious and rechecking your manual don't resolve the problem, here are some more common things that can go wrong with a CD-ROM drive and how to fix them. But, before you start thrashing around, hooking and rehooking everything up again, take a sanity break. Watch ten minutes of a Monty Python rerun on Comedy Central, have a laugh.

Methinks the Drive Doth Protest Too Much

The first thing you should do—after checking the obvious and before trying to see what might be wrong with your installation—is grab your CD-ROM drive's manual. See if the drive has a self-test or diagnostic mode. Some do. If it does, use it.

Instead of leaping to the conclusion that whatever is wrong is your fault (especially since we eliminated all the obvious things that could be wrong), take two minutes to check the drive itself. You may have gotten a bad one. (If the drive doesn't spin when you insert a disc, it's a bad 'un.)

Running a CD-ROM drive's diagnostic usually involves turning the drive off, then back on, while holding down a button (or buttons) on its control panel. It will then check

By the Way... There's advice on how to deal effectively with technical support later in the chapter. You should probably read it before you pick up the phone. Hey! It couldn't hurt.

itself out and report its findings to you on its display. Keep your manual handy. The diagnostic messages are usually in codes you'll have to look up to interpret—sometimes it's like casting runes or reading Tarot cards.

If the drive gives itself a clean bill of health, you can carry on checking out other things. If it doesn't, well, time to call the drive manufacturer's technical-support number.

IBM-Compatible Complaints

Here's how things work: When you start up your PC, a command in your CONFIG.SYS file tells your computer to load the appropriate device-driver software from your hard drive. When the driver loads, the first thing it does is look for a SCSI adapter (or other expansion card) where the CD-ROM drive will be connected. You'll get a message during the *POST (Power-On Self-Test)* saying the card has been found, or not found. If it finds the card, the driver will then look for the CD-ROM drive, and you'll get another message saying the drive has been detected (or not).

MSCDEX Microsoft CD-ROM extension for DOS, a program that allows DOS to talk to the CD-ROM device driver, which talks to the drive itself. The drive passes information back to the device driver, which hands it to MSCDEX, which passes it off to DOS.

Your computer knows you have a CD-ROM now, but DOS doesn't know what to do with it. That's where *MSCDEX* (Microsoft CD-ROM extension for DOS) comes in.

MSCDEX is loaded when your AUTOEXEC.BAT file is executed, and you should see a variation of the following message appear on your screen (depending on what versions of DOS and MSCDEX you have):

```
MSCDEX Version 2.22
Copyright (c) Microsoft Corp. 1986-1992. All
rights reserved.
Drive D:= (an abbreviated form of your drive
name) Unit 0.
```

It tells you that MSCDEX has loaded properly and has assigned your CD-ROM drive the drive letter D, so you know that when you want to access a CD, you'll tell your computer to read that drive letter.

The vast majority of CD-related problems you'll have will occur when you're starting your system, when you're trying to read a CD-ROM disc, or when you've got more than one SCSI device attached to your PC.

Starting on the Wrong Foot

If your computer will not start (or you get an error message on startup) after you installed the SCSI adapter, sound card, and/or other controller card, the card(s) are either installed incorrectly or conflicting with each other. Check to see that the card (or cards) are seated properly in their slots. Check your CD-ROM drive's connection to the card(s). Be sure you powered on the CD-ROM drive (if external) before you turned on the computer.

If everything looks okay, you may have a card conflict problem. Different combinations of cards conflict in different ways, so I can't help you. If your system crashed, it's probably an IRQ problem. If one or more of your cards just don't work now, it's probably something with a DMA setting. Or it could be something wondrous and strange, like pixelated pixies popping your processor. (*I'm sorry, Mr. Burke, but your Pentium has a nasty case of elf infestation.*)

Check the manuals of the suspect cards for suggestions on resolving the conflict or call the companies' technical-support numbers.

"No Devices Respond"

How rude, not to speak when spoken to. The CD-ROM drive did not respond when queried by your adapter card, so the computer doesn't think there's a drive there. Be sure you powered on the CD-ROM drive (if external) before you turned on the computer. Check to see that the drive's cables are properly (and securely) connected at the drive and computer ends of the cable.

"Incorrect DOS Version"

This error, at startup, indicates you've got a conflict between your installed version of DOS and the MSCDEX—one of them is too old. MS-DOS 6.x requires MSCDEX version 2.22. Luckily, version 2.22 comes with DOS 6.x. You'll find it in your /**DOS** subdirectory.

There's No DOS Like an Old DOS

If you're running an older version of DOS, you'll probably find the appropriate version of MSCDEX in the /DOS subdirectory on your hard drive.

Odds are, an older version of MSCDEX got installed from your CD-ROM's driver software (those disks can sit around a long time before someone buys them). Most installation programs will automatically alter your AUTOEXEC.BAT and CONFIG.SYS files to load device drivers from their own software's subdirectories, rather than from the \DOS subdirectory.

Steel your nerves; you'll need to modify your AUTOEXEC.BAT file so it loads from \DOS. Here's how:

1. At the DOS prompt, type **EDIT C:\AUTOEXEC.BAT** and then press **ENTER**. The MS-DOS Editor will open a copy of your AUTOEXEC.BAT file.

2. Locate the line that looks something like the following: C:\SCSI\MSCDEX /D:NECCDR /M:10. The \SCSI will vary, depending on the kind of controller you have, and the driver software—check your manual just to be safe.

3. Edit the path statement so MSCDEX will load from the /DOS subdirectory. The one in Step 2 would be changed to C:\DOS\MSCDEX /D:NECCDR /M:10.

4. **SAVE** the file (press **Alt+F+S**), **EXIT** from the EDIT program (press **Alt+F+X**, and restart your computer by pressing the **Control+Alt+Delete** key combination).

That should fix it.

"Not Enough Drive Letters"

Right out of the box (or right off of the disk), DOS only recognizes five logical drive letters (A through E). If you've used those letters for disk drives (or hard drive partitions) and wound up having your CD-ROM drive assigned a letter after E:, you'll need to alter or add a LASTDRIVE statement to your CONFIG.SYS file.

The LASTDRIVE statement can go anywhere in your CONFIG.SYS file. Here's how to do it:

1. At the DOS prompt, type **EDIT C:\CONFIG.SYS** and then press **ENTER**.

2. On any line, type **LASTDRIVE=F** (or whatever higher drive letter you want/need).

3. **SAVE** the file (pres **Alt+F+S**), **EXIT** from the EDIT program (**Alt+F+X**), and restart your computer by pressing the **Control+Alt+Delete** key combination.

Network Alert!

If your computer is on a network, you have to be very careful using the LASTDRIVE statement. Check with your network administrator before you do anything.

"Invalid Drive Specification"

If you get this error message, it means that for some reason or another, MSCDEX did not load properly when you started your system. There are a couple of possible reasons.

First, if you have your AUTOEXEC.BAT file written so that Windows (or some other DOS shell) loads automatically at startup, the line that loads MSCDEX may come after the line that opens Windows (or whatever). If the shell program opens first, MSCDEX gets cut off at the knees and does not load. Easy to fix: simply move the statement that opens MSCDEX (something like: **C:\DOS\MSCDEX/D:(CD-ROM name) /M:10**) to a location *before* the statement that opens your DOS shell. Alternatively, you can move the line that opens your DOS shell (or whatever) to the end of the AUTOEXEC.BAT file, so it's the last thing that happens at startup.

MSCDEX will also not load if your CD-ROM's device driver did not install properly. You'll probably see a variation of one of these error messages:

```
Bad or missing: C:\SCSI\(driver file name).SYS
Error in CONFIG.SYS line #
```

Something got boogered up in the line that tells your computer where to find your adapter card (or CD-ROM drive's device driver). Check the appropriate manual for how to fix the line.

```
No SCSI adapter found
Aborting device driver
```

Your system found the device driver, but couldn't find the device (in this example, the SCSI card). Your computer will beep and pause in the startup routine for this sort of error. Check your adapter card to be sure it is installed properly (sometimes they work loose in the slot). Consult your card's manual, too. You may also need to refresh yourself on the SCSI ABCs, discussed back in Chapter 15.

Finally, all the drivers may load properly, the adapter card is adapting, but your PC can't seem to locate a CD-ROM drive. Check the obvious: plugged in, power on, cables tight? It's probably just a loose connection. Don't panic. If checking the obvious doesn't solve the problem, your drive may be having some sort of nervous breakdown. Run its self-test, if it has one, and see what happens. You should check for damaged cables, too.

"CDR-101 error"

You'll get this message when there's a problem with your disc, your connection to the CD-ROM drive, or hardware.

First be sure you've inserted your disc correctly, especially if your drive is the kind that seats the disc on a little hub. Make sure it's pushed completely down over that hub: the disc should snap securely into place. You may have a bad disc; try using a different one. If the second disc works, either the first one was inserted wrong (try again), is defective (it can happen), or you're having a hardware problem.

If it seems hardware is to blame, check your connector cable at the back of the drive and where it connects to your computer. If the cable is okay, check your SCSI drive's termination. You may have it set wrong, or in the process of—I don't know, dusting around it—you may have accidentally changed the termination setting. Stranger things have happened.

If that's not it, it's time to run the drive's self-test or to check the connector card (they also come with diagnostic software). Check the appropriate manual for details.

"CDR-103 error"

You'll get a **CDR-103** error when you try to use an incompatible disc in the drive (one not meant for an IBM-compatible system). Someone didn't read their labels closely while shopping.

If the disc *is* appropriate to your system, your disc may be damaged, or your SCSI (or other) adapter card may be conflicting with another interface board (like your sound or video cards). Check the appropriate card manuals to help resolve the conflict.

When All Else Fails...

Read your manual. If that doesn't get it, skip ahead to the section on calling technical support for some advice on getting good customer service from the weasels who sold you such a difficult-to-set-up drive.

Macintosh Miseries

That's "miseries" not "mysteries," because Macs are pretty good about letting you know (in no uncertain terms) that something screwy is going on with your CD-ROM drive—or any attached peripheral, for that matter.

X Marks the Icon

The first indication you might get that something is wrong is at startup. When the little icons start popping up across the bottom of your monitor, if the CD-ROM driver software's icon has a big ol' X through it, something is wrong. (It looks just like the icon for the driver extension—see Chapter 14 for details.) It could be:

➤ Your CD-ROM drive isn't turned on. Turn it on and restart your Mac (using the **Restart** command in the **Special menu**).

➤ A loose SCSI connection. Check the connections at your drive and at your SCSI port (in an external SCSI chain, also check any intermediate connections you might have, at an external hard drive, say).

➤ A SCSI ID number conflict. Check to be sure that all your SCSI devices, including your internal hard drive(s) and your Mac itself, have different SCSI ID numbers.

➤ Chapter 15 will help with SCSI hassles.

If it isn't a problem with your SCSI cable or ID numbers, you may be experiencing a problem with your termination. Check out the SCSI ABCs in Chapter 15.

Startup Icon? What Startup Icon?

If you don't see a CD-ROM driver icon at startup, you've probably installed the software incorrectly. You should have extensions for the driver for your particular drive, Foreign File Access, High Sierra File Access, ISO 9660 File Access, Audio CD Access, and perhaps others (depending upon your drive). Check your manual for a complete list.

These extensions should be inside your System Folder, either in your Extensions folder (System 7 and later) or loose inside the System Folder (System 6 and earlier). If you can't find them at *all*, reinstall them from your original CD-ROM driver disk, according to the directions in your CD-ROM drive's manual.

Disc Icon? What Disc Icon?

When you insert a CD in your drive (either a -ROM or audio CD), no icon appears on your desktop for

Probing Your SCSI Chain If you do have multiple SCSI devices connected to your Mac, you should really lay your hands on a copy of *SCSI Probe*, a control panel by Robert Polic. It will give you some detailed information about all your SCSI devices (like their ID numbers), and it will let you mount some of them (it doesn't work with CD-ROM drives) while your Mac is turned on; no more having to restart when you want to turn on a SCSI device that wasn't on at startup. You can find SCSI Probe on most online services (like America Online or CompuServe), or get it from a Macintosh User Group (like BMUG), or even from a friend who owns it—it's free!

Mount When any sort of a disk (a hard drive, floppy, or CD-ROM) is inserted or acknowledged by your Mac, its icon appears on your desktop so you can access its contents. That disk is said to be mounted. If no icon appears, you say, "The disk won't mount."

it—the disk doesn't *mount*. Something got boogered up when you were starting up, and you just didn't see it happen. Try the suggestions in the last couple of sections.

"This Is Not a Macintosh Disk... Initialize It?"

Ack! No, don't!

You've gotten hold of a disc that is not Macintosh-compatible, like an IBM MPC disc. Now who forgot to read the label? If it is a Macintosh disc, you may be having SCSI difficulties: check your CD-ROM drive's termination. It could also just be a bad disc; try mounting one you know works.

You may also be suffering from a software conflict—especially if you have an extension or control panel installed to allow you to mount DOS-formatted disks on your Mac. Try turning the control panel off (or removing the suspect extension from your System Folder) and restarting your Mac.

Managing Those Extensions

If that fixes the problem, you might want to invest in an extension manager (something like Baseline Publishing's *INIT Manager* software, or the Extension Manager control panel that comes with System 7.5) so you can turn sets of extensions and control panels on and off at startup. They're especially handy if you need to free up memory when you run greedy multimedia software from the CD-ROM drive. It will also save you a lot of extension-juggling and Mac-restarting down the line.

Something's Scuzzy in Denmark

In addition to the symptoms mentioned above, SCSI difficulties can manifest themselves in any number of ways: One or more SCSI devices will disappear when a new device is added; your Mac won't start at all; disks in SCSI devices won't mount. All kinds of nonsense.

Run, do not walk, to the SCSI ABCs section in Chapter 15 and review the rules of SCSI. Remember to be methodical in trying to resolve SCSI difficulties. Don't just thrash around trying stuff; you'll go nuts.

When All Else Fails

Read the manual.

Uncle Wiggly's Technical-Support Tips and Tricks

You did your best. You tried everything I suggested here, read your manuals. You even read your manual's manuals. No go. It's time to pick up the phone and call for help. Like anything else, there's a right and a wrong way to ask for help.

RIGHT: *Hi, I'm having trouble getting your CD-ROM drive, model XYZ3, up and running with my (computer make and model). What am I doing wrong?*

WRONG: *You idiots! It's not working! Why isn't it working?! Kill you all! Kill you all! Arrrrggggghhhhh!*

In addition to approaching the technical-support people with the proper attitude, it will help if you call from a phone near your computer (so you can try the things they suggest right away), and have the following information handy—write it down so it's all in one place:

➤ All of your pertinent system information. The kind of thing you wrote down back in Chapter 10 to take shopping with you. (You can use the same list, if you still have it.)

➤ **PC users:** A hard copy of your CONFIG.SYS and AUTOEXEC.BAT files.

➤ **Mac users:** A list of all the extensions and control panels you had loaded to run when the problem occurred. (An easy way to get these lists is to open the Extensions folder and then select the PrintWindow command from the File menu. Repeat the process for your Control Panels folder.)

➤ The make and model of the CD-ROM drive.

➤ The exact problem: When I did this (started up, inserted a disc, and so on), that happened (nothing, specific error message, and so on).

➤ The steps you took trying to resolve the problem before you called (described briefly, but in detail).

The technician you speak to will probably want some of your system information as a starting point and the description of the problem. It will go on from there—you may need the rest of the information, and you may not, but it's better to have it handy.

When the tech-support person answers, identify yourself by name. Ask his or her name if it isn't given, and write it down. You may have to call back later, and it will save you time if you keep dealing with the same person. While on the phone, remain calm. Remember, the tech-support people don't manufacture the product, they answer questions about it. They answer a lot of questions.

Sometimes tech-support types will leap to conclusions because the problem may be new to you, but they've seen it 50 or 100 times a day. If he starts leap-frogging around so you don't follow his reasoning, stop him and say, "Slowly please, I'm writing this down." You should really write it down, too. It provides you with a written record of what didn't and (hopefully) did work so you have it for future reference.

If suggestions are made, repeat them back before you try them so you're sure you're doing the right thing. When things get resolved, thank the person who helped you and go on your merry way. If things don't get resolved, ask to speak to a supervisor. You'll probably have to start the process all over again, but if it solves the problem...

With any luck at all, you won't have to bother with technical support, but if you do, be prepared for it.

The Least You Need to Know

➤ When problems occur, first check the obvious, then check the drive and make sure it's working okay. Finally, you can check everything else.

➤ CD-ROM problems occur in one of three places: at the drive (hardware problem, bad disc, and so on); at your computer (driver software, adapter card problem); or somewhere in-between (loose connections, no power).

➤ Be methodical so you know what you've tried and what didn't work—that way you won't waste time trying it again.

➤ Be prepared with vital information (computer, software, drive, problem, and so on) before you call technical support.

➤ Calm yourself down before you do anything. It won't help, and all that thrashing about could cause more problems.

A LITTLE PINCH OF OREGANO...

Chapter 31

Tidbits You Can Add... Later

In This Chapter

➤ Scanning scanners

➤ Ins and outs of video

➤ Skirting MIDI

➤ Adding mass (storage)

Throughout this book, we've looked at the basic stuff you need to get into the wonderful world of CD-ROM. We even looked at some of the nice-but-not-absolutely-necessary stuff.

What if you're the kind of person who won't be satisfied with "enough" or "more than enough"? This chapter is for you because it goes to extremes.

Think of this as a postscript to the rest of the book, a big, fat "By the Way," in case you aspire to more than just using your CD-ROM drive to look at stuff other people put together. Your drive, along with some other hardware, can put you in the producer's chair.

The Art of the Scan

If you get heavily into this multimedia thing and think it might be fun creating your own (or watching your kids create their own) multimedia masterpieces, you may want to scan images or words from printed pages so you can display and/or use them on your computer. To do that, you need to add a *scanner*.

A scanner is a device that works something like a photocopier. It takes a "picture" of a page (containing either words or pictures) and instead of printing it to another page, it sends it to your computer so it can re-create the page on your monitor (the figure below shows a picture being scanned). Very cool.

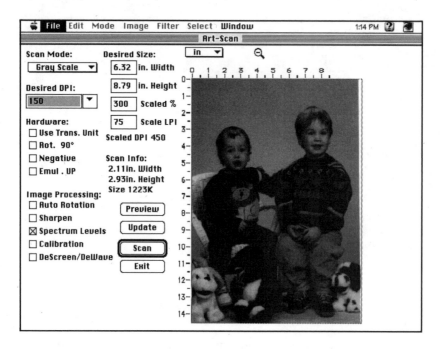

Scanning the nephews for later, teen-years embarrassment.

Scanners come in two main flavors: *hand-held* and *flatbed*.

Hand-held models are (get ready for a major revelation) small enough to hold comfortably in your hand. Flatbed models sit on your desktop and look a lot like small photocopiers. The one I used to scan the photograph above is of the flatbed variety (a Relysis Avec Colour 2400, using Adobe Photoshop to receive and edit the scanned images).

The hand-held models are less expensive than the flatbed variety, but they are small, so they can mean more work for you.

If you scan an item that's larger than the scanner, you'll have to scan it in two or more passes, then put the image's pieces together like the pieces of a jigsaw puzzle.

Scanners also come in two, I guess, sub-flavors: *color* and *grayscale*, but if your goal is to produce dazzling multimedia junk (or should that be *junque*?), you'll want a color scanner that can reproduce color photographs, illustrations, and text.

OCR (to pronounce it, just say each letter) The abbreviated form of **Optical Character Recognition**. It's software that "reads" scanned text images and (one character at a time) turns it back into editable text. Nowadays, most scanners come with some sort of software bundle, including OCR software.

If you are considering a scanner, you should look for one that comes with *OCR* software.

If you scan in a page of text, your computer will treat it like a picture of a page of text. You can't edit it unless you first run it through OCR software to change it from a picture into an editable text file. Then you can load the text into your favorite word processor and play around with it.

Lights, Camera, Action!

If you want to add original, live-motion video to your creations, you'll need to add a *video-capture card* to your computer.

Unless, of Course...

Naturally, if you happen to own a computer with video sampling built-in (like the AV line of Macintosh computers and one or two of the latest PC-compatibles), you don't need to add a capture card; you just need to plug in your video source. More on that in a moment.

A video-capture card is like a scanner, except it deals with *moving* pictures. With one of these, you can plug a camcorder or VCR into your computer and transfer video-taped images to your system.

The video card turns the moving pictures into digital information your computer can store. You can edit and enhance them, add effects and fancy titles, then include them in a presentation or program of your own creation.

Some video cards also give you the ability to send digital movie information from your computer and record it on video tape. This is handy if you want the presentation you create to be easily distributed and viewed by a wide variety of people who may or may not have computers.

Video-capture cards come in a wide variety of styles, from simpler ones for home use, to very expensive models that will create videos suitable for broadcast. (How do you think your local TV stations get those really cool, computer-generated logos and images from their computers to your television?)

Naturally, if you want to add a video-capture board to your computer, you should already have (or plan to buy) a video source: a camcorder, laser disc player, or VCR.

Adding a color video-capture card to your computer can be an expensive proposition—from $250 to as much as $3,800— and probably too expensive for average, at-home dabblers. However, there *is* a (relatively) inexpensive alternative: Connectix Corporation's *QuickCam* (shown below).

Connectix's QuickCam—believe it or not, that's a digital video camera.

With a mail-order price of $100, the QuickCam is easily the least expensive way I know of getting live-action video (with sound) into your computer. It also doubles as a still camera.

The QuickCam, the round part in the figure, connects to any serial port (nicely sidestepping the need for a video card), comes with simple-to-use software, and is a real *hoot* to play around with. I lost *hours* to it (you'll find some of the results of my lost hours on the CD at the back of the book).

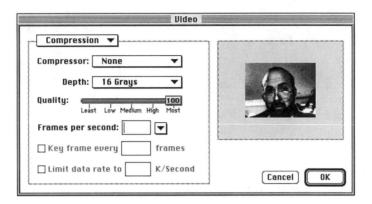

Toying with video... and my face. Gosh, I look so serious.

The only drawbacks to the QuickCam are: It only works in black-and-white (although a color version is expected by the end of the year, with an easy upgrade available to owners of the black-and-white version), and it's only available for the Mac. The PC version is supposed to start shipping... probably by the time you read this, so that's one drawback out of the way.

The toy-brain in me can't say, strongly enough, how much fun this little (and I do mean little—the camera part is less than three inches in diameter) doohickey is, and it's certainly an inexpensive way to get into digital video.

Say It Again, Sam

At the risk of sounding like a broken record, I'm going to blather about sound cards again. Mac owners, because your sound support is built-in, you may skip merrily ahead—the most you'll need to add is a microphone, unless you want to add more high-powered sound support.

One of the most attractive (if subliminal) aspects of multimedia software is that it can include a good bit of audio data, in addition to everything else.

Many high-end (read: expensive) sound cards will allow you (with the addition of a microphone/audio-in jack) to record your own spoken words or music either directly or from another sound source (like prerecorded cassettes or audio CDs).

Ask Any Lawyer

Be aware that copying copyrighted music or spoken words (or scenes from your favorite movie with a video board) from prerecorded sources for use in a commercial product is highly illegal without permission from the copyright holder. You must ask, "Mother, may I?" You usually have to cough up a fee, too.

If you see yourself venturing into CD software creation or multimedia presentations, you should buy yourself a high-end sound card and learn its (sound) ins and outs.

Maestro, If You Please...

Those of a more musical bent, who wouldn't be satisfied with someone else's music spicing up their work, might want to consider adding MIDI equipment to their shopping lists.

No, MIDI isn't equipment used to design moderate-length skirts, although it *is* pronounced the same. *MIDI* is another one of those annoying computer-geek acronyms; it stands for *Musical Instrument Digital Interface*.

It allows you to hook a music synthesizer up to your computer to record, tinker with, and play back your original compositions. Think Stevie Wonder or Wendy Carlos, both masters of the MIDI.

Your computer keeps track of all the notes you play (on the synthesizer's keyboard) and then plays them back on demand. With the proper software, you can then speed up, slow down, change key, all of those good musical things that I can't do. (I have a tin ear, froggy voice, and two left feet. I'm the one they're talking about when they say white folks don't have rhythm.)

My brother's got all this MIDI stuff. His studio looks like a set from Star Wars: the Musical. Me, I don't play anything. I'd need to get one of those Miracle piano teaching systems (which also are MIDI devices and hook into your computer). It'd be a miracle if it could teach me to play.

If you're part of an aspiring rock (or whatever) band, you could pair your MIDI equipment with your video-capture equipment and produce and edit your own music video right on your desk—what a concept!

Mass Appeal

All of the junk we've been talking about plugging into your computer takes stuff from one form and transforms it into digital information.

The one other thing they all have in common is that the computer files they create take up lots and lots of storage space—enough to choke the average hard drive.

If you plan to indulge in multimedia excesses, you're going to need to build an addition to your computer in the form of a *mass storage* device.

Hard drives are mass storage. You can buy them so they hold *gigabytes* of information (that's billions of bytes of data, in case you forgot).

If the stuff you produce never leaves your home or office, a big, fat hard drive might be enough. If you have to *shlep* your digital decadence around with you (like to a service bureau to have it converted to a CD-ROM disc), it may be easier for you to buy a hard drive with removable media.

A regular hard drive is considered a *fixed-media* drive; you can't remove the magnetic platter where all your data is stored and pop in another one. With a removable-media drive, you can. Removable-media drives give you virtually unlimited storage space.

It's Like Closet Space

Even if you're as rich as Croesus and can afford to spend a few thousand dollars on a recordable CD drive, you're still going to need somewhere to store a CD's worth of data (over 600MB) until you're ready to copy it to a disc.

Removable-media drives are available in a wide variety that will fit a wide variety of budgets. The details and technical distinctions are (technically speaking) boring as heck. Do your homework before you go shopping (the tips in Chapter 15 will help).

But Wait, There's More

There's a ton of hardware you can add to your computer to create spiffy multimedia presentations and professional-quality CD-ROM discs. But the hardware just can't do it alone.

Naturally, you need inspiration (though there's a lot of decidedly uninspired doo-doo filling software shelves), and talent helps, too, but you also need something to assemble the various sounds, images, movies, and text into a pretty package.

That's the realm of authoring and presentation software. You can read all about it back in Chapter 27.

Why Bother?

You're probably thinking, why would I want to buy all this crap? I'm not going to be producing CD-ROM discs any time soon. There are some practical applications for everyday folks like you and me.

For Kids

A lot of kids are learning to create multimedia projects on their own in school. The availability of the hardware and kid-friendly software (like HyperStudio, to name one) in schools makes today's students multimedia-mavens waiting to happen. Imagine their grades if they were able to do projects at *home* for homework and extra credit. And not just kids, but students of *all* ages.

For Family

Already, a lot of people use their home computers to do family newsletters—if there are enough computers in the family, why not send presentations built around your family photographs and video. Scan your kid's latest Crayola masterpiece. Add sampled sounds of your baby's first words to video of her first step. Share the important moments of your life.

For Business

I've got a lot of friends who are self-employed (mostly theater-types: actors, designers, directors) who are always looking for new ways to promote themselves. They're always suckering me into doing computer-stuff for them: actors who want scans of their head-shots so they can put their pictures on postcards and resumes; directors who need computer-generated newspaper headlines and photographs.

The most challenging project has been coming up with a digital version of a designer's portfolio, with photographs of his sets, copies of reviews, and other material so it can be distributed easily and cheaply. We're still working that one out—and probably will wind up going with a presentation printed to video tape for easy distribution.

Whether you're self-employed, run a business, or just work in a small business, you can use this assortment of hardware and software add-ons to create multimedia promotional tools just like the major corporations use to sell their wares.

Think About It

Multimedia at home is a relatively new concept. Right now, it's mostly used by big corporations and software companies, but there's no reason why people with limited resources can't make use of the same tools in new and innovative ways to educate, promote, or otherwise enhance their lives and businesses. Just think about it. You may find yourself one day saying, "I wish there was a way I could..." and for all you know, there may already be a way.

The Least You Need to Know

Nobody, but nobody, should come away from this thinking I want you to run out and buy all this expensive stuff on a whim. If you need it, sure. Otherwise, just be open to the idea of someday adding on and expanding your system with other cool toys.

➤ A scanner will get pictures and words from a piece of paper into your computer without your having to retype or redraw them.

➤ A video-capture board will let you digitize moving pictures from another video source (like a VCR or camcorder).

➤ A sound card with audio-in capability will let you record spoken words or music in a form you can use on your computer.

➤ A MIDI setup will let you write and perform your own music, and record it digitally so you can incorporate it into your multimedia productions.

➤ All this digitized stuff takes gobs and gobs of storage space, so you may want to expand your storage capacity with a huge fixed- or smaller removable-media drive.

➤ Be open to new and creative uses of your computer equipment. It's more than just an expensive typewriter/boom box combination.

Speak Like a Geek: The Complete Archive

1X   A mystical abbreviation applied to a CD-ROM drive that operates at only one speed.

2X   A mystical abbreviation applied to a CD-ROM drive that operates at two speeds, one of them twice as fast as a 1X drive. Also known as (AKA) double-speed drives.

3X   (Haven't you nailed this concept yet?) An abbreviation applied to a CD-ROM drive that operates at three different speeds, one of them three times as fast as a 1X drive. AKA triple-speed drives.

8-bit   A confusing term, with multiple uses. A bit is the basic (smallest) unit of digital information. Eight bits equal one byte. An 8-bit sound card plays and records sound one byte at a time. 8-bit video, on the other hand, is a video monitor and card capable of displaying a maximum of 256 colors. For video, it's called 8-bit because each pixel or dot on the monitor has 8-bits of memory allotted to it.

16-bit   A term twice as confusing as 8-bit. 16-bit sound cards play and record 16 bits (two bytes) of audio information at a time, giving you fuller, richer sound. It's the standard for audio CDs.

24-bit   A term three times as confusing as 8-bit. 24-bit video is a video monitor and card capable of displaying over 16 million colors. It's called 24-bit because each pixel or dot on the monitor has 24-bits of memory allotted to it.

access time   The average time it takes a CD-ROM drive to jump to the location of the next bit of data it needs. You'll usually see it measured in **ms**, as in "the drive has an access time of 300ms," for milliseconds.

active speakers   Speakers, usually intended for CD or CD-ROM use, that come with a built-in amplifier, so that audio volume can be boosted to a level beyond what the CD-ROM drive can produce on its own. "Active" because they do something more than let sound pass through. See also *passive speakers*.

amplifier   An electronic doodad that boosts the audio signal from an audio source to comfortable listening volumes and beyond.

audio CD   A commercially recorded compact disc primarily intended for use in a home stereo, but you can also play them in most CD-ROM drives. (In case you're still keeping track, I'm listening to Rickie Lee Jones' "Traffic From Paradise" audio CD right now.)

audio-out jack   The plug or port socket that allows you to connect speakers or headphones to your CD-ROM drive or sound card.

bay   See *expansion bay*.

binary   The language of computers is called binary, in which everything is said in combinations of zero and one.

bit   The smallest amount of information a computer can deal with (a zero or a one). Bits get sent to your computer in eight-packs called bytes.

bootable device   A computer storage device (such as a hard drive, floppy drive, even, in rare instances, a CD-ROM drive) that contains all the information (such as DOS, or System 7) your computer needs to function. Therefore, starting a computer may be called "booting" or "booting up."

bootleg   An illegal copy of software sold by someone other than the original manufacturer. Sometimes called "pirated software." I think the term comes from folks who used to distill and sell illegal alcoholic beverages during prohibition—they must have walked around with bottles of the stuff down their bootlegs.

buffer   See *cache*.

bundle(d)   Literally, a bunch of stuff lumped together in a single package. Computers and other hardware often come bundled with software. Sometimes other software gets bundled with a particular piece of software.

byte   Eight bits. A basic unit of computer memory or storage. Not to be confused with a shave and a haircut, which is only two bits.

byte-head   A term used to describe someone fascinated by the technical details of computing. Byte-heads think nothing of popping the hoods on their computers and fiddling with the innards just to see what will happen. Also known as tweaks.

cache   A chunk of memory set aside to hold frequently accessed data to speed up your system's operation. For a CD-ROM drive, it's memory used only for storing information from a disc. The information is fed to the computer from one end of the cache, while new information is fed into the cache from the other end. It smooths out the data access so there are fewer pauses.

CD   Compact disc. A storage medium originally developed by the Sony and Phillips corporations for music, but is now used for movies and computer data as well.

CD-R   Compact Disc-Recordable. A special computer CD that can be written to, but only once, by an appropriate CD-R drive and read in a normal CD-ROM drive. They're very expensive.

CD-ROM   Compact Disc Read-Only Memory. So named to distinguish computer CDs from audio CDs. They're "read-only" because data can only be read from, not written to, them. Also applies to the drives that read the discs.

CD-ROM drive   A computer attachment for reading data from a CD-ROM disc and sending it to your computer for interpretation and/or processing.

CD-WO   Compact Disc-Write Once. Same as CD-R, above, just more letters.

chutzpah   Yiddish for nerve, bravado, testicular fortitude. It can be good or bad, depending on the context and the vocal spin you put on it. I love Yiddish—so many great words that are fun to say (a lot of glottal sounds)—but I need a good Whitebread-to-Yiddish dictionary so I can get the spellings right.

CONFIG.SYS   A text file on IBM-compatible computers. It contains instructions that **config**ure your computer **system**'s hardware components (keyboard, memory, mouse, printer, and so on) so all of your applications can use them. When you start up your computer, one of the first things it does is carry out the commands in the CONFIG.SYS file.

control panel   A bit of software that lets you customize its behavior (and, therefore, your computer's behavior) to some extent. On a Mac, you access it by selecting **Control Panels** from the   menu. On a PC with Windows, you'll find your control panels in the **Main** program group by double-clicking the **Control Panel** icon.

customer service   The people whose job it is to straighten out their company's mistakes, and to tolerate yours. A good company will fix their own mistakes with no additional hassle to you. A great company will fix your mistake with no additional hassle.

daisy chain   A string of from two to six SCSI devices, connected to each other and (ultimately) to your computer.

device   In this context, a computer add-on that does something. Usually, you'll see "device" paired with another word (like SCSI device) so you'll know what kind of device you're talking about.

disc caddy   A plastic container for CDs that protects both the disc and the drive from dust and other hazards. Some CD-ROM drives require the use of disc caddies.

disk/disc   Two different spellings of the same word. When you see it spelled "disk," it refers to a computer floppy disk. When you see it spelled "disc," it refers to a compact disc (CD), which can be either the audio kind (like a music CD), or the computer kind (a CD-ROM). Some folks don't make the distinction at all. Go figure.

DMA   DMA stands for **Direct Memory Access**. An expansion card with DMA is assigned a particular path for funneling information directly to your computer's RAM. No two cards should have the same DMA setting.

DOS   Disk Operating System. Generically it means the set of instructions that tell a computer what it's supposed to do. Most often, when people say DOS, they mean MS-DOS, Microsoft's version of the operating system for IBM-compatible machines.

double-speed   A descriptive term for CD-ROM drives that can access data at two speeds, usually 150 and 300 kilobytes per second. It's abbreviated 2X.

drive bay   See *expansion bay*.

driver   A small bit of software that tells your computer how to deal with a new piece of hardware.

expansion bay   An open area set aside in the front of most computers for the addition of internal computer peripherals (such as hard, floppy, and CD-ROM drives). There's usually a support structure in place to secure these peripherals in the bay. It's sometimes referred to as a drive bay.

expansion card   A printed circuit board that, when added to your computer, "expands" its capabilities.

export   When one application saves your document in a format that can be used by another (different) application. When the second application uses that file, it "imports" it.

extension   A small bit of software that adds extra capabilities (like using a CD-ROM drive) to your Mac. They go in the Extensions folder inside your System folder on your hard drive.

female   A type of port (or business-end of a cable) that has an arrangement of holes that match up with the arrangement of pins in a male connector or port.

floppy disk   A basic computer storage media. It's a plastic wafer with a round disk of magnetic material inside. A computer's floppy drive writes and reads data to and from the magnetic media. See also *disk/disc*.

font   A digital/computer typeface of a particular size and shape. They come in a lot of varieties, as well as in different formats for use with different computers, even computer programs.

freeware   Software that you can just have and use, and it doesn't cost you much of anything (maybe the price of disk). The authors, in their beneficence, give a little gift to the computing world. You can find freeware in most of the same places as shareware.

gigabyte   A billion bytes. It's abbreviated GB or Gig.

graphics   A fancy computerese way of saying pictures.

grayscale   A type of computer monitor that substitutes shades of gray for all the other colors.

hard boot   See *reboot.*

hardware   The solid, tangible, three-dimensional stuff of computing: computers, monitors, printers, disk drives. As opposed to software.

HFS   Hierarchical File System. The Hierarchical File System is what allows a Mac to have a folder inside of a folder inside of a folder inside of a folder and so on.

Hierarchical File System   See *HFS.*

High Sierra Format   Or HSF, for short. High Sierra Format is a method of formatting CD-ROM discs so they can be used with different computer systems. Don't confuse HSF with HFS.

HSF   See *High Sierra Format.*

IBM-compatible   A DOS-based computer built to work in much the same way as the computers originally developed by IBM.

INDEO   The Intel Corporation's take on digital video for IBM-compatible computers. See also *QuickTime* and *Video for Windows.*

integrated   A single software package that includes word processor, database, spreadsheet, painting and/or drawing, outlining, charting, and telecommunications software. These packages are called "integrated" because you can use features of many of the different programs in one document. They're sometimes called "something" Works because they come with the works.

interactive   Buzzword meaning that the course of whatever you're doing (for example, learning a foreign language) is not fixed—that is, it will proceed differently depending upon your input. It reacts to your input, while you react to it. Since each reacts to the other, it's called inter-active.

interface   How two things interact. In people-to-computer terms, it's how you interact (give commands) to your computer, whether with a mouse, or by typing commands. In peripheral-to-computer terms, it's how information is passed back and forth (through a SCSI cable, and so on) or how they are physically connected to each other.

internal drive   A disk (or other) drive that is installed inside a computer's main housing. See also *expansion bay.*

IRQ   IRQ stands for Interrupt ReQuest. IRQ settings give an expansion card a particular way to interrupt whatever your PC is doing so you can get information sent in from the CD-ROM drive or other device. No two cards should have the same IRQ settings.

ISO   International Standards Organization. They create and set world-wide standards, to help assure consistency between manufacturers and their products.

ISO 9660   Standard for formatting CD-ROM discs for DOS PCs. See also *ISO.*

jewel box   The plastic storage case that most audio, and many CD-ROM CDs come packaged in.

kilobyte   A thousand bytes. It's abbreviated K or KB.

Kodak PhotoCD   The new way to get your photographs developed. When you turn in your roll of film, instead of getting a stack of prints back, you get the images on a CD-ROM disc (see Chapter 5).

male   A type of port (or business-end of a cable) that's got an arrangement of pins that plug into a female connector, or port, of similar configuration.

megabyte   A million bytes. It's abbreviated MB or Meg (like the nickname for Margaret).

memory   The amount of RAM, or Random Access Memory, your computer has. It's the amount of space your computer has for holding the program(s) you are working with, as well as the file(s) you are working on. See also *SIMMs.*

memory cache   See *cache.*

MIDI   Another one of those annoying computer-geek acronyms; it stands for Musical Instrument Digital Interface. It allows you to hook a synthesizer and all manner of musical goodies to your computer to record, tinker with, and play back music compositions.

millisecond (ms)   One thousandth of a second.

monitor   A television-like device that lets you see what your computer is up to while you're working with it.

mount   When any sort of disk (hard drive, floppy, or CD-ROM) is inserted or acknowledged by your Mac, its icon appears on your desktop so you can access its contents. That disk is said to be mounted. If no icon appears, you say, "The disk won't mount."

MPC   The first standard set for a Multimedia Personal Computer. It specifies the hardware requirements you must meet to call your computer and/or peripherals MPC-compatible.

MPC2   The revised, higher standard for Multimedia Personal Computers, updated to include advances in CD-ROM and computer technology. See also *MPC*.

MSCDEX   (MicroSoft CD-ROM EXtension for DOS) Allows DOS to talk to the CD-ROM device driver, which talks to the drive itself. The drive passes information back to the device driver, which hands it to MSCDEX, which passes it off to DOS.

multimedia   A big, fat, juggernaut of a buzzword, used so many different ways it's almost meaningless. When I say "multimedia," I mean software that combines several kinds of data: plain text, photographs, drawings, sounds, and other dynamic data (like animation or video clips).

multisession   Term applied to Kodak PhotoCD discs and the CD-ROM drives that read them. It indicates that a disc can be written to more than once, or that the drive can read a multisession PhotoCD.

OCR   The abbreviated form of Optical Character Recognition. Software that "reads" scanned text images and (one character at a time) turns them back into editable text.

oogy   Highly technical term for images of the moist and nasty persuasion—the kinds found in books like 1001 Sores and Pustules, or every other scene in a *Friday the 13th* movie.

parallel interface   A computer or peripheral port which passes information in sets of eight bits. IBM-compatibles come with at least one parallel port.

passive speakers   Computer (or other) speakers that do not have a built-in amplifier. "Passive" because they don't do anything but let sound pass through them. See also *active speakers*.

PDA   An abbreviated form of Personal Digital Assistant. They're pen-based (as opposed to keyboard-based) devices that let you write information on a pressure-sensitive screen, converting handwriting to a text or picture file for storage and later retrieval. Apple's Newton and Sharp's Expert Pad are both PDAs.

Pentium   The very, very, too, too chic name created for the 586 chips (and the computers that use them) designed by Intel for IBM-compatible machines.

PhotoCD   Name for the new photographic medium developed (no pun intended) by Kodak. Instead of paper prints, you get your photographs back stored digitally on a CD-ROM disc, called a "PhotoCD."

pins   The little metal posts inside a computer cable's connector, they are what conduct the data from the cable to the receiving computer or device. The pins correspond to wires inside the cable.

pirated software   Arrrgh, see *bootleg*, mateys.

port   A techno-geeky way of saying where computer-type things plug into each other.

power supply   The (usually) silver box inside of your computer that receives and distributes electricity to the rest of the internal components. Never try to open it—it will hurt you.

QuickTime   A software doodad for Macintosh and Windows computers, developed by Apple, to allow you to display video clips on your computer.

RAM   Random-access memory. The place where your computer temporarily holds program information while you work with it. See also *memory*.

RAM cache   A bit of your computer's RAM set aside for a specific function. Not to be confused with a CD-ROM drive's built-in cache (discussed in Chapter 4), even though they are similar. A drive's cache is a permanent thing, and part of the CD-ROM drive. A RAM cache is temporary, and created in your computer's RAM.

reboot   Restarting a computer. A hard reboot involves turning the power off and then back on again, and is bad for your computer. A soft reboot involves restarting without cutting off the power (pressing Control-Alt-Delete on a PC or using the Restart command under a Mac's Special menu). A soft reboot is better for your computer.

SCSI   Abbreviation that stands for Small Computer System Interface. It's a way of connecting up to seven SCSI devices to a computer in a daisy chain.

SCSI ID number   A number (usually 0–7) assigned to a SCSI device to identify it to the computer that controls it. No two SCSI devices attached to a computer should have the same ID number.

SCSI II   SCSI the next generation. It's a later version of SCSI that is faster than the original.

serial interface   A computer or peripheral port that passes information, in order, one bit at a time. Many IBM-compatibles come with one serial port.

shareware   Software that you can try (in the comfort of your own home, on your own computer) before you pay for it. The money goes right to the software's author, instead of filtering through a huge (or even tiny) corporation. You can find shareware in some software catalogs, all over online services (such as CompuServe, America Online, and eWorld), and from users groups. It is very, very tacky to keep and use shareware without paying the fee.

SIMMs   (Single Inline Memory Modules) Collections of memory chips on small cards. When installed in your computer, they increase the amount of RAM available for computing tasks.

SND   The format for Macintosh alert and other Mac sounds. SND, as in, well, sound.

soft boot   See *reboot*.

software   The complicated sets of instructions (the ghost in the machine, if you will) that tell your hardware what to do. While it is stored on a tangible medium (a floppy disc, and so on), the actual "software" itself is very ephemeral and esoteric. Thinking about it gives me a headache and makes me want to read Nietzsche in the bath.

sound card   An expansion card that gives an IBM-compatible a variety of audio capabilities, including sound playback and recording. Macintosh computers have basic sound support built-in.

SoundBlaster   A brand of sound card made by Creative Labs, Inc. It's a very common brand with which many other cards are compatible.

System 7.5   The current version of the Macintosh OS. See also *DOS* (generic definition).

system requirements   The hardware and software you must have before you can use another piece of software, like a CD-ROM game, and so on.

terminator/termination   An electronic widget that tells your computer it has reached the end of the SCSI line, that there are no more SCSI devices for it to look for. The last device in a SCSI (daisy) chain should always be terminated. (A SCSI terminator never says, "I'll be back.")

transfer rate   How quickly a CD-ROM drive can move information from a disc to your computer. It is measured in KB/sec, for kilobytes per second.

triple speed   See *3X*.

users group   A club that focuses on the needs and concerns of a particular computer, software, or aspect of computing. They're all over the place, and they're great to join.

uvula   That little punching-bag-like thing that dangles down at the back of your throat.

VGA   A shortened form of Video Graphics Array. It's a type of monitor and video card for IBM-compatible (and some Macintosh) computers.

Video for Windows   As the phrase implies, it's the software extension that makes it possible to view video clips within Windows and Windows applications.

WAV   The format for Windows and other alert sounds. WAV, as in sound wave.

WORM   An acronym for Write-Once Read-Many, most often associated with high-capacity optical drives, like mutant floppy drives. Occasionally, it gets applied to CD-R and CD-WO drives.

XA   A shortened form of eXtendended Architecture, XA is a formatting standard that interleaves audio and video segments on a CD-ROM disc. Think of "interleaving" like shuffling a deck of playing cards. The cards in one hand are video, in the other hand, audio. When you shuffle the two stacks of cards, you're interleaving them.

Index

PLUG YOURSELF INTO...

THE MACMILLAN INFORMATION SUPERLIBRARY™

Free information and vast computer resources from the world's leading computer book publisher—online!

FIND THE BOOKS THAT ARE RIGHT FOR YOU!

A complete online catalog, plus sample chapters and tables of contents give you an in-depth look at *all* of our books, including hard-to-find titles. It's the best way to find the books you need!

- STAY INFORMED with the latest computer industry news through our online newsletter, press releases, and customized Information SuperLibrary Reports.

- GET FAST ANSWERS to your questions about MCP books and software.

- VISIT our online bookstore for the latest information and editions!

- COMMUNICATE with our expert authors through e-mail and conferences.

- DOWNLOAD SOFTWARE from the immense MCP library:
  - Source code and files from MCP books
  - The best shareware, freeware, and demos

- DISCOVER HOT SPOTS on other parts of the Internet.

- WIN BOOKS in ongoing contests and giveaways!

TO PLUG INTO MCP: ➔ WORLD WIDE WEB: **http://www.mcp.com**

GOPHER: gopher.mcp.com

FTP: ftp.mcp.com

Who Cares What YOU Think?

WE DO!

We're not complete idiots. We take our readers' opinions very personally. After all, you're the reason we publish these books! Without you, we'd be pretty bored.

So please! Drop us a note or fax us a fax! We'd love to hear what you think about this book or others. A real person—not a computer—reads every letter we get, and makes sure your comments get relayed to the appropriate people.

Not sure what to say? Here's some stuff we'd like to know:

- ➡ Who are you (age, occupation, hobbies, etc.)?
- ➡ Which book did you buy and where did you get it?
- ➡ Why did you pick this book instead of another one?
- ➡ What do you like best about this book?
- ➡ What could we have done better?
- ➡ What's your overall opinion of the book?
- ➡ What other topics would you like to purchase a book on?

Mail, e-mail, or fax your brilliant opinions to:

Barry Pruett
Publishing Manager
Que Corporation
201 West 103rd Street
Indianapolis, IN 46290
FAX: (317) 581-4669

CompuServe: 75430,174
Internet: 75430.174@compuserve.com